PODCASTING FOR BEGINNERS: VALUE EDITION

HOW TO START AND GET YOUR FIRST THOUSAND DOWNLOADS, FEATURING PODCASTING MADE SIMPLE + PODCAST MARKETING

DANIEL LARSON

AT PUBLISHING

CONTENTS

DEAR VALUED READER...

Grab your 4 free bonus resources and discover how my friend Jake got to 300k/monthly downloads in under 7 months without using social media via the link below.

https://daniel-larson.com/pmbonus

Daniel Larson

Podcasting Made Simple: The Step By Step Guide On How To Start A Successful Podcast From The Ground Up

INTRODUCTION

Podcasting is the rewarding medium we've been missing for decades that allows you to discuss your passions, share your message with the world, and have a massive impact on people's lives. With more than 6.5 million weekly listeners in the UK and over 72 million weekly listeners in the United States, there are literally millions of people waiting for you to impact their lives with your message. Additionally, podcasting is a trending business model that carries as much bite as it does bark. The fact that more than half of listeners are interested in buying products they learned about through a podcast, renders it a hobby with a highly profitable potential.

The fact that you are here proves that I don't need to sell the idea of podcasting to you. You have already decided that you want to start podcasting. Now, you are looking for details on how to do it! Fortunately, *Podcasting Made Simple* contains everything you need to get started.

There are many reasons why you may be interested in starting a podcast right now. You may desire to build a passionately engaged audience that is inspired by what you talk about, just as much as you are. Even if you are not entirely sure of what that passion is yet, you can feel in your heart that there is something worth talking about that is longing for your attention, and capable of having a huge impact on your listeners. Or, you may have an idea of a podcast that should exist but doesn't yet, so you want to be the one to get it to market. Maybe, your number one focus here is to market your existing business or create a brand new business through your podcast that will earn you an incredible profit. No matter what your reasoning is, you can be sure that podcasting is a great way to fulfil your needs and that you will discover exactly how to do that right here.

In this book, I'm removing every inch of uncertainty from your experience so that you know the exact steps to take to create your podcast and reach all of your podcasting goals, every single time. With the steps I share, you can develop your own professionally produced, highly captivating show that nurtures your passion for sharing while capturing the attention of listeners everywhere.

The comprehensive guides inside *Podcasting Made Simple* will cover everything from creating a viable plan for your podcast, branding and marketing your podcast, what equipment you need for the best sound and experience, how to edit, produce, and share your podcast, and more. Even if you are not particularly outgoing, you will discover how to find your unique voice and share it with the world through your podcast. Each chapter is full of specific strategies and instructions that will help you minimize the hurdles and launch your podcast into success in minimal timing. You will discover that, although this can be a business model, podcasting is a fun experience that can bring a lot of joy to your life. I, myself, have experienced the magnificent joy of sharing my own passion through podcasts, and I can vouch that there is something so wonderful about being able to show up, talk about something you love, and experience the fascination of everyone who listens to your show on a regular basis.

Over recent years, I have grown to love and care for the ever passionate podcast community. Despite the growing size and popularity of podcasts, very few guides exist that go into great detail about the specifics around creating a highly successful and profitable podcast. I want to change that. I want to provide you with an excellent launch pad so that you can take your enthusiastic beginner's mentality and turn it into your own ultimate success story. My goal here is to provide you with specific action steps you can take, free of any contradictory information, and thoroughly researched so that you know you are doing everything it takes to generate a successful podcast. Whether you want to have a solo podcast, a talk show, or a hand over-fist profitable business model, you will discover everything you need to generate success right here in *Podcasting Made Simple.*

I must admit, writing this book is as much for my pleasure as it is for your benefit. Over the past years, I have become obsessed with finding new, innovative ways to develop a podcast, as well as understanding tested and respected methods that get results. Having an outlet for me to put this all together while developing a cohesive and comprehensive guide for you has been a blast for me. I hope you will find it to be a great asset for you as you take on the exciting process of creating, recording, publishing, and promoting your podcast.

I suggest you read this book over ten days, reading one chapter per day, so you can fully absorb all of the valuable information here in this book. The more you understand the secrets of brilliant podcasts, and all of the steps that go into making one, the easier it will be for you to turn your podcast into a great success. By the end, you will have an excellent understanding of what it takes to develop a successful podcast from start to finish. This way, not only are you aware of what you need to do, but you also understand how and you can feel confident in achieving your goals through a simple step-by-step process.

It is important that you understand that podcasting can be highly profitable, but it is not a get-rich-quick scheme. You must be willing to take the necessary action to turn it into a success and push yourself to reach all of your goals. If you do, however, you can make an incredible profit off of your podcast. Not only that, but you can also take your entire brand and transform it into multiple profit streams, effectively growing your income-producing abilities. Once you have an established audience, money *can* be made, and you can achieve financial stability through your podcast. The trick is, you have to genuinely love what you are doing and be willing to do it without any revenue coming from it, as this level of joy ensures that you have the passion and devotion required to turn a profit. With this deep level of commitment to something you love, you will have the energy to show up with passion and consistency, enough so that your audience stays engaged. When your engaged audience begins to form, the opportunity for earning an income starts.

After years of researching podcasts of all sizes, and investing time in understanding the ins and outs of what it takes to develop a successful podcast, I am confident that I can show you the way to success with your own podcast. The methods I unveil to you in this book have been used by the most successful podcasters who are both profitable and wildly in love with the work they do and work in a low-stress way.

If you implement everything instructed to you in this guide, you will be able to turn your podcasting vision into a reality. Whether your goal is big or small, you will be able to transform it into an enriching journey that amplifies your life in many ways. This book is the most well-informed source of information to guide you to make the best decisions that will best serve you and your audience through your podcast. You already know this is something you want to do, so now you have to put your head down and make it happen. With podcasting, you truly will get out what you put in, so don't let your dreams remain idle ideas that stay untouched in the depths of your mind. Release them, research them, and turn them into your reality. The time is now.

In case you are worried about being late to the podcasting party, I want to assure you that you are not. You have made it just in the nick of time! However, podcasting is a rapidly growing medium, and thousands of new podcasts are popping up every single day. Everyone wants to have their share of success in the podcasting world, while also getting to have a say on the things they are most passionate about! If you really want to strike it large, you must not put it off. You must start developing your podcast right away and get it to market as soon as possible. The quicker you are to jump into action now, the larger your podcast will be. The longer you wait, the more saturated the market gets, the quieter your voice gets amongst the thousand others and the more challenging it becomes to climb your way to the top. Let everyone else sleep on this incredible opportunity while *you* become one of the ones who made it happen.

As we dive into this book, for the sake of transparency I'd like to preface something. Daniel Larson is in fact a pen name, and there are two of us operating behind it. I know, weird huh? And maybe a little confusing. We (Taig and Anthony) are recent university graduates who've owned a publishing company for years - since we were students, in fact. We learned a lot about marketing and immersed ourselves in the podcasting community for months before writing and launching this book (and we even have our own podcasting communities now, with a total reach of over 7000 members). From then to now, we've seen common themes and trends of the struggles and challenges people go through...and also of what seems to work really well time and time again, for different shows. We wanted to compile all the best proven practices in one resource to help passion driven but confused individuals looking to start and grow their podcast, become clear and confident on the best way to turn their idea into a successful show and build a loyal audience. *Podcasting Made Simple* is more than just the title of this book, it's our brand. For simplicity, the book will proceed from the perspective of a singular Daniel Larson. I think all parties can agree here that a book written in the plural first person would be...distracting.

Action is the first step in reaching your goals, so buckle up; you're about to start a thrilling journey that will transform your life. Let's begin!

ENVISIONING THE DREAM AND KNOWING WHY

IF YOU ARE NOT ALREADY CONVINCED, PODCASTING IS AN incredible medium to get into. The unique power of a podcast is that it captures your audience's attention, creates a unique and personalized connection between yourself and your audience, and connects you with your audience at any time. Unlike blogs or videos, where your audience must have time to actively read or watch your content, podcasts can be consumed on-the-go. As you likely already know, our modern world is all about *go*.

Aside from fitting your business into their busy schedules, podcasting gives you the opportunity to provide an abundance of benefits to your audience. You can offer entertainment, education, interviews, or any other number of unique listener experiences that provide your audience with a wonderful reason to tune in for every episode. Truly, there are many great ways that you can benefit your audience through the power of your podcast.

Your audience isn't the only one benefitting from your podcast, though. Although you may be creating your podcast for your audience, and promoting it so that you can connect with your audience, there are many benefits that you stand to gain from your podcast, too. One great value you gain from your podcast is offered in the form of therapeutic value. Therapeutic values such as learning to become a better individual through giving people a voice, feeling a sense of personal accomplishment for something you put together yourself, and being able to express yourself and your thoughts all have highly therapeutic values. The level of pride you feel in yourself as you celebrate your own successes is wonderful for your self esteem, self-confidence, and overall sense of self-worth.

Another benefit you gain from your podcast is known as a parasocial relationship. Parasocial relationships are one-sided relationships that form between media personas and their audiences. The easiest way to understand a parasocial relationship is to consider a media persona you adore, such as a singer, actor or actress, or other media personality. Now, consider the way you feel about that person. Chances are, you feel like you have some form of meaningful connection with them, despite the fact that they have no idea who you are. Still, because you are a part of their overall audience, they care about you and add to the relationship, just not on a personal level. Parasocial relationships can be healthy to an extent, offering a sense of belonging and creating a wonderful sense of community. However, it is important that you do not rely exclusively on parasocial relationships in your life, or you will begin to feel lonely and disconnected from the world around you. As you grow, continue to nurture interpersonal relationships you develop through your podcast. This will not only support you with growing your podcast but developing your sense of wellbeing, too.

BEFORE YOU CAN TAP INTO ALL OF THESE BENEFITS YOU AND your audience both gain, you must know *why* you are here building your podcast in the first place. What specifically has drawn you to podcasting, and why is this such an important dream of yours? What about this dream makes it worth pursuing, and how are you going to use this to compel you to keep going? The answer is in the details...

One of the biggest mistakes new podcasters, or business owners in general, can make is failing to clearly define what their dream is and why they want that dream. Without these two elements, you are setting yourself up for failure. A dream gives you a clear sense of direction and a tangible measuring stick to monitor your results with, while a reason why gives you the fuel you need to reach those results and fulfill your inevitable dream.

To define your dream requires a two-pronged approach. You must first let yourself go, free of any expectations, to write down everything you truly want for your podcast. At this point, you want to imagine that your podcast is already a massive success and that it has become everything you hoped it would be and more. Use this imaginative game to define what success looks like for you. Be as specific as you possibly can, as details help drive success. Vague statements like "I make $10,000 a month and people like me" are not going to provide you with a clear vision to work toward. If anything, these indecisive statements will actually drive you away from putting effort in because it leads to you feeling overwhelmed by the statement you have made, and confused with how to proceed. Rather than giving you an "open-ended dream to run toward," it ends up boxing you in, making you feel like there is no point trying because your dream is too big to achieve.

Instead, try creating statements like "I easily earn $10,000 through advertisements, sponsorships, and affiliate marketing deals, and I feel relaxed and confident doing it. My followers are engaged, enjoy listening to me, and contribute to the community that I am building through my podcast with their own anecdotes, willingness to participate, and loyalty to listening." Dream about what your studio will look like, where your podcast will be produced, and what it will feel like to vocalize your opinion on things you are passionate about. Consider the relationship you share with your audience, what it will be like, and how fun it will be to partake in that relationship with the people who are following you. Even allow yourself to dream of your brand, and how your brand will represent you and your podcast, and come to be a point of excitement for your audience.

If you already know what you want to speak about, you can also write down what you want to speak about in a specific manner. Again, do not be vague about this. Get clear on what your podcast will be about, and how your podcast will benefit your listeners. Understand what value you will be giving them and how this value will transform their life. These specific statements are invaluable when it comes to launching your own podcast, starting with a crystal-clear dream.

If you do not yet know what you want to talk about, see if you can define what it will feel like to be producing content for your podcast. Do you want to feel inspired? Passionate? Entertained? Intrigued? Curious? Mysterious? Define what the content will feel like, how it will feel creating it, and how that fits into your overall vision of having a podcast.

I cannot stress enough the importance of being specific throughout this entire process. The clearer you can be when dreaming up these early stages, the easier your podcast development will be because you have a clear sense of direction and focus. The value you gain here is immeasurable, as it truly will direct you straight toward your success. Imagine giving yourself a literal roadmap to where you are going. Rather than giving vague directions like "head west for twenty minutes, then turn slightly south," give yourself clear directions. Your specific description creates a specific set of guidelines and a clear destination, and as a result, you are far more likely to actually get there.

After you have defined your dream in broad terms, the second step is to quickly compare your dream to a S.M.A.R.T goal. S.M.A.R.T goals are the most powerful goals you can develop, as they truly turn your plans into a measurable destination that you can use to drive your actions. Always transform any dream into a smart goal before attempting to fulfill said dream, as this will make it far more attainable. To compare your dream to a S.M.A.R.T goal, you need to make sure it is Specific, Measurable, Attainable, Realistic, and Timed, or able to be given a deadline for when you want to achieve it by. If you can see these five elements defined in your dream, you have an excellent foundation to launch from.

Knowing where you need to go is crucial, but having the fuel to get there is equally as important. After all, it does not matter if you know where you need to go if you have absolutely no fuel to get you there. It is true for a road trip, and it is true for your podcast, too! The fuel to this whole experience is your desire, resiliency, strength, courage, and willingness. In the business, we call it your "why." In other words, why are you even doing this? Knowing why you are doing something, and having a truly meaningful reason for doing it, enables you to motivate yourself and keep your energy up as you work through the process of getting yourself to your dreams. Without a clear, meaningful reason behind why you are doing something, you will surely give up the second things look challenging or seem to require more energy or effort than you have to give them. In any industry, the most successful people all have a clear reason for their actions. They know that this clear reason is the most important thing because without it they never get anywhere. With it, they get everywhere.

Defining your why is a process that must be highly personal to you. You must know exactly what matters to you, what has the power to move you and drive you, and what is going to get you going even when times get challenging. Most times, people with great success decide to turn their why from a "what?" into a "who?" In other words, it's not what they're working toward; it's who they're doing it for that matters most. Marathon runners, for example, run for the people they love by dedicating their races to them, which gives them the energy and strength to keep going. This is the secret to really giving yourself a reason that is beyond powerful, and that will keep you going all the way until you reach your dreams and beyond.

See, people who go after a "what" instead of a "who" often attach their meaningful association to something that is not particularly responsive, or worthy of pursuing. A major driving factor many people believe they have is money, for example. You might think that the reason why you want to do something is money. Perhaps you have decided you want to be a six-figure income earner, or a millionaire, or even a multi-millionaire. The thing is, though, money is non reciprocated. You will work hard for your money, and your money will fluctuate. Sometimes it is there; sometimes, it is not there. Sometimes it is easy to come by, sometimes it eludes you, and you cannot seem to get your hands on any. Even if you do have a lot and you master maintaining high levels of money, money will not keep you company, behave like a friend, or offer you anything beyond financial security and opportunity. While it may seem worthwhile at first, the reality is that money is a fickle lover, and so it should be seen more as a by-product or a part of the motivator, and not *the* driving "why" itself.

The same goes for financial security, the house of your dreams, the city of your dreams, the vacations you long for, the wardrobe you think will make you happy, or anything else that exists in the material world. A material desire will always let you down because the moment you acquire it, the emotional drive is gone. While you may continue to appreciate it and be fond of it, the novelty wears off, the emotional high disappears, and you are left by yourself looking for that next emotional high in yet another material item. As soon as you fulfill your next emotional high, you will be left feeling unfulfilled all over again. The sense of fulfillment from material goods will always be finite and quick to drain. Never motivate yourself with these, as you will struggle to maintain your motivation and keep going, which can drastically reduce your momentum and your success.

A more powerful way to motivate yourself and a way that is deeply engraved in the medium of podcasting is to motivate yourself with a "who." Your "who" might be someone in your life that you love very much, someone who you have yet to meet, or the very people you want to represent with your podcast. Make sure that whoever you choose is important to you and will continue to motivate you, even in challenging times.

When you associate your "why" with a living being, you become far more likely to achieve your why because you experience a powerful, sustainable, and fulfilling back-and-forth exchange of emotions that drives you. For example, if you start a podcast because you want to give a voice to an underrepresented part of your community, the relationships you build within that community will flourish and thrive through your efforts. As a result, you will receive positive emotional fulfillment, which will inspire and drive you to keep going. The more you go, the deeper the relationships become, the more powerful your work is, and the more you are driven to keep going. This creates a sustainable source of energy that drives you to continue through any obstacle you face so you can get your podcast on the airwaves.

One thing I do want to note is that while it may seem endearing to choose yourself as your "who" to represent your "why," this is unlikely to be a sustainable approach. The reason behind this is that we have a tendency to be able to quickly and easily justify why we are no longer pursuing things, or why we are letting ourselves down, and we can rapidly forgive ourselves for quitting. When no one else is involved in the process, the only person you are "letting down" is yourself, and if you decide you are okay with that, then there is no real motivation to proceed. If your "who" is someone outside of yourself, though, you will be far less likely to let them down because justifying *that* becomes much more challenging. While the opportunity to let them down always exists, you will be far less likely to take that action because you know it would ultimately make you feel terrible, too.

DESIGNING THE PODCAST THAT SUITS YOU

Developing a dream and defining the fuel to that dream is essential to begin any new endeavor. Unfortunately, many people stop there because they think a dream is enough, or they become overwhelmed with the idea of bringing that dream to life. You won't stop there, though. You want this way more than that.

The very fact that you clearly defined your dream and developed a specific why is evidence that you have the ability to take the necessary steps to fulfill your podcasting dreams. As you witnessed yesterday, small actions can turn into big results, rapidly. After just a few minutes, you were able to go from a vaguely defined vision and drive, to a clearly defined goal and a meaningful source of fuel to get you there. That is ultimately what the entire journey is comprised of: consistent, small steps that move you in the right direction. The more you take these small steps, the further you are moved in your desired direction, and the more success you will develop in a shorter period of time.

Today's focus is going to be on designing a podcast that suits you so that you are sure to truly enjoy podcasting and get everything you desire out of it. If, until now, you were looking into *other* people's formulas for success and trying to figure out how you might apply their approach to your success, chances are you have found a lot of contradicting information. Everywhere you look, people are providing different details on what it means to podcast, how podcasting works, how your show should be developed, and how frequently you should be sharing with your audience. The reality is, while we do have statistics that give us a general guideline as to what works, *there is no one-size-fits-all approach.* Designing a podcast that suits you ensures that you are developing a formula that fits what you can offer your podcast and what you are looking to get out of your pod cast. Remember, with podcasting you get out of it what you put into it. This means if you put nothing into it, you will get nothing out of it. Alternatively, if you put stress, overwhelm, and confusion into it, *you will get stress, overwhelm, and confusion out of it.* The real system for success is to find a way to pour passion, excitement, and joy into your podcast in a practical way that turns results, so that you can get passion, excitement, and joy out of your podcast, as well as your desired results. When you can combine a positive attitude *and* a proven method, you have a fool-proof design for success.

The three parts of designing a podcast formula that suits you and gets the results you need include: having a captivating intro, nailing the shape and size of your podcast, and having the right output frequency. The key to successfully designing these three elements is to pay attention to the statistics and use them to guide the development of your own formula so that you have something that works for you *and* provides you with the security of proven effectiveness.

CREATING A CAPTIVATING INTRODUCTION

The first element of designing your own podcast is creating a captivating introduction that sells something you are able, and excited, to deliver on. Your show will actually contain two elements where you can shine here: an intro and an outro. Both can contain music, which creates a memorable show with a clearly defined identity. Your introduction, however, can go even deeper. Most podcasts have an introduction that consists of 2-5 brief sentences defining who you are, what the podcast is about, why you are making it, and what people can expect to gain from it. Explain all this in as few words as possible, so your audience does not grow bored and back out of your podcast before ever getting to the actual episode. You want to be concise, lively, and ready to jump into the episode.

Before you get into scripting your introduction, start by deciding what type of music you want to be associated with your podcast. By now, you might already have an idea of a little tune you want to use to help introduce your show. If not, that's okay; you can always take your time to think about it or browse royalty free samples of music that are available for your use. It would be best to start with a good idea as to what energy you want the music to have, or at least one aspect of sound that should be included so that you have a starting point. From there, you can start searching for soundtracks with that sound until you find the one you like. PremiumBeat-.com, Ben Sound.com, and FreeMusicArchive.com are all great places for you to look if you want to get royalty free soundtracks for cheap. Once you have found one that you like, listen to it a few times to make sure it is a sound you would be interested in listening to over and over again, every time your podcast starts and ends. As well, consider how it relates to your podcast's energy, and whether or not it is something that can be easily recognized and memorized by your audience. A good podcast has consistent music in every podcast. A *great* podcast has music that can be memorized to the point where your audience hums it to themselves or gets it stuck in their head for a little while because it is so catchy. A great example of this is not actually in a podcast but is associated with the fast-food franchise known as *McDonalds.* Even if you don't eat there, you can likely sing the "Ba da ba ba ba, I'm lovin' it" jingle to yourself. Catchy jingles have been used for decades, possibly since the beginning of advertising itself. That is because these are memorable, making it easy for them to get stuck in your head so that you think about them over and over

PODCASTING FOR BEGINNERS: VALUE EDITION

again. Even if the brand is not immediately in front of you, you might catch yourself humming the jingle and thinking about them. Thus, you are more likely to search it out and interact with it once again.

That is exactly what you want to create with your intro and outro music. The last thing you should consider about your music is whether or not you can reasonably talk over it. Podcasts are well known for their briefly descriptive introduction, and that is because this method of introducing the show *works*. You should do it for your podcast, too.

Introducing your podcast through a brief description requires you to quickly summarize your podcast in 2-5 short sentences and record it. Then, you will lay that over the introduction music and play that as your introduction for every single podcast you create. This specific introduction is not introducing the episode of the podcast, but your podcast as a whole. Introducing the specific episode can be accomplished at a later point in the development of your show.

Scripting your introduction should be as simple as saying a brief yet concise and meaningful description of your show for your followers. Since you have already put effort into defining your dream podcast yesterday, fulfilling this task should be simple! You want to quickly answer who you are, what your podcast is about, what they can expect to gain from it, and why it is worth listening to. For example, you might say, "Welcome to the Podcasting Podcast, where we dis cuss practical, actionable steps for new podcasters to achieve their big-time dreams without the confusion, hassle, or stress." This quick introduction describes who you are ("Podcasting Podcast"), what your podcast is about ("podcasting"), what they can expect to gain from it ("practical, actionable steps for new podcasters"), and why it is worth listening to ("to achieve their big-time dreams without the confusion, hassle, or stress.")

Create your introduction by scripting the answers to these four questions. Then, begin looking for ways to write them together, so they flow and create a catchy and interesting introduction. If you find you have a particularly long introduction, see if you can shorten it by getting more concise, eliminating unnecessary descriptions, or even transferring some of the introduction into the podcast episode introduction with a simple one-liner that fills in the details that your podcast introduction misses.

A few great examples of podcast introductions might include:

"Welcome to the Todd and Randy show, where we discuss everything sports related. If you're looking for a splash of entertainment mixed with some cold hard truths, you've come to the right show!"

"Welcome to the Mommy Wine show, where the focus is on wine, babies, and scratch-your-head or pee-your-pants stories of uncensored motherhood experiences."

"You're listening to the Music Podcast, where our number one focus is on the latest tracks and the brilliant minds who laid them out for us. Are you ready to be entertained?" "Ready for an hour of mystery, thrills, and downright spooky fun? Welcome to the spooky story podcast, I'm your host Jennifer, and I'm ready to slay your day."

These introductions are short, concise, and provide quick insight about your show to a new or long-time listener. Essentially, they are the perfect introductions to spark someone's interest and get excited to share time with you!

YOUR PODCAST'S SHAPE AND SIZE

Designing your podcast is not just about designing an intro and outro; it is also about designing the bulk of the podcast itself. At this point, we're not talking about specific individualized episodes. Instead, we are talking about the general formula each episode will follow to ensure that it fits into the greater theme of the podcast you are creating.

The first thing you need to cover when it comes to designing your podcast is to decide what format you are going to follow. Six specific formats that, according to *Voices*, have the greatest impact on your audience. These formats will provide excellent content within each episode, as well as a cohesive flow across your entire channel. The six main formats include nonfiction narrative storytelling, hybrid, interviews or panel discussions, repurposed content, educational, and conversational. Of course, you can also blend these formats together to help you get the exact podcast you desire.

To help you understand these formats a little more, let's discuss what they are and how they work. Nonfiction narrative storytelling is a format where you actually read nonfiction stories to your listeners. These could be stories written in books, or they could be stories you come across or have submitted to you by your audience. This one is more tricky because you have to have an excellent storytelling voice that will allow you to entertain your audience, while also conveying the underlying messages of your stories.

A hybrid podcast is one that has a set podcast host, but that also frequently rotates between guests, guest hosts, and speakers who contribute to the show so that there is plenty of diverse content from a number of different people. The difference between a hybrid and interview or panel discussion is how the show is recorded. In a hybrid, the show is rotated frequently. In an interview or panel, the host(s) always remains the same, but the people being interviewed or questioned will change from episode to episode. One can be more conversational, while the other comes off as a more traditional interview.

An interview or panel discussion format allows you to leverage others' to help you get even more content onto your show. With inter views, you might interview one person or one unified group of people (such as a band or co-owners of a small business or nonprofit group) to answer questions you have curated. For a panel discus sion, you would sit on a panel with others and answer pre-chosen questions ahead of time. In this situation, you would also be answering the questions, not just asking them. These are great for getting many opinions circulating, and for encouraging discussion on important topics.

Repurposed content is a format where you essentially repurpose content you have created for other mediums. For example, if you are already hosting a YouTube channel or a blog, you might use repurposed content as an opportunity to repurpose videos or blog posts. This way, rather than having to come up with brand new content, you can share the excellent content you have already created. Plus, you can start using this as an opportunity to transform your content into a format that is easy to listen on the go, or while your listeners are doing other things.

Educational podcasts are formatted to educate the audience on something over a set period of time. These range from bite-sized or short podcast episodes that provide the audience with a number of facts on a specific topic, to full-sized or longer podcast episodes that discuss certain topics in-depth. The intention is to teach the listener something new through the duration of the show. Some educational podcasts aim to provide interesting or unusual information, while others aim to educate people on something specific such as social justice or farming practices.

Conversational podcasts are formatted to include a conversational experience. The purpose here is essentially to speak into the podcast as though you were sharing a diary entry with your audience. They would then listen along to feel as though they are closer with you, while also getting a snapshot into your life. This is common among people who are developing a personal brand, or who have a life that may be particularly interesting and worth sharing about. For example, if you travel a lot, a traveling diary type podcast may be fun to share.

It is important that you choose a format that not only serves popular content, but that also fulfills your passion. You should feel as though you are genuinely connected to the content you are creating, as you want to develop a show that you will look forward to making for years to come. The more you enjoy your show, the easier it will be to make a show that everyone else enjoys, too.

AFTER YOU HAVE CHOSEN THE FORMAT FOR YOUR PODCAST, YOU need to decide what the actual podcast episodes are going to look like. This means you need to decide on the length of each podcast episode, what you want to offer through that episode, and how you are going to make the episode worth listening to while also making your show worth returning for.

Deciding on the length of your podcast episodes may be tricky, as you may not feel entirely confident in what is likely to work for you. It can be easy to get caught up in defining the exact number of minutes, but the reality is that the minutes themselves are not what truly matters. What matters is what you are offering in those minutes, and whether or not they are worth listening to. If you have a show that is 60 minutes long, but the content of each episode could have been offered in as little as 20 minutes, meaning the rest of your show is really just unimportant and unexciting filler, you have a terrible podcast episode. If, however, you have a show that is 60 minutes long and full of engaging, inspiring, and exciting content that people are genuinely enjoying tuning into and that they want to keep tuning into, you have a show that is worth listening to.

One rule of thumb when it comes to podcasting is if you have a show that is going on for longer than 30 minutes, you should have at least one, if not two entertainment segments that help break up the show. Serious or deep topics that are discussed for more than 30 minutes can be dense and heavy to follow. Your audience may have a hard time consuming all of your information because you are providing it so rapidly that they start to lose focus. Breaking your show up with a small break where your audience is given a chance to mentally absorb everything you have said ensures that when you start talking again, they are more focused and actually gain immense value from your show.

Your entertainment segment could be a quiz, interesting facts, a listener engagement game, a shout out to loyal fans who have been following you for any period of time, a story submitted by a listener, a story or anecdote you heard at some point that week, or anything else. As long as you have something enjoyable that your audience looks forward to listening to, you have a great segment to help break up your show, keep it fun and interesting to listen to and keep your listeners engaged for longer.

Segments are actually an incredibly powerful tool to leverage when it comes to providing audio content on a medium such as podcasting. With segments, you can offer plenty of high-value content in a single podcast, over specific periods of time on your show. A great example of how you could segment your show is as follows. The first ten minutes could be spent discussing current events, the next ten minutes could be about actionable steps your audience can take, and the third ten minute segment could be about inspiring your listeners. You could also include a small segment that encourages your audience to engage with you. By breaking your show up into segments, people know what to expect, they look forward to each segment, and you are able to more clearly organize your show script and experience.

OUTPUT FREQUENCY

The last thing you need to focus on when it comes to developing your podcast is to decide how frequently you are going to upload new podcast shows. Most podcasts upload at least once per week, though others upload as often as daily or as little as once per month.

Decide on your frequency by considering your audience, your topic, and the length of each episode. If you will be uploading 15 minute episodes and you know your audience can easily digest that on a day to day basis, you might want to upload new shows daily. If, however, you will be uploading 30 minutes to hour long episodes, or longer, you will want to reduce your output frequency. Uploading fewer longer episodes means that your audience has more time to get through each episode before you upload a new one. It is also more realistic for you to create this content and sustain your output frequency.

It is important to note that despite the fact that monthly podcasts exist, they are not an ideal way to go. Monthly podcasts often have to be rather lengthy to create enough content to make up for having to wait an entire month between episodes, plus they happen so infrequently that people tend to forget about you. As well, just because you are posting monthly does not mean you can get away with a 3-4 hour episode. It would be better to break that up and deliver it weekly, rather than deliver something incredibly long once per month.

You can also determine your frequency by considering the type of content you are creating. How frequently are people interested in consuming your specific type of content? Do they want to consume it multiple times a week, once a week, or once every other week or every few weeks? The answer to these questions largely depends on what type of content you are creating. For example, if you are hosting a podcast that reviews new music, you may want to host it just once or twice per week so that you have time to listen to new music and produce thoughtful feedback on the music you have listened to. If you were hosting a podcast about the latest tech updates, though, you might want to share shorter daily episodes. This is because every day, new tech developments are being announced, and you do not want to fall behind on these trends and lose your audience to someone who is more up to date and quick about sharing.

After you have considered the average length you want your episodes to be and how frequently you will be uploading, you want to compare it to the following chart to see if you are within the right ballpark for your preferences and your audience's preferences.

The following chart compares the length of the episode to output frequency to give you an idea of what works best, and what is most realistic for you to create on an ongoing basis:

- Semi-daily episode (two per day): 1-5 minutes per episode. Daily episodes: 1-15 minutes per episode, up to 30 minutes. Weekly episodes: 15-60 minutes per episode, up to 90 minutes.

- Bi-weekly episodes: 60 minutes per episode, up to 90 minutes.
- Monthly episodes: 60-90 minutes per episode, no more.

If your chosen length and frequency are not matched up in the above chart, I highly recommend you adjust either your length or output frequency. It may seem intimidating or unmanageable right now, but you will find that with the right length and frequency, you will be able to offer plenty of high value content to your audience and frequently enough to stay relevant. If you look at this chart and feel like you have absolutely no idea what you would say or where you would begin, fear not! Starting tomorrow, we will be digging in on ways that you can maximize the quality of your show so that you have plenty of high-quality content to share, and your listeners are captivated by everything you have to say.

One last thing I must point out that it will save your sanity as a beginner is the power of batching content. Podcasters batch content as a way to streamline their time spent on each stage of producing a podcast, which results in a much less stressful podcasting experience. To batch your content, you will first determine how much time you can consecutively spend in the studio recording your podcast. Then, you will figure out how many episodes you can reasonably create in that timeframe. For example, if you have 8 hours in the studio and you are creating 15 minute daily episodes, you could reason ably create around 25 episodes in a single session. While you could technically get as many as 32, you would want to factor in time for rest, eating, bathroom breaks, and do-overs in case you make mis takes (and you will.)

During those 8 hours, you would then record all 25 podcast episodes. Next, you would edit all 25 podcast episodes at the same time. Then, you would upload them into your production suite and schedule them for their launch dates. By doing this, you streamline the process, have plenty of content made in advance, and don't have to go back and forth between recording, editing, and publishing all of your content. In the above scenario, you would only need to record for 1 day every 14 days to create enough content for a daily show.

UNDERSTANDING AND IMPLEMENTING THE CATALYSTS FOR AN IMMERSIVE SHOW

THE DESIGN OF YOUR SHOW SHOULD BE YOUR FIRST FOCUS. ONCE you have that down, you need to be focused on creating high-quality episodes. Your episodes need to be captivating and inspiring so your audience enjoys them and comes back for more each time you release a new one. If you are new to using the power of your voice and spoken content to create engaging content, it may seem strange to rely on your voice and your content to create strong relationships with your audience, while inspiring them to come back for more. Fortunately, it is much easier than you might think, and if you let yourself relax and rely on high-quality catalysts for an immersive show, you can actually have a lot of fun with this entire experience.

I find with new podcasters that their fear and tendency to hold back their voice and minimize the quality of their expression comes from not entirely understanding what gets your audience excited, or what makes them want to listen. You might also feel silly when you realize that the more expressive you are, the better, which can sometimes be the opposite of how you communicate in your day to day life. When you learn exactly what your audience needs to hear, and how they like to hear it, your audience becomes insatiable because the quality of your show explodes. This is the best way to grab the attention of your audience and keep it.

An excellent way to quickly get over the fear of sounding silly, or the discomfort that leads to you keeping your voice small, is to truly talk about something you are passionate about. Never underestimate the power of your own passion. When you are passionate about what you are talking about, you will have a hard time *not* showcasing that passion in your voice. As a result, all that expression and energy will come naturally, and you will not have to work so hard to make it happen. Plus, you will carry natural confidence with you. All of this will translate into an incredible show that people are thrilled to tune into for each new episode.

The four catalysts to developing an immersive show that will capture your listeners and bring new listeners to your show with each new episode include: using the power of your voice, writing a compelling script, building parasocial relationships, and adding explosive flavor to your podcast. The more you can incorporate these elements into your podcast, and do so with excellency, the more each episode will take off and help you truly launch into the glory podcast success.

WRITE COMPELLING SCRIPTS

Writing scripts for your podcast is the secret sauce for making each episode as stress-free as possible. If you have already planned out what you are going to say and how you are going to say it ahead of time, there is no reason to feel pressured to figure it out on recording day. This way, on recording day, you can focus more on the power of your voice and keeping things running smoothly.

How you script your show will depend on what type of show it is. Some shows do better with a small script that keeps the host organized and focused, while other shows may be scripted all the way through to ensure the podcast is perfect from start to finish. Generally speaking, podcasts with more conversational tones or ones that are run by people who are highly confident in their recording skills are done with minimal scripting. The scripting is solely to keep the host on topic and to prevent them from spending too much time talking on any given subject. On the other hand, if you are new to podcasting or if you are talking about something that is particular, or that may require you to remember very specific information, scripting is a powerful way to help yourself along. With a proper script, you can keep yourself from having to think through what you are going to say, and instead focus solely on your delivery.

Writing your script in advance also helps reduce the amount of time you spend in the studio, as it allows you to focus solely on recording, rather than on creating content and recording it at the same time. In order to achieve this, though, and leverage the power of a script, you must write the perfect script. A proper script should follow a specific formula that allows you to cover all of the necessary content for your show, and that provides you with the ability to keep the show engaging and captivating. With the right formula, you also seamlessly flow from one point to the next, generating a cohesive and enjoyable podcast.

The general formula you should follow, per *Castos* "Podcast Script 101" is as follows:

Sponsor Message

Introduction

Musical jingle/sound effects

Longer explanation of what is in store

<u>**Topic 1**</u>
Main point
Supporting point

30

Supporting data
Supporting quote

Segue

<u>**Topic 2**</u>
Main point
Supporting point
Supporting data
Supporting quote

Sponsor message

<u>**Topic 3**</u>
Main point
Supporting point
Supporting data
Supporting quote

Segue

Outro

Call to action

Sponsor message

Musical jingle/sound effects

AS YOU WRITE YOUR SCRIPT, IT IS IMPORTANT TO KEEP IT conversational and to write it in a way that supports your delivery. Creating a conversational script ensures that your script does not come across as being too stiff or stuffy, and prevents you from developing a monotonous sound that causes people to immediately tune out. Another benefit of creating a conversational script is that it allows *you* to feel more relaxed in your delivery, and it creates more room for you to truly share your passions with your audience. Creating notes to support your delivery makes it even easier to liven up your voice and deliver a great show. This ensures you follow the proper pauses, emphasis, laughs, sighs, and other dramatic effects to brighten up your energy and make your show more enjoyable to listen to.

Even if you are brand new, you should still leave space in your script for you to go off on improvised tangents. Being able to chat on what ever comes naturally in that moment is a great way to keep the podcast more authentic and present to the moment that you are recording. Plus, this can make the recording process far more enjoyable. Remember to keep your tangents on topic so they are relevant, and don't forget that you can always edit them out at a later date if you do not particularly like them.

As you record your podcast, be mindful of descriptions and pace. Descriptions allow you to bring the listener into your experience by actually describing the experience to them in a way that draws them in. For example, if you talk about your recent trip to the grocery store, describe what grocery store you go to or offer a few descriptors to help your listener picture the scene in your mind. Don't be too extensive or in-depth, just say enough to give your audience a clear vision in their mind. As you do all of this, maintain a reason able pace, so you do not rush through the episode, or put listeners to sleep by going too slow. Speak using a conversational pace that allows you to get information across in reasonable timing, without rushing through so people miss everything you said.

FINALLY, BE YOURSELF. THERE IS NOTHING WORSE THAN listening to a podcast, or consuming any content really, and realizing that the person is behaving as a pre-canned persona, rather than their real self. If you find yourself trying to live into a personality that does not fit you, or trying to make your personality seem more "likable," you are likely trying way too hard. While you do want to encourage yourself to have a charming and captivating persona, there is no reason to try to force yourself to be anyone other than who you are. Trust that your personality is plenty and that people will love listening to you as you are!

When your script is well-designed, it showcases your personality with excellency, and this ensures that your listeners fall in love with your content because they develop a relationship with the personality of the person sharing it... in other words, you! Being yourself and showing up in a positive impactful way is the ultimate key to gaining true fans that are willing to subscribe to your show and listen on a regular basis.

USE YOUR POWERFUL VOICE

Your voice is what people are listening to. Even if they are listening for the content you are sharing; they have to receive that content through your voice. Do everything in your power to ensure you are exciting to listen to while matching the tone that best reflects your podcast's topic. You can do this by energizing yourself, smiling while you are talking, annunciating your words, and expressing yourself with great enthusiasm. Of course, be sure you do so in a way that is entirely respectful of the content you are producing. While this upbeat energy is excellent for most shows, it may not be appropriate to a show where you talk about tragedies, mysteries, or anything that might require a more serious or questioning tone. For example, if you talk about unsolved or unusual crime mysteries, you do not want to sound upbeat and cheery because that will sound completely out of place for the content. Instead, you want to sound serious, questioning, and concerned. Adjust your tone to match the content you are producing, as this allows for a much more immersive show where you've instantly captivated your listeners, delivering a podcast experience that they'll be excited to come back to. This helps your listeners to develop a deeper level of attraction to your show because of how interesting your tone makes it.

Podcast creators will often use an incredibly animated voice in their intro or outro and then will use a more muted animated voice for the bulk of their content. This is because a more animated intro immediately captures the attention of your audience and gets them curious about what you have to say. The energy you pour into your intro also transfers into your audience, getting them excited for your show and building their own energy. In this sense, it is like developing an infectious energy that your audience can't help but feel themselves. In doing so, you not only excite them for each episode but have them looking forward to listening again because they look forward to a pick-me-up during their day.

For the bulk of your episode, you do not need to speak with quite such an animated tone, but you still need to speak with energy and enthusiasm. In doing so, you continue to develop that infectious energy and support people in feeling positive while listening to you, while also encouraging them to want to listen in again for that very same reason.

Encouraging your audience to match your energy and develop excitement around your shows is not the only benefit you gain from sharing your content with enthusiasm, either. In doing so, you also create a positive association between yourself and your audience, which leads to you being able to begin to feel as though they are developing a positive relationship with you.

This relationship, called a parasocial relationship, is the foundation for massive success in your role as a media producer.

BUILD PARASOCIAL RELATIONSHIPS

As I mentioned previously, parasocial relationships are relationships that are largely one-sided, and they describe the relationships that audiences share with media figures. When you develop a podcast, whether you like it or not, you are going to be engaging in a parasocial relationship with your audience. This can be uncomfortable and even weird to get used to at first, especially if you value equal and fair treatment in relationships, as you may feel like your audience deserves more from you. The problem with this is that you cannot reasonably offer your 1:1 attention to every single person in your audience, and pressuring yourself to *have* to is a terrible idea. What will end up happening is you burn yourself out in an effort to try to maintain 1:1 relationships with your growing audience, which is never sustainable.

Rather than feeling guilty or burning yourself out, reframe parasocial relationships and understand your role within the one you share with your audience. Understanding this role will allow you to show that you value and are grateful for your audience in a way that feels meaningful for them, without draining yourself or placing unreasonable expectations on yourself.

The first way to build your parasocial relationship is to develop a persona. Your persona is a fictional representation of who you are, and the purpose of it is to create an entire "person" for people to relate with, while still giving yourself room to respect your personal privacy and life. Personas are essential in successful brands because they allow you to drive your design decisions, develop your brand, and grow your audiences without creating unhealthy demands on your personal character.

Your persona includes:

- Your host name
- Your title and major responsibilities
- A quote that defines you
- Your demographics (age, education, ethnicity, family status, etc.)
- Your goals and tasks you want to accomplish
- Your pain points or frustrations
- Your technical experience and background
- Your working environment
- Photographs of you that portray your persona
- The things you find funny, and the things you dislike Your favourite food, colour, and season
- The way you spend your time when you are not recording

As you develop your persona, I strongly encourage you to think about a persona that genuinely reflects who you are, and that can easily be promoted to your audience. Again, it all comes back to passion. You need to feel truly passionate about the persona you are creating, and you need to feel the ability to genuinely connect to your persona so you can feel deeply connected to the brand you are creating. This is key. People with personas who explode in popularity while also loving every aspect of what they do are people who have created their persona to accurately reflect who they are. This make it easier for people to believe in the persona and enjoy being around that person.

Once you have developed your persona, you need to learn how to leverage your persona and your interaction measures to create and nurture your parasocial relationships. You can do this by first understanding your role in the parasocial relationship. Your role is to be yourself, or your persona, and portray yourself in a way that allows your followers to feel personally connected with you, as they would with a friend. However, you are not giving them direct, one-on-one attention. Instead, you are offering certain aspects that allow them to know you are aware of their presence and you respect and value them, while also respecting and valuing the fact that a media persona cannot reasonably keep up with that many 1:1 relationships. It would not be healthy nor feasible.

Your role is to show up, create engaging content that people love, and continue to do so over and over again. As a result, people consume your content and "live with" you as a part of their daily lives, which creates a sense of personal connection between them and you. The bond of intimacy that is created through these relationships is an illusion, but it is a good illusion. That is, assuming that you are using it for positive purposes. As people develop this sense of connection with you, you have the power to motivate, inspire, entertain, and support them in many different ways. While it may not be 1:1, there are still plenty of valuable ways you can support people.

In order to leverage parasocial relationships to develop a powerful connection with your audience, you need to accomplish one thing over five different steps. That is, you need to accomplish the illusion of having a face-to-face experience with your audience. That is exactly why descriptive podcasts, expressive voices, and corresponding social media presences are so important. They all help build your perceived face-to-face interaction with your audience.

The first way to build your face-to-face experience is to speak directly to your audience. Use words like "you" and "us," as these words inspire a sense of belonging within your audience and encourage them to feel like they are a part of your world.

The second way to build your face-to-face experience is to share real stories. Your real stories create a sense of connection between your audience and yourself because they offer your audience the ability to resonate with you and feel a sense of emotional connection to your experience. Tell your audience's stories, too. Especially when your audience submits their own stories to you, share them, as this deepens the dynamic between you and your audience and creates an even more relatable experience for other listeners.

The third way to build your face-to-face experience is to mingle with your audience. Comment back, hang out where your audience hangs out, and become a part of the group as much as you possibly can. Even if you are not able to personally connect with everyone in these engagements, connect with as many people as you can. This way, you are a part of them, and not shouting at them from a distance. A great way to hang out where your audience hangs out, aside from offline locations, is to get into online communities where there is an active audience 24/7. Facebook groups are a great example of these audiences, as they allow you to hop on and start building relation ships with people in those groups. Make sure you engage in these groups in a way that encourages genuine engagement, and that allows you to have real, down-to-earth conversations with the members. Do not just drop a link and run, but actually participate and become a valued member of the group, as this is how you will actually capture the attention of your audience and have them interested in listening to your new podcast episodes. Now, they feel connected to you, and they want to listen to you and everything you have to say.

The fourth way to build your face-to-face experience is to create an idealized version of what your audience wants. Your audience wants something very specific in life, and you have the ability to mirror back to them that experience. For example, Liberace mirrors back the gentle and understanding husband that the audience doesn't have, or Nancy Berg shows off the idea of being the perfect housewife. You essentially want to create an image within your own life of what your audience wishes they had, and then you want to market that to them. Then, they live vicariously through you.

The fifth way to build your face-to-face experience is to become a part of everyday life. That is precisely what you are going to do with your podcast, by creating content that they can listen to while they go about their daily experiences. You will also do that by creating a social media presence that corresponds with your podcast and has people following you across multiple platforms. And, of course, you can do this by attaching your persona to a specific symbol or correlation so that whenever your audience sees that correlation, they think of you. For example, the Kardashians are heavily associated with magazines, so anytime you see magazines or similar tabloids, you will likely think about the Kardashians and wonder what they are doing. Or, at the very least, you will think about them.

Finally, I strongly encourage you to put your own spin on all of this. Do not think about it too hard, and do not make it too much of a professional choice. If you treat your persona and parasocial relationships like a business, it is going to feel extremely false for both yourself and your audience. You need to pour your passion into this and show up authentically so that it feels true to who you are and how you genuinely want to show up, as this will allow you to nurture these relationships in a meaningful way that feels good. That energy will inevitably translate into your audience and result in a back-and forth relationship that is exhilarating to uphold, and that supports you with creating everything you desire in your business, without making it feel too professional. Remember, the entire goal is to have fun! The finances are just a benefit of you having the most fun you can possibly have.

If you can create that face-to-face illusion through these five methods, you will create a persona that people immediately connect with and that they want to continue to connect with because it feels special and positive. They will relate with you, resonate with what you have to say, and genuinely begin to care about you and everything you are doing because it allows them to feel connected to someone they care about. In their eyes, they see you similar to how they would see a friend, and they care about you just the same. In your eyes, you respect and value them because they are the very reason you have the position of success you have, since your audience is what gives you the attention you need to grow your brand to successful lengths. Make sure you consider this and include it in both your show script and in your social media presence when it comes to developing your platforms and advertising your podcast to your audience.

LEVERAGE EXPLOSIVE FLAVOR

The one thing every successful persona is phenomenal at that others aren't taking advantage of is explosive flavor. Strong personas have a powerful capacity to infuse serious energy into everything they do, even if it is just talking into a microphone. For a podcast, that means conveying your aura through your voice, your content, and your approach. Believe me, when I say, this one thing matters *a lot* when it comes to generating success. In fact, I can virtually guarantee that you will not be successful if you do not add explosive flavor to your podcast from day one.

Your jaw-dropping personality is what turns someone into a viral sensation overnight. This is how brand new podcasters turn their shows into the most-listened podcasts in record timing, and it is how you can get yourself toward all your goals as fast as possible.

Developing an explosive flavor for your show may seem intimidating, especially if you think you have to copy someone else's flavor or do things that seem wildly unrealistic for your personality. Fortunately, that is *not* how the creation of your own signature energy and persona works. Creating the "pop" for your own personality is achieved by taking the most likable parts of your personality and turning them all the way up. If you tend to be a funny person, turn the dial up. If you are charismatic, turn the dial up. If you are charming, expressive, honest, excellent at explaining things, passionate, curious, great at asking questions, inspiring, or anything else, *turn the dial up.* Be who you are, in a loud and bold manner, and use this as your unique flavor for your explosive content.

Aside from becoming a louder version of your already awesome self, there are other practical ways you can turn the flavor up on your podcast, too. These proven methods will have your show growing rapidly and your goals being achieved with record timing.

Firstly, get incredibly clear on your persona and play into that character to the best of your ability. Always go beyond your comfort zone, and expand who your persona is so that you develop an infectious and attention-grabbing personality that captures listeners' interest. You could also find yourself a co-host that you get along with, and who you share great chemistry with, that you can create your show with. Getting two flavorful personalities together is a great way to liven up your show even more. Plus, you will likely find that you start expanding off of each other's energy and blowing your flavor up to incredible proportions. This will make you both extremely fun to listen to.

One podcaster actually exploded his viewership on his hip hop show by having a 3 minute segment where he would freestyle rap for his audience. To create his rap, he would use comments his audience had left on his content from the previous week and turn it into a freestyle rap in that moment. This was an incredibly engaging experience that highlighted his viewers, made them feel as though they were a part of the experience, and that expanded his viewership because it was such a fun, interactive experience for the audience. While many may have come to the show to listen to his raps, the reality is that they were also growing fond of the show itself, and therefore they became devoted listeners, and it all started with a fun experience with explosive flavor.

Another great way to explode your flavor is to create a listener's spotlight. A listener's spotlight is a spot where you can promote your listener's work. This can be accomplished during the end of an episode as an opportunity to showcase your listeners and their talent, while also showing your appreciation for them. By doing this, you create a sense of back-and-forth interaction with your audience, too, in a way where you are able to give back to them. As a result, they see that there is a positive and valuable relationship being built between your listeners and you, and they are more likely to remain committed to your show, and to you.

Listener's spotlights are not the only way to create engagement, either. You can create engagement through many different methods. The more you create engagement between your listeners and your show, the better, because the more they actively listen to your show and participate in a parasocial relationship with you. One simple way to get more engagement is to ask people questions and then report their responses in your shows. For example, if you have a thriving Instagram presence where you promote your podcast, you might ask questions on Instagram and then share that question and the answers you received on your podcast. This is a great way to give your listeners a voice and allow them to partake in the development of your show.

Another great way to create engagement with your podcast would be to invite listeners to verbally share stories with you. This would work similarly to radios having callers call in and share stories, except you would have your callers send you an audio file of their story, and then you would edit it into the show. While this may seem more advanced, if you have an engaged audience and they fall with in a demographic that is fluent with technology, this can be a great way to amplify your engagement and create a fun, interactive segment of your show. If you want to go even further with this, you could invite listeners to apply to share their opinion on the show; then you could record part of the show over a platform such as zoom, or have the listener come to your recording studio if possible, and include them on your show that way. This offers your audience unique perspectives and gives your listeners a chance to chime in. At first, you will not have a large enough audience to share from or spotlight, so you will not be able to do this. A great alternative is to discuss interesting stories or highlights of general people that relate to your niche. Simply tell the stories of people you heard about on line or through friends, and use the same "spotlight" approach. This way, as your audience grows, you can start swapping out these general stories for stories directly out of your audience, which will make for a smooth shift that grows your audience and increases viewer loyalty.

EVERY SINGLE EPISODE SHOULD HAVE SOMETHING SIMILAR TO ALL of your other episodes. Not just your intro and outro, but a segment of the show that is the exact same on every single episode. This could be a freestyle rap, a funny limerick, interesting facts, or anything else that entertains your audience and relates to your show. Try to make this segment short enough that it can be saved as an audio clip and use it to promote your show on other social media platforms. This way, your audience, and new listeners can all get a tiny sample of the new episode before it comes out, effectively building their interest and getting them excited to hear more. This is a great practice from the get go; although you might not have many listeners, getting into the habit of this off the bat will help you in the long run. In addition, you're stocked up on content that you can use for promo and now have great content for listeners who might decide to binge your content.

THE COMPLETE AND CONCISE GUIDE TO THE TECHNOLOGICAL SIDE OF PODCASTING

THE PREPARATION IS COMPLETE, AND NOW IT IS TIME TO GET into actual podcasting. This is the part where most people believe you are supposed to start, but as you now know, it is actually something that comes a little later on. Before you can get to the actual process of setting up your equipment and software and getting your podcast recorded, you need to have the right vision, fuel, plan, and show design to get you going. With all that done now, you can focus on more technical things, such as setting up your studio and preparing yourself to actually record the podcast!

If you do not come from a rich tech background, or if your background does not include audio recording, you might feel totally confused when you start looking into all of the equipment and software that is required for you to run a podcast. With so many different pieces of equipment, types of software, and steps to be completed, it makes sense that you might get confused. I want to make sure it is incredibly simple for you to understand, and that you are able to get started with equipment that will make your show pop from the start. We can do that by covering the recording studio setup, the editing and producing setup, and the setup for getting your podcast published.

RECORDING

Before you begin investing in any equipment, I want to make it very clear that your focus should be on buying the highest quality equipment that is within your budget. Do not purchase the cheapest equipment you can find and wait until your podcast takes off before investing in better stuff. That is a terrible approach, as it results in you investing in low-quality equipment and then growing frustrated with trying to make that equipment work. Alternatively, do not stress your budget out and buy equipment that is far beyond what you would ever actually need for your podcast. Overspending is equally as bad, as it leads to you finding yourself out a lot of money in exchange for something that you could have accomplished for much less. Find a happy medium by creating a reasonable budget and affording the best quality equipment within your budget.

The equipment you will need includes: a microphone, head-phones, and a quiet place for you to record your content.

Never rely on the microphone built-in to your computer, cell-phone, or headphones. These microphones will not give you clear audio that is free of interference, and it will not convert well onto higher quality speakers. A great microphone for any starter, which will serve professional-level sound quality at an affordable price, is a Blue Yeti USB Mic. It plugs directly into your computer, and is a condenser microphone as opposed to the standard dynamic type. Another great condenser mic to look into would be the Rode NT1A or NT2A, both of which are excellent for recording with. However, to use non USB condensers like such, you would need a mixer or audio inter-face to connect these devices to your computer, which can make this route more expensive.

It is not recommended that you get a dynamic microphone, as they are just simply not as suited to podcasting as a condenser - the reason being, to put it simply, that condenser micro-phones are more sensitive in picking up sounds, so they are better quality for recording things that either aren't too loud or have more intricate sounds through a variety of frequencies - both of which apply to the human voice. Since the listening experience is the entire purpose of a podcast show, it is impor-tant that you focus on buying an excellent quality mic to create that high quality listening experience right from the start. The investment will be well-worth it in the long run.

Regardless of what type of microphone you invest in, it is important that you get a pop shield. Pop shields go over your microphone or sit in front of your mic and prevent it from picking up the plosives on p's and b's, which both give sudden bursts of high pressure into the mic as you are speaking. The pop shield is incredibly inexpensive and will improve your sound quality exponentially. If you can not purchase one, consider making one by taking a wire coat hanger and pulling it apart, so it creates an "O" shape, then covering it with nylons. You can then set that about an inch or two in front of your mic, keeping it close enough that it works, but far enough away that it does not touch your mic and destroy your sound quality.

When you are recording, headphones are important as they will allow you to clearly hear your recordings and create higher quality recordings right away. It is important to get over the ear headphones, and not just earphones, as these will give the best surround sound and will allow you to immediately pick up on any sound errors or strange background noises that may be interrupting your recording. A pair of Audio-Technica ATH-M30X would be great, as they are inexpensive and provide excellent sound quality. Another benefit of over-the-ear sound blocking headphones is that you can wear them while you are recording, which allows you to drown out any background noises. The less you hear yourself, and the more you can focus on recording, the better quality your show will be. Not wearing your headphones and listening to yourself can become very distracting and may cause you to become self-conscious, minimize your expressions, or otherwise reduce your overall recording quality due to distractions or excessive self-analyzing. Leave that part for later when you are editing.

The final element of recording is to have a proper recording space. Your recording space should be sound-proof, relatively small, so your voice does not echo, and where you will not be interrupted. If you have to record at home, consider using a walk-in closet, or even a smaller room in your home such as a smaller home office or a bed room. If external noise is a concern, consider lining the walls with egg cartons or cardboard, or surrounding yourself with heavy-duty curtains to keep external noises out. If you do not have access to that, consider going to the middle of a field in a large park where you are unlikely to be interrupted by people or traffic and record there, on a day when there is no wind.

Once everything is set up and ready to record, you will only require one piece of software to get you recording. That is, a piece of software that allows you to record and store your audio locally to your device. Skype is an excellent tool, as you can record yourself talking and store it, or you can record a conversation with a guest you may have on your show and store that. I recommend Skype for this because it is inexpensive, works in the most straightforward manner, and allows you to store your sound locally. If you want something a little more advanced, try Ringr, which is anywhere between $8-19/month and offers excellent recording abilities, too. I like

Ringr because it is made specifically for podcasters, which means you get high-quality sound, a straightforward platform, and excellent storage options so you can store any audio you record over the platform. Your guests can download Ringr, too, which allows them to call in to your Ringr account and gain access to all of the same great benefits, meaning it is also wonderfully easy for your guests to take advantage of, too.

It is important to keep things as simple as possible, especially early on, as you will already have a lot of things that are fairly new to you at this point, and complicating any step of the process will only make your podcast a challenge. Instead, keep it simple, focus on producing high-quality content with what you have, and worry about advancing different parts of the process later on.

THE EDITING AND PRODUCTION SETUP

Your editing and production setup relies more on software, which is used to improve your sound quality, add in your intro and outro, and edit out any parts which you do not want to be presented on your episode. If you have an Apple computer, you will already have Garageband installed. This is an excellent platform for editing audio on. If you are using a PC, look into Adobe Audition, Audacity, or Reaper. These are all free platforms you can use to edit audio that will provide you with excellent tools at no expense. If you want something more advanced, Logic Pro is a great platform that offers semi-professional features, though it will require an investment on your behalf since it costs around $250 in the United States. For either Mac or Windows I would also recommend Avid Protools, which is the industry standard for Music and Film Production is the most powerful software available and ranges from £250 all the way up to £2500.

While editing your podcast can help you polish it up, it is important to understand that you should not be aiming to spend hours in the editing process. Instead, you should be investing in high-quality equipment so that your recordings are already high quality from the start. The editing process should be a quick, simple process where you polish the sound, add your intro and outro, include any sound effects that you may want to use, and cut out any clips of audio that you do not want in the final rendering of your episode.

You can simplify your editing process by following these exact steps:

1. Apply a fade to the beginning and end of any audio clips in your project, as this provides a smoother transition from clip to clip. If you have just one audio file, you will only need to do it at the beginning and end. If you have clipped out parts or placed multiple files together, though, you will need to apply fades to the beginning and end of every single file. If you add

sound effects, you will add fades to the beginning and ending of those, too.

2. Render your audio through a high-pass filter. High pass filters eliminate unwanted low frequencies from your audio so that it does not have a "muddy" or "boomy" sound to it. All high frequencies will pass through the filter, but everything else will be eliminated, giving you a much higher quality finished sound piece. Set your filter between 80-100 Hz, as this ensures nothing lower gets through. The human range is 20 to 20,000 Hz, and the average human voice range is 85 to 180 Hz for a male or 165 – 255 Hz for a female. Setting your filter around 80-100 or even a little higher if you are a female ensures that nothing aside from your voice gets through to the final rendering of your audio.

3. Compress your audio file so that you do not have such a dynamic range of audio in your final rendering. Compressing your file ensures that no matter what type of speaker your audience is listening through, they can hear you properly. Not doing this can result in certain parts of your audio being cut off or difficult for your listener to hear, depending on what type of speaker they are listening on.

4. Export your audio using the bounce feature so that your final audio file is stored locally to your computer and able to be uploaded to your website, social media,

or any platform where you might be hosting your podcast.

I must repeat one more time that it is essential that you get a high quality recording first, then edit your already-high-quality file. You cannot edit quality into a podcast recording; you can only improve existing quality. Attempting to perfect a low-quality piece of audio will result in you still having a low-quality piece of audio in the end, even if you have begun to see some improvements with your audio.

It is also important to take some time to get acquainted with your editing software so that you are able to use it effectively with your sound files. These days, most software is quite intuitive, meaning they are capable of providing high-quality sound with little effort. As well, the interfaces are extremely user-friendly and can help you develop excellent sound without all of the confusion or a need for extensive technical experience. If you do find yourself struggling, YouTube offers great videos on how to use most software so that you can figure out how to work your software properly and achieve excellent results.

GETTING YOUR PODCAST PUBLISHED

The last setup you need to know about is the part where you get yourself published. You can either publish yourself to social media, to your website, or to a platform that airs podcasts on platforms such as Apple's Podcast app.

YouTube can be an excellent spot to upload your podcast, as it supports audio and is able to be embedded on most other platforms. Since this is a video-based platform, you will want to either record video at the same time or create some sort of visual for your audience to look at. While YouTube is a great starting platform, I do recommend moving to a better audio platform as soon as possible so you can host your podcast on platforms like Apple Podcasts, Spotify, iHeartRadio, or TuneIn.

If you want to upload your Podcast to your website, turn it into an MP3 or WAV file and upload it directly to your self-hosted website. Many podcasters will do this by creating a blog page and then up loading files into individual blog posts with a short description of what that day's episode was about and what they can expect to find. This is also an excellent option if you plan on marketing products for sponsors in your videos because you can share links to those products in the blog post so listeners can easily grab those links at the end of the show.

SoundCloud, Blubrry, BuzzSprout, Anchor, and Podbean are also great platforms that you can share your podcast on. These platforms will allow you to share directly on an audio based site, and you can direct your listeners over to your profile on that platform so they can find and listen to you. If you want to get your podcast on iTunes, Spotify, or any other similar provider, you will need to create an account with that provider, submit your podcast for approval, and then wait for it to happen. Once it is approved, it will go live, and you will have your show hosted natively within these apps. Doing this is worthwhile if you want your podcast to be easily accessible, as these larger platforms are already massively popular among the podcast listening community, which means that they will be far more likely to find you and listen to your content.

THE 4TH DIMENSION: GUESTS, RESEARCH, AND ESSENTIAL INTERVIEW SKILLS

THE 4TH DIMENSION OF HOSTING YOUR PODCAST INCLUDES having guests on your show, or bringing others into the creation process. Many beginners will skip over the 4th dimension, as they want to create their shows for themselves, which is perfectly fine. You can absolutely run a show entirely solo and have an excellent turnout. However, adding guests from time to time, or even on a regular basis, can help your show experience rapid growth, while also providing even more value to your listeners. Plus, hosting guests can be incredibly fun as you get to engage in real, back-and forth discussion with others who are passionate about the same topics as you are, and then hear the feedback from your audience as they listen to the episode.

To create a high quality 4th dimension for your show, you need to expand your ability to research and interview others so you can create a high quality episode with your guest. Knowing how to ask the right questions, drive the show in a positive direction, and create a clear outcome for your audience is an important part of bringing guests onto your show.

Even if you are 100% new to hosting any form of online content, you can be an incredible host and interviewer right from the start. All it takes is some knowledge, practice, and a willingness to do your best from the start.

ATTRACTING AND HOSTING GUESTS ON YOUR SHOW

Step one: delete the idea that beginners cannot attract and host guests on their show right now. Just because you have a brand new show or a show that has not even been released yet, does not mean that people are not interested in being guests on your show. Although you may be doubting yourself or feeling inferior based on your lack of completed episodes to serve as proof, *many* people are going to understand your vision, believe in you, and get excited about collaborating with you. Even if no one knows who you are, this will be true. The key is to get yourself into groups where people want to have a chance to speak about what they are passionate about, and who are speaking about content that is relevant to your podcast, and then put the offer out there. *They. Will. Come.* You can be confident in that.

The more you host guests and provide excellent shows, the more guests will come around, and the more opportunities you will have to host more guests. I strongly advise that even if you intend on hosting a solo show, you create a segment or special episodes devoted to hosting guests. Guests offer an exciting, new, and unique perspective for your audience, and if they have their own audience they may bring even more viewers to your show. While they may come for the episode that your guest is in, they will stay when they realize how enjoyable your show is.

Your guest can be anyone from a friend to someone in your industry who can offer content for your audience. Early on, you may feel more comfortable interviewing friends or people that you already know as this helps you feel more confident talking with them, which can create a more enjoyable show to listen to. Even if you do not have any friends to host, though, you can still create excellent chemistry with any guest by being willing to talk to them like they are a friend. You can also develop that chemistry by researching your guests before the interview, which we will talk about in a moment.

Once you have a show on the go, you can also intentionally market your desire to host guests on your show. Include a quick blurb at the end of your show, write about it on social media platforms, and let your audience know the opportunity to be a guest is available. This encourages them to reach out to you so they can apply for a guest opportunity, rather than you always having to reach out to potential guests. This way, you have a steady instream of guests who are ready to share and bring their audience with them.

GUEST PREPARATION THAT GUARANTEES A SMOOTH SAILING INTERVIEW

Researching your guests before the interview, even if you are already familiar with them, is a great way to get yourself prepared for the interview. As you research your guests, you give yourself the opportunity to develop a greater sense of charisma between yourself and their persona before the show. The show also becomes more enjoyable to record because you are not spending time on superficial conversation but instead connecting on a deeper level right from the start. Now, rather than asking the basics, you can invite them to maybe state a summary for your audience, and then you can dig into the juicy details.

Having the capability of getting your interviews into juicy details means that you will create both an exciting show to record and an exciting show to listen to. For you, you will feel a natural sense of energy, charisma, and excitement washing through yourself and your guest as you both dig deeper into your passions and share in them through a lively conversation. This means that while the process of recording your show may be more of a fun appointment with a friend, and a great learning opportunity, rather than a strictly business type meeting.

For your audience, they will naturally pick up on that energy of you going deeper with your guest and sharing that passion with each other. As they listen, they will feel the excitement and synchronicity flowing between yourself and your guest, which creates a feeling as though they are right there with you, listening to that conversation live. This breaks down the wall between your audience and yourself, making it feel like they are having a live experience and deepening the connection between them and yourself.

To develop this lively energy through research first, there are three steps you are going to take. First, you are going to get a general sense of who your guest is so that you understand what they have to offer your show. Next, you are going to decide on your angle of focus and research them in a way that allows you to really narrow in on a topic and energy that will serve your show. Then, you are going to finalize your questions and arrange them in a way that draws the energy of the show into deeper and deeper levels of passion as you go.

Ideally, you should have a general sense of who your guest is *before* you invite them on the show. Not knowing who they are or what they have to offer can lead to you bringing on a guest that may be rather boring for you to interview, or it may result in you having an interview that barely, if at all, gets into a positive synchronicity. If you are approaching people to invite them to be on your show, make sure you take the time to research them first so that you know if they will be a good fit. First, research their industry and niche of knowledge to ensure they know what you will be talking about and that they will have plenty to bring to the table. Then, consider their personality. Do they have a personality that you mesh well with? Will you have fun interviewing this person? Does it seem like you would be able to get plenty out of an interview with them? If you were to spend one hour on a call together, would it be enjoyable, or do you think you would have to pull the conversation along and really push to get that show where you wanted it to go? Always consider the fun factor because if that chemistry does not exist between you and a guest member, it will make the process of recording your show extremely boring, and possibly even frustrating. You might also have a hard time standing behind the content you have created because it does not reflect your usual energy and passion. Make sure every possible guest is qualified, passionate, and that you share chemistry *before* you bring them on the show.

Some of the questions you should ask yourself as you research your guest include:

- Who are they, where are they from, what is their story? What is their personality like?
- How can you structure the interview to draw out the best of their personality, making the show more enjoyable for your audience?
- How or why are they relevant to your niche?

- Why will your audience be interested in listening to them?
- What specific topic do you want to discuss with them? Why? How are they able to contribute to this topic?
- What can they teach your audience? Why are they qualified to teach this?

If you open a forum for people to apply, this is the best way to ensure that you are getting qualified people who are eager to be a part of what you are doing. This also puts you in a unique position where you can ask for their bios and conduct small interviews with them to see how your shared chemistry feels. Since you are inviting people for interviews and not promising positions right away, you can use this as an opportunity to be a bit picky and only host guests who are truly a great pairing with your show. Again, look for passion, chemistry, excitement, and a fun time talking about topics that are highly relevant to your audience.

After you have researched the general bio of a person, you need to get more specific and decide on the topic for your show, and the angle you will take when interviewing someone. Chances are if you have picked a great guest, the two of you could happily go on for *hours* talking about your passions. The problem is, podcast episodes are finite in length, and while you can certainly host a two or three part series with one guest, you do not want to go overboard and take away from the purpose of your show. This means you need to go into the interview with a clear focus and understand how that focus is going to deepen the passion and excitement in the interview itself.

Let's say you run a podcast about personal development for entrepreneurs, for example. You could talk to anyone about any personal development topic for hours, however you only have a set amount of time to talk about something in your episode. You need to find a specific topic that your guest can passionately discuss and discover how that particular topic will fit in with your show. By choosing this one aspect, you give the show a focus, have the opportunity to build the episode up as something educational and complete for your audience, and gain the opportunity to let your guest really dig into what they are experts at. Knowing how to do this ensures that your episode really digs into juicy details, rather than floating around on a surface level.

If you can provide that deep level of knowledge to them through each episode, you will keep your listeners focused. It may feel uncomfortable or like you are alienating certain listeners from time to time to be so specific in your episodes, but remember that they are all flowing together as a part of a bigger picture. Your audience would rather have fewer excep-tional quality episodes they can relate to, rather than many that are not detailed enough to be worth listening to.

FINALLY, YOU NEED TO FINALIZE YOUR QUESTIONS. WHEN YOU are conducting an interview, many questions will occur naturally in the conversation, and you should let them. The more authentic the conversation is, the easier it will flow, and the more you will enjoy recording interviews. Aside from authentic conversational questions, ask specific questions that keep the interview rolling, too. These specific questions should be developed in a way that allows you to direct the interview so you stay on topic so you can teach your audience something specific, while deepening the discussion, and while giving plenty of room for authentic conversation to take place.

Your average interview should have one structured question for every five minutes, as this allows plenty of time for authentic discussion to happen around the answers. Of course, you may need to adjust this if you have limited time to conduct an interview, such as if your shows are 20 minutes or less. In this case, you may want to arrange for one question every 3 minutes, which would give you more questions to answer, making the interview more efficient.

The questions should be broken down into three groups. The first group will happen over the first 2-5 questions, depending on the length of the interview, and they should invite your guest to offer some form of back story or information about themselves. Remember that your audience will already know you are a credible source, but your guest will need a few minutes to build up rapport and establish credibility.

Answering these questions gives them a chance to do so while also introducing them to your audience.

The bulk of your questions, which should make up around half of the total questions, should be about digging into their knowledge base or essentially picking their brain. You want to ask as many questions about their unique field of knowledge as you can, as this allows you to deepen the conversation and extract great levels of information for yourself and your audience. For example, if you were hosting a parenting podcast, you might ask a stay at home mom about how she structures her day, decides on activities to do, and overcomes daily challenges. This method of specific and deep questioning would apply to any topic you may be talking about. You want to get into the meat of the topic by digging deep, asking questions, and stringing them in a cohesive way so that it makes sense when you move from one question to the next.

The final group of questions you ask should be an inviting summary, while also encouraging your guest to leave your audience with a lesson of sorts. This is their opportunity to give your audience 1-3 take away points that they can apply to their everyday life starting right away so that they can begin to see results in their own lives based on whichever topic you have been discussing. It is important that your audience is always left with some form of action steps, as this allows them to feel like they have actually gotten something out of the interview, and they can start to see the results from those action steps. As a result, they are more likely to come back and listen to even more episodes, because they realize that your podcast is not only a blast to listen to, but it actually helps them get more out of their lives, too, either by teaching them something, or by providing them with a wonderful means of entertainment.

CREATING A CONVERSATIONAL INTERVIEW STYLE THAT FLOWS

Creating a conversational interview style that flows is not just about creating a podcast that is easier for your audience to listen to; it is also about creating a podcast that you actually enjoy recording. There is nothing enjoyable about finding yourself sitting in a booth feeling trapped in a requirement to talk in an overly stuffy manner, as though you were inter-viewing people for a medical study. In fact, if you are not care-ful, a stuffy interview style could lead to you *resenting* your podcast because it makes it so unenjoyable, and could lead to you feeling like there is no way you can keep going. Since this is all about developing your passion, it is important that you never create this sort of resentment for yourself within your show design.

Creating a conversational interview style starts with proper research and preparation for your show, which you have already completed. Now, you need to make sure your chosen questions nurture conversation, and that you actually ask them in a way that encourages it, too. This will start to come more naturally as you continue practicing, so be patient with yourself and give yourself a chance to relax into the experience and go with the flow. The more you settle into the conversation, the easier it will be to have an actual conversation al type interview.

Some great conversational type questions you might ask include:

- Tell me about the overall journey that got you into this passion, what did that look like?
- Who are your biggest role models in this industry?
- What gets you really excited about the work you are doing?
- What are some of the biggest mistakes you made while learning what you have learned so far?
- If you could do anything to make this industry even better, what would you do?

These types of questions are open-ended, invite for a conversation to form, and leave for many secondary questions to be spontaneously included as that authentic conversation develops. For example, if your guest responds to who their biggest role models are, you might ask them why those are their role models, or when they started looking up to those individuals as role models. These are great ways to really expand on the interview and make it feel like a positive back and-forth experience while learning more about your guest and having a great deal of fun.

Another way to make it conversational is to keep your eye on the clock to make sure you ask your next questions on time but to not make it feel rushed. About one minute before you need to ask the next question, let your guest wrap up what they are saying and then respond with something in a short summary of what you have just discussed. Then, lead into your next question. If you have organized your questions properly, they should naturally flow one into the next. If you do end up going in a totally different direction, make sure you highlight that fact in the conversation. This way, your guest and audience know that you are changing topics and do not get confused by the switch. This makes your show easier for people to follow and makes it feel like you are still enjoying a conversational experience.

If you are going to do conversational interviews on your show, strive to make sure that the episodes are long enough to allow for plenty of enriching discussion. While you can definitely fit 15 minute interview segments into a larger show, that may not always be enough if you want to dig deep into a certain discussion. If you prefer shorter interview segments like this, consider having special episodes every so often, which is a full-episode interview. This makes these episodes extra special, as they are different from your usual pace and offer a lot of valuable content to your audience. This is a great way to mix it up and give plenty of added value, without entirely straying away from a structured show with different segments, if that is the design you prefer.

Lastly, make sure you listen to your interviews after you conduct them and look for opportunities to relax and conduct more fluid and conversational interviews. However, do not listen to them immediately after you record them or you might find yourself judging yourself too harshly, which can lead to you actually feeling even more self-conscious in your next interview, and growing more uncomfortable with your interviewing style. Instead, give yourself a day or so, then listen to the interview with the desire to look for opportunities to improve. Choose 1-2 things you can improve on after each interview, and make a point to improve on those things the next time you are interviewing someone. This way, your interviews improve over time, and you are able to feel more comfortable and confident along the way. You will find you enjoy interviews far more if you take this approach, as you are making it more about having fun and enjoying yourself than anything else, and that will shine both in your experience and the final episode that you put out for your listeners to enjoy.

LAUNCHING MADE SIMPLE

GETTING YOUR PODCAST READY TO PUT OUT THERE IS AN exciting time, and then comes the launch. In the digital world, launching is often talked about as being a stressful and over-whelming time that can leave you feeling like a mess after-ward. While inefficient launch strategies can certainly make you feel like you have bitten off way more than you can chew, launching does *not* have to be that challenging. Launching can be as effortless as you make it, and, in fact, it should be effort-less. The idea is that your launch, and any marketing you ever do, should always be an extension of your passion and a part of the fun of running your podcast. Yes, at times, you are likely going to find yourself feeling somewhat stressed out or over-whelmed by the different operations of your podcast. However, the majority of your experience should be fun, and that includes launching.

Before you get into any specific details about launching, resolve to choose a strategy that suits your personality and your persona, and that matches the energy of your podcast. You must do this before you do anything else because everything that comes next will be built on this foundation. If you fail to do this first, you will find your branding and marketing strategies do not fit your podcast accurately, and the whole thing feels "off." The more personalized this experience is to you and your podcast, the more joy you will have in it, and the more attention you will attract to your podcast through your energy. You read that right: *joy sells.* Joy is the number one ingredient of getting people to pay attention, and the more you enjoy what you are doing, the more success you will have.

EVERYTHING YOU NEED TO KNOW ABOUT DISTRIBUTION AND HOSTING

Let's get the stressful parts out of the way, first. Distribution and hosting may seem stressful because there are so many different platforms out there. It is likely that you want to get your podcast on all the major platforms, as this is where you are likely to reach the widest viewership. The easiest way to get your distribution and hosting system set up is to break it down into independent steps and go from there.

The first step is to create your podcast. Develop your intro and outro, record your show, and get the audio ready so that your podcast can be uploaded to a system.

Step two is to turn to your primary host. You *need* a primary host, as this host is going to make it easy for you to upload your podcast to every single platform. They are essentially designed for the distribution process. If you do not already have one, Libsyn, Buzzsprout, and Podbean are all great platforms you can use to get your content in front of your audience. When you have your host chosen, you will register your new show and set up the information regarding your show into your host. Each platform will have you do this slightly differently, but the general idea will always be that you upload the name of your show, the show description, the web address and slug for your show, and other information regarding the type of show you are producing. Some of this information is going to include information that is relevant to major distribution sites, such as iTunes. It is recommended that you input this information, as this will allow your host to interact with the distribution channel, effectively making your show easier for viewers to find.

Once you have set up your host, you need to find your main feed or your RSS feed. Your RSS feed is important, as it contains the link you will require when it comes to sharing your podcast with distribution platforms. The link of your primary podcast, such as your personal website link, is *not* the link the directories will be looking for. They want the RSS feed link for the show you are hosting, as this is how they validate it and allow your podcast to be hosted on their platform.

Step three is to upload your mp3 media file for your podcast. This is where you are going to upload the final version of your podcast episode to the platform. Once everything is set up, you will skip step two and jump straight to step three as you upload your shows to your host, because everything else will already be set up for you.

Step four is to let all of the directories, such as iTunes, know that your show exists. It is important that you get your show on iTunes right away, even if you only have one episode so far because this ensures that your connection is working. Even if you load everything up to iTunes right away, you do not have to do an official launch yet. You can use this as an opportunity to adjust everything and get it ready. Meanwhile, you can continue promoting your podcast for launch.

In order to get your podcast up on iTunes in particular, you need to go to iTunes and set up an account with them. Then, you need to go to podcastsconnect.apple.com so you can set up a new show. There, you will include your RSS feed by adding the URL for your RSS feed. Remember, this is not your personal website feed, but the RSS feed from your podcast hosting website. After you submit it, you will hit "validate," and Apple will validate your podcast. This should only take a few minutes. You will immediately see a display of your podcast on the screen, where it will show your podcast's image and all of the information regarding your podcast such as the title, language, and description. If there are any errors, these will be displayed as well so that you can fix those errors. As soon as you have, you can validate the RSS URL again, and then Apple should say "submit" so you can actually submit the show for distribution. At that point, your show with all of your current episodes will be available for live viewing on iTunes.

The same general process works for Stitcher and Google Play, as well. For Stitcher, you will go to the Stitcher website, create an account, and then go to Stitcher.com/content-providers, which will allow you to follow the exact same process to get your podcast live on Stitcher. For Google Play, you will create an account and then go to G.co/podcastportal to get your Podcast live on that platform, too. It is important that you get your podcast live on all three, as these are the major podcasting websites where you are most likely to get found. As well, this makes your podcast easily accessible to your audience as they can enjoy your content on apps they already have downloaded on their smart devices.

After everything has been set up the first time around, the hardest part is over. The only thing to do now is to upload future shows to your host site so they can go live. All of your newly uploaded episodes should become available within an hour of them being uploaded to your hosting account.

THE MOST EFFECTIVE LAUNCH STRATEGIES (GRAND OPENING VS. SOFT OPENING)

Once you have your podcast properly linked to your host and distribution channels, you need to start thinking about your actual launch strategy. Your launch strategy does not just define your process of getting your podcast out there, but your process of actually marketing your podcast to an audience so that people know where to find you.

There are two different types of launch strategies when it comes to getting your podcast out there: a grand opening and a soft opening. A grand opening is a wonderful way to drive a lot of attention to your podcast from day one and to help get your viewership up right away. A soft opening is excellent if you want to get started and then build attention later, when your podcast already has some episodes up and ready to go. There are pros and cons to each launch method; you will need to decide what is accurate for you and your launch.

A GRAND OPENING IS WONDERFUL BECAUSE IT GETS A LOT OF attention on your podcast right away. However, if you tend to be shyer, or if you are worried about people not necessarily liking your podcast, it may make you feel intimidated by your own launch as you realize suddenly you have a lot of eyes on your content. Grand openings are a great way to generate a lot of traffic from day one, so it is important that you are ready to impress that traffic and give them a reason to stick around from day one, too.

Soft openings are wonderful because they help you develop a greater sense of confidence in podcasting, while growing your personal style. They do, however, result in minimal attention on your podcast from the start, which can make it more challenging to grow your podcast over time. Despite this, a soft opening can be excellent if you are just getting into podcasting as a hobby or for fun, and it can help decrease the pressure from you as you do not have to worry about a consistent uploading schedule or marketing. At first, you might find yourself struggling for a while to get algorithms to realize that your podcast is sought after and worth listening to. Once you get the momentum rolling, though, it should be excellent for getting your content out there.

If you want to follow a grand opening strategy, the most important thing you can do is create a presence for your podcast and start driving as much traffic there as possible, before your podcast even launches. Your presence for your podcast should consist of pages on major social media platforms, such as Facebook, Instagram, or Twitter. You can also have a self-hosted website where you create a landing page and invite people to opt-in to a newsletter so you can email them updates about your podcast, including about the launch itself. Once your presence is set up, post about your upcoming podcast, let your friends and family know and invite everyone to share the news about your new podcast with everyone they know. You can also run advertisements to generate more attention, as this will get more traffic to your pages. The idea here is to get as many people excited about your podcast as possible so that when you do launch it, you have a major audience to launch it to. Through this, you should get a lot of traction from day one, and your primary focus will be to keep that engagement going as you continue to launch new episodes.

IF YOU PREFER TO DO A SOFT LAUNCH, YOU SHOULD STILL CREATE a presence for your podcast, but you do not necessarily want to promote your presence. Rather than doing everything in your power to drive traffic there and get everyone excited for your podcast, your focus should be on just putting out podcasts and getting a small circle of people listening to it. For example, your friends and family and any recommendations you may get along the way. Once you get comfortable with the entire process of hosting a podcast and launching episodes, then you can start ramping up your advertising, so get yourself even more traction. At this point, you would want to start looking at advertisements and getting yourself out there as much as possible.

It is important to understand that the grand opening is always the best idea for your podcast, as it will give you the best opportunity to get yourself out there and let your passions be seen and heard by the world. If, however, you find that you do not have the experience, you are not yet comfortable with a huge audience, or you do not have the budget to support advertisements and such, you can always start with a soft launch first. As soon as you feel comfortable advertising in a bigger way, that should become your primary focus.

Regardless of what I, or anyone else, says is the best route, *do what is right for you.* Let this podcast be as enjoyable as it can be. If that means making a big bang and jumping into the podcast scene with lots of excitement, do that. If it means taking the soft opening approach and giving yourself time to warm up or save up a greater budget to get yourself out there, do that instead. There is no right or wrong answer here, as long as you are putting the energy into getting yourself out there and growing your audience.

THE 7 DO'S AND DON'TS OF LAUNCHING YOUR NEW PODCAST

To make launching as easy as possible, I have comprised a quick list of 7 do's and don'ts you should know about before you get into the launch process. These rules apply whether you are launching a new show or new episodes. When it comes to promotion in any format, it is important that you always adhere to strict guidelines to avoid promoting in a way that comes across as tacky, or that drives your audience away. Tasteful promotion is actually simpler than any other strategy and will get you the best results every single time.

DO Leverage Your Existing Communities

First and foremost, always leverage your existing communities. If you are already in Facebook groups, hanging out on forums, or even partaking in offline communities, leverage them. Talk about content related to your podcast, be an active member of these communities, and build strong relationships with the people you meet in them. Make your number one point to be about engagement, not about talking about your page, as engagement is what will get you the best results. Show up as a human and a friend first, and then use the interest people have in you as an opportunity to share your podcast with them. This is an excellent way to get to your first 100 listeners.

DO Add Valuable on-Topic Content to These Communities

When you are partaking in these communities, make sure everything you do is on-topic. Avoid coming into any community and trying to "take over" or sharing about things that are entirely irrelevant, as this will lead to two highly unwanted experiences. First and foremost, you will not be talking to your target audience in a way that captures their attention and gets them excited about your show, which means your energy will be wasted. Second, it makes you look tacky because it makes it seem like you cannot participate in a group and stay on topic, so they no longer want to be a part of your audience. Always join groups that are on-topic and relevant to your niche, and then stay on-topic in those groups. That is the fastest way to grow your audience in a tasteful, attraction-marketing based manner.

DO Join MULTIPLE Facebook Groups That Are Relevant to Your Niche

Never limit yourself to just one or two spaces. Always join multiple groups that are relevant to your niche, and if you can join them as your podcast's business page, rather than your personal page. Make a point to participate in all of them. If you can, set aside several 15-30 minute blocks of time every single week and then get into those groups and start participating. Even just a few minutes in each group, commenting, posting engaging content, and sharing your knowledge with people is a great way to build those relationships and get yourself out there. The more you engage, the more people will want to know about you and will pay attention to your podcast, too. Another platform to look into outside of Facebook would be Reddit or Tumblr, both full of threads with people seeking information that is exactly what you have been sharing on your podcast.

Whenever you join a social media group to share about your podcast, there is one golden rule you MUST follow. That is: do *not* spam the community with your content. Posting too much content about yourself and your podcast, dropping links and ignoring the rest of the group, or generally failing to participate except to talk about yourself and your podcast is a terrible way to get attention on your podcast. You must participate in these groups, build up relationships and rapport, then share your content if you want to generate success with this marketing approach. Otherwise, people will think that you are too spammy, and therefore your show is likely also spammy or low-quality and will not want to listen to it, no matter how good it may actually be.

DO Learn How To Leverage SEO

SEO, or search engine optimization, is a necessary tool to understand if you want to get your podcast out into the world and develop a massive following. Everything from Google to Facebook and even Reddit uses a search engine algorithm to help decide what types of content to show to their audience, and you need to know how to leverage that algorithm to get views. There are three key steps when it comes to content SEO, regardless of where you are posting that content. The three steps include: relevancy, keywords, and quality.

Your audience is already looking content up and interacting with specific types of content online. Algorithms recognize this and show content that is relevant to these specific topics or search terms, so having relevant content ensures that you show up within your audience's feed or search results.

Keywords are specific words that your audience is looking up or using. Algorithms find these keywords either based on the fact that they were specifically searched, or based on the fact that the posts your audience is paying attention to all share these words in common. Having these keywords in your post, in moderation, ensures that search engines see you as being relevant and show your content in their posts. This is different from overall relevance because here you are targeting specific words, while with relevancy you are targeting a specific overall topic.

Lastly, the quality of your content matters because search engines and other algorithm-based platforms do not want to be showing low-quality content to their viewers. Using language that is easy to read, written in a correct manner, and that offers value to your audience ensures that your content is high quality so algorithms will be more likely to show it.

DO Upload 3 Episodes on Day One

On the first day, you launch your podcast, regardless of whether you do a grand opening or a soft opening, you need to upload 3 podcasts. 3 podcasts give your listener a variety of content to listen to so that they can choose their favorite episode and then binge watch the rest. Although modern people have a shorter attention span than ever before, if they do find themselves thoroughly enjoying something, they will want to consume as much content from said thing as possible. Having episodes for them to choose from, and additional episodes for them to listen to right after, gives them the opportunity to fall in love with your content enough to binge on it.

Having new listeners binge on your content is actually important to your SEO, too. The steps you took previously with relevancy, keywords, and quality were all done in an effort to get people to consume your content. The more they consume your content, the more algorithms will assume they enjoy your content and will show you in their feed. This means you will show up consistently throughout their feed, rather than just every so often, which means you will get more engagement. As your engagement goes up, so will your reach and therefore your following will grow, too.

DON'T Follow a Weak Uploading Schedule

In your first weeks after launching a podcast, you should be uploading at least three shows per week. Even if you intend on uploading fewer than that in the future, three per week is an important place to start as it allows you to accumulate plenty of great content, and fast. This means that your existing audience has plenty of content to listen to, and any newcomers who stumble upon you have plenty of great content to binge on. The more you upload, the more you have something to promote, and the easier it is to get eyes on or back on your podcast. You want people to continue thinking about your podcast, hearing about your podcast, and talking about your podcast as often as possible so that you become etched in their memory. This way, if you do decide to go to a slower-paced output frequency, people still have plenty of content to listen to, and they know and like you enough to be patient for your new content to come out.

DON'T Drop the Ball on Your Promotional Activities

Even after you launch your podcast, you still need to be ready to engage in promotional activities. SEO is an extremely important tool you should be using, in particular, when it comes to promoting your strategies as SEO is how you increase your likelihood of being found. SEO strategies will work on Google, as well as search engines such as the very distribution platforms you are hosting your podcast on. If you rank well when people search for new podcasts in your niche, you will be more likely to come up over anyone else. You can increase SEO by using keywords, filling out the details of your episodes on every episode, and creating high-quality promotional materials on other platforms that direct back to your podcast. Getting featured on high-ranking websites and having them link to your podcast is also a great way to increase your SEO rankings.

It is extremely important to use timing to your advantage. You can do this by checking with other successful podcasts and seeing what their uploading patterns look like. What time of day are they generally uploading at? If you notice a pattern, use this to help you create your own uploading pattern, too, by uploading at those times of the day. Over time, your show will have enough data of its own, which will allow you to see when people are consuming your content most, so that you can upload new content when people are most likely to listen to it. The sooner you get a higher number of viewers, the better your podcast will rank, and the more viewers you will accumulate over the coming hours and days.

Another great promotion you can use is to make shareable content. Taking snippets from your show and turning them into tiny videos that can be shared online, or taking quotes from your show and turning them into pictures that can be shared online, are great ways for you to share your content out as far as possible. You can share this content on your social media platforms, with your email list, and anywhere else where you might be able to access a new audience. However, make sure you are following anti-spam practices to avoid having people think that you, and your podcast, are spamming them. You want it to come across as genuine, authentic and engaged. It is a good idea to turn this snippet-sharing process into a strategy by sharing a few clips in the days leading up to the release of your new episode. Play around with dropping these clips to see what times your audience is most receptive, then continue to share your clips at those times. Sharing a clip or two each day on the days leading up to your new episode releases ensures that you always have high quality content to share, and that said content is growing interest and excitement with your audience. This way, they will be far more likely to listen when you launch the show.

Lastly, make sure you are not writing paragraphs upon paragraphs of content about your show. People like podcasts because they don't want to be reading too much, and you need to keep that up across your digital promotions, too. Write small captions and posts and link snippets of your podcast or quote pictures into those posts. This way, people can quickly look at it, determine if they like it, tune in, and share it if they are impressed.

Make sure that you use every single place imaginable to your advantage to find new listeners. Share these posts out to Facebook groups, blogs, Reddit, and Quora. Join conversations that are relevant to your podcast and share relevant podcast episodes whenever you can. This way, people who are curious about content relevant to what you are creating will find you and listen to your show. Always be transparent when you market your podcast in this way, too, so that people are aware of the fact that you are self-promoting, as they will appreciate you being transparent more than they will appreciate you link-dropping and pretending it was a "random episode" you found. Be honest, have fun, and let your passion shine, and you will be far more likely to grow a wide listenership for your podcast.

HOW TO BRING YOUR PODCAST TO THE IMMEDIATE ATTENTION OF HUNDREDS, THEN THOUSANDS OF EAGER LISTENERS

THERE IS AN OCEAN OF PEOPLE TRYING TO GET NOTICED IN THE podcasting community, and each one of them is fighting to stand out more than the rest. Every method you can think of has been used in an effort to get in front of your audience so your competitors can have their podcasts heard, as they want the same success you are aiming for. If you are going to generate success with your own podcast, you need to know how to promote it properly so you can get massive attention on your podcast as soon as possible.

I want to make one thing very clear to you right now: your passion *matters*. There is a world full of people trying to get in front of every audience imaginable, including yours. They are all pounding pavement, showing themselves in the faces of their audiences, and doing everything they can to earn their attention and loyalty. Do you know what happens when you pound pavement and force yourself in front of people? *They tune you out.* Think about it... do you like it when people are hollering in your face from every angle, and trying to get you to pay attention to them? Probably not. At best, you ignore them. At worst, you get annoyed and possibly even quite angry toward them. Don't be that person. That person is only in it for one thing: money.

Be the person that is in it for passion. Host a podcast because you love doing it, because it is fun, and because you are wildly passionate about what you are talking about. Host your podcast because it is something you genuinely want to be doing, and not because you feel like this is the only way to stay relevant. When you host your podcast, be the kind of person who's energy speaks for them, and let everything else fall into place with *ease.*

It may sound challenging, but it is a lot more simple than you think. There are hundreds, if not thousands of people out there doing it successfully right now, and not one of them is forcing their way in front of a crowd and demanding their attention and loyalty. They are all sitting back, enjoying themselves, having fun, and presenting themselves and their podcasts to the people who are most likely to be interested. The entire energy is different, and it works to *attract* an audience, rather than *demand* an audience. In the end, these are the podcasters who have thousands, if not millions of obsessed fans who listen to every single episode they ever put out.

BRING THE MARKET TO YOUR PODCAST

Bringing the market to your podcast means that you pour your heart and soul into making your podcast the best podcast possible through the power of your passion, and then you make it possible for people to see your podcast. A great way to think about this process would be to think about a car. Imagine you were passionate about sports cars, and you wanted to enjoy the experience of owning and caring for a sports car. Because of your passion, you would likely take your time, find a beautiful car, and take great pride in it to the point where it is always clean and shiny, and it possibly has a few upgrades that make it look even fancier. Your passion for your car shows. Every time you drive down the street (present it), people turn their heads. You did not demand them to turn their heads by yelling out the car window screaming at them to pay attention or by honking your horn obsessively until they started paying attention. Instead, you simply took pride in it, poured your passion into it, and presented it. The attention you gained was a natural reflection of the passion and energy you poured into it.

THIS IS PRECISELY WHAT YOU NEED TO DO WITH YOUR PODCAST. You need to pour so much passion and energy into it that when it comes to marketing, the only purpose of your marketing is to present it, so your audience has the chance to see it. The quality speaks for itself, so there is no reason for you to jam that concept down everyone's throats. In order for this to really work, though, you need to make sure your promotion posts pour just as much passion into your project as your actual recordings do, too. Create graphics or share snippets from each episode that highlight the passion you have poured into your podcast, and invite people to become a part of that. They won't be able to help themselves; they will become so curious that they quite literally turn their head to see your advertising. Or, at least, they scroll back up on their phones or pause on their desktops to see what is being advertised to them.

One of the most important things to understand about promoting through passion this way is that an advertising budget is optional. Of course, if you can afford to pour money into an advertising budget and get your content out there faster, this is a great way to push your podcast up through the rankings and get as far as you possibly can. If, however, you cannot afford to put any money toward advertising, you can still market through passion and make an incredible impact with your promotions. By sharing your promotional posts in as many locations as you can and encouraging your audience to share it, too, you become far more likely to get your content out there. Again, your passion will shine through, and you *will* be heard above the crowd.

ADVERTISE YOUR PODCAST EFFICIENTLY

Aside from letting your passion speak for you, there are many efficient methods you can use to help get your podcast out for the world to see. These practical steps are excellent for spreading the news about your podcast, increasing your listenership, and gaining traction as your podcast continues to grow. It is important that, in order to grow your podcast as large as possible, you leverage the power of *efficient* marketing. Working smarter, not harder, gets your content out there so your audience can see it and fall in love with your show.

Efficient advertising means taking as few steps as possible to reach as many people as possible, and that these are the only methods you are focusing on. When you find methods that are not working, you should cease using them immediately. Pour your energy into the things that work.

There are four excellent methods you can use when it comes to getting a bigger audience for your page, and these methods are effortless to complete. If you pour your energy into these methods, you will be far more likely to grow your audience and get a greater listenership for your page.

The first method you can use to efficiently advertise your business and bring the market to you is paid advertising. Facebook and Instagram offer prestigious marketing opportunities which allow you to get yourself in front of a much larger audience as fast as possible, without having to do anything yourself. Instead, your money is working for you. On Facebook, the best advertisement would be one that features a quote from your podcast shown on an image, with a short 1-2 sentence description of your show and a link for listening. On Instagram, a short audio clip of your show pasted over an image of your show's logo or a snapshot from you recording your show would work excellently. With either platform, adequate targeting is imperative. You need to identify what your likely demographic is for your audience and define that in your advertisement's creation. If you are not entirely sure who is listening, yet, choose the most likely gender that would listen to you, or both, and then choose the most likely age group(s) that would listen to you. Then, choose a fairly narrow geographical region, such as *just* your country where you currently live. You can always target larger later, but going any larger now will result in you struggling to get a wide enough reach since it is unlikely that you have a budget that can reasonably support that large of an audience. It is important that, while you target your audience, you define a few interests your audience has that are relevant to your podcast. You could also search for some of the major podcasts in your niche to see if they come up as interests, and tag them if you can. This gives Facebook or Instagram a clear description of who you are trying to get in front of and ensures your ads are seen by people who are most likely to enjoy your content.

The most successful advertisements for podcasts have been episode clips with promotional videos attached to them, in the design of a trailer. Alternatively, an image of yourself as the host, and any other hosts of your show if you have multiple, works as this helps place a face with your podcast. The image of yourself either as an introduction to the host, or in the trailer, should be full of personality so people are immediately interested and want to learn more.

Google uses the same steps for targeting followers for your show, though it is not always the most practical method for advertising podcasts, especially newer ones, as it requires larger budgets and relies on excellent wording to grow your following. If you have a lower budget or cannot create a captivating enough written summary for your podcast, it would be best to rely on Facebook or Instagram for your podcast advertisements. If you do have a large budget of at least $500+ and the ability to summarize your podcast in a captivating manner, then Google is an excellent place to promote your podcast, too.

The second step for growth is to get on Instagram and find people in your industry who are successful and well-respected, with the same audience you have. They can be fellow podcasters, or they can be other members of authority in your industry. Go through their followers and start engaging with their followers using comments primarily, with a few likes here and there. Follow any of the accounts that look as though they would enjoy listening to your podcast. Those followers will take notice, and if they like your account, they will follow you back. If someone does follow you back, send them a thank you message for their follow and to introduce them to your podcast in that message. You can also let them know there are a few clips on your page to give them a taste of what you have to offer, in case they want to check that out before committing to an entire episode. This is a great way to gain followers, engage with them, and turn them into actual listeners for your podcast. To optimize your conversion rate, go to that person's page, find their first name (typically by either working it out from their username or their bio), and use that when addressing them as it is far more personalized than a generic introduction, or using their username in place of their name (and also that you're not one of these pesky bots!). After a few days, unfollow any account that did not follow you back and then start again.

The third method for growing your audience is using every single place on the internet to your advantage so that you can find as many potential listeners as possible. Get on blogs, Facebook groups, Reddit and Quora, and find conversations that are relevant to your industry. Get involved in those conversations, offer your answers, and let people know you have a podcast episode that answers those questions, or that you have an upcoming episode that answers those questions. This is not only going to show the original poster your podcast but will also show every other person who had the same question and was looking for an answer, too. Getting yourself out there as much as possible, and doing so in a way that respects the user guidelines of the community, is an imperative part of growing your podcast through social networking.

HARNESSING THE POWER OF NETWORKING

Never underestimate the power of growing your network. Networking is hands down one of the most impactful marketing strategies you will ever tap into, especially when it comes to growing your audience with a system of loyal followers. Your network will significantly boost your show by offering you many different opportunities that you simply could not create on your own. The caveat is that you need to be prepared to give back to your network as much as, if not more than, you receive from it. That is how you tap into the abundance of opportunities and grow your audience large enough for your network to genuinely support your podcast. This may sound like a lot of work, but networking is a non-negotiable when you are growing your podcast or any other platform for that matter.

"YOUR NETWORK IS YOUR NET WORTH." – PORTER GALE. YOUR network can offer you the ability to grow your podcast rapidly. You can appear as a guest on different shows, host guests on your show, and get featured in prominent marketing areas, just through knowing the right people. For example, if you build out your network and someone within your network happens to run a highly successful blog, they may wish to talk about your podcast on their blog, which earns you direct access to their major audience. In return, it is important that you support them in having plenty of high-quality pieces of content to add to their blog so you are well-represented and their audience receives the high-quality content they have become accustomed to.

Networking with other podcasters is an excellent marketing tool to exploit because it gets you in front of their audience, too, and the fact that you are a guest on their show means their audience is similar to yours. As soon as their followers listen to you, if they like you, they will seek out your podcast and become active listeners of your podcast, too. This works vice versa, too. The more you bring visitors onto your show, the more they will bring their audience with them, and your listenership will grow. This works both ways, as well, since you will also be turning your listener's attention to other podcasters, meaning they will be growing their audience, too. This creates an excellent win-win situation! It is important to have other podcasters in your network, but expand beyond them and find others' relevant to your industry, too. This expands your opportunities even further by connecting you with people who are passionate about the same things as you are but fulfilling those passions in different ways.

As you grow your network, ensure that you consider reality alongside strategy. Many times, people get caught up in the idea of using their network as a tool to leverage their growth, to the point where they routinely fail to stop and consider whether or not they actually enjoy the network they are building. Always be protective of your time and energy, even when you are investing in the growth of your podcast. You came here to do something you are passionate about, and that should leak into every aspect of your growth. If you realize that you do not mesh well with certain people in your network, do not be afraid to invest less energy in those relationships. Do not abruptly cut them out, but invest less energy over time so that the connection slowly fades. Structure your network in a way that feels like you are building a circle of friends around you who understand and share in a common interest of yours, whether it be podcasting or the specific industry you are addressing with podcasting. It should feel fun and exciting to hang out with your network of people. If it doesn't, you need to detox your network.

As far as your audience goes, your network has the capacity to turn friends and members of your network into loyal fans of your show. Likewise, you will probably also become a fan of many of theirs, too. It is important to nurture these relationships even more, as these individuals are likely to become major champions of your content. Chances are, they will share your content out, celebrate you, talk you up to their friends and family, and help get you in front of your target audience. This is because they know in return, you will offer them excellent attention and support, as well.

THE BEST WAY TO NURTURE YOUR NETWORK IS TO ALWAYS DO your best to genuinely get to know each person in your network. Then, anytime you can offer them the same opportunities that you yourself would love to receive from your network. If you hear of opportunities that you think people in your network would fit well in, recommend them for that position, or let them know about it. Always spread the opportunities around to your network, as this ensures that you are all winning as often as possible. It also means they will be far more likely to recommend opportunities to you later, too. This also helps grow your reputation, making you the person that people love to talk about and recommend because they genuinely enjoy your generous and caring personality. It is important to understand that, in networking, you get what you give. Just like you cannot expect friends to carry your friendships as you coast by without contributing anything, you cannot expect your network to give you opportunities as you coast by without offering anything back. When you give abundantly to your network, you receive abundantly, too - like in all aspects of life, actually.

The more you contribute to your network, the more they are going to support you in growing your podcast, too. Together, you will all rise much faster. Even though you may be going at something alone, or with just one or two partners, you can still enlist the support of tens or hundreds of people, while offering support back to those individuals, too. Build your network like a strong community around you, and that network will support you in every way imaginable.

BUILDING YOUR BRAND: HELPING YOU STAND OUT IN THE VAST OCEAN THAT IS PODCASTING

BRANDING IS AN ESSENTIAL PART OF ANY BUSINESS, WHETHER IT is intended to be a professional business or a hobby outlet. Podcasting is no different. If you want to stand out in the ocean of podcasters and get yourself noticed faster, you need to have a brand that is as unique as you are, and it needs to be as memorable as possible, too. By now, branding is a well-understood concept, and the steps that are required to make a stand-out brand are well-known by marketing experts. I have gone to the very sources of these marketing and branding experts and brought forward only the best tips to help you brand like a pro. In doing this, you will stand apart from everyone else. The best part is, these strategies are incredibly simple and will serve as a crucial driving factor behind your podcast becoming a success.

WHEN IT COMES TO BRANDING LIKE A PRO, THERE ARE THREE main areas you need to focus on: emotional familiarity, a distinct presence, and an invaluable audience relationship. If you can create these three factors through your brand, your brand will start with a solid foundation that allows it to explode with growth as you continue to pour your energy into building your podcast.

CREATING EMOTIONAL FAMILIARITY THROUGH VISUALS

Branding guides frequently highlight the importance of having a coherent brand kit with defined colors, fonts, a well-created logo, and certain graphic themes. While this is part of it, if you rely exclusively on this information for building your brand, you will be building a brand that is superficial and disconnected from the root of what your audience really wants. True branding is not *just* about how your company looks; it is also about how your company persona is represented. Your appearance is just a part of that.

Branding is not the process of putting together a coherent, color-coded brand with consistency across your fonts and images. Those steps are all tools that you use to create the more important aspect of branding, which is emotional familiarity developed through the power of visuals. Pause for a moment and think of Coca Cola. What comes to mind? Maybe the color red, the infamous white scripted font, the cuddly white pandas, or the sodas with your name on them. Dig deeper, though. I'll bet you also get a feeling associated with the branding, even if you are not an avid supporter of the brand itself. Maybe you get a feeling of comfort, relaxation, and community. Perhaps you feel a sense of cuteness or warmth in your heart when you think about the little panda bears. It is likely that some sort of positive feeling that washes over you anytime you think about this brand. The same can be accomplished by thinking about any major brand. That is not because they have a coherent, color-coordinated brand, but because they have developed their brand in a way that generates emotional familiarity.

Yes, you need to pick colors, fonts, a logo, and decide on a theme of what your pictures will look like so that when you post everything, it looks coherent. All of that, however, should be used to encourage your audience to feel the way you want them to feel when they think about your brand. Do you want them to feel empowered? Curious? Comfortable? Seen? Cared for? Entertained? Happy? Define some feelings you want your audience to feel every time they look at your brand. Then, choose colors that are known to encourage those feelings, fonts that match that energy, and graphics that create an emotional familiarity with those unique emotions. This will become your well-designed brand, which is not only coherent and uniformed but developed in a way that actually stands out from everyone else. The easiest way to choose your colors and design is to research what feelings are associated with the colors you are using, so you can leverage the right emotions through your brand colors. It is important, too, that these colors look neat together as you want a simple yet eye-catching brand that is different and unique from everything else. All of your branding imagery should have that same overall look to it so that you have a cohesive, attractive brand.

DEVELOPING A DISTINCT ONLINE PRESENCE

Creating a distinct online presence is an absolute must if you are going live with your podcast. You need your own website, as well as a presence on the major social media platforms. Your website is a non-negotiable when it comes to running a podcast. While you could go for a hosted website on a site building platform, I advise you to go self-hosted with Word-Press. The reasoning behind this is simple: it is a bare-basics platform that has everything you need, it is fully customizable, and it will support your growth better than any other plat-form. Hosts like Site Ground or Host Gator can be used to host your website online, and then you can download a simple theme for your platform, or you can use a click-and-build plugin like Divi or Elementor to build your page in an even easier manner. Your website is important because it is a hub where you can share your podcast, capture emails, and actually own the entire platform you are creating.

Your website should contain archives of your previous posts, SEO in your posts to encourage Google to showcase you to new listeners, and a comment section on your posts so listeners can interact with you. You should also have an excellent home page that acts as a landing site for you to drive promotional traffic to from your Google, Facebook, or Instagram advertisements. Your home page should include a captivating image about your show, a bio about yourself and a host image, and a directory for where your page visitors can find your posts with your episodes.

Social media is a powerhouse when it comes to developing your online presence. Social media platforms' sole focus is to attract users, and they want to connect those users with other users or brands that they are likely to enjoy. As soon as you launch an account, you can start making content, and those platforms will work to connect you with potential viewers. This is a vital step in driving traffic to your podcast, as well as to your website. Your end goal should *always* be to get people to your website, then to your podcast. However, you can encourage people to skip your website and go straight to your podcast as well, to increase your listenership. It is essential that you drive traffic to your website as often as possible though, and that you capture emails because your email captures are important. Email captures are those opt-in sections where visitors can input their emails so they can receive promotional emails from you, and they are one of the best promotional tools out there. Through your newsletter you can promote your show, find guests, and get feedback on what types of content do best for your podcast. On social media, algorithms are constantly changing, and this can be a tumultuous experience for your brand. Some changes will be excellent and will drive greater traffic your way, while other changes will be difficult and could actually take traffic away from your content. At times, when platforms are down completely, you can lose total access to your audience, which results in you not being able to promote your podcast and keep your listenership up. This has happened a couple of times within the last five years, so recognize that this is a real possibility, and it can throw a damper into your business. If you own your website and have an email capture, however, you can still access your listeners even when social media is down, which means you are not required to start from scratch and work your way back up from ground zero.

As you develop your presence on your website and social media, incorporate your branding elements, so everything looks coherent and uniform. Then, take it a massive step further. Look at the emotional aspects of everything you post and ask yourself if those aspects match the emotional familiarity you want to be creating with your brand. Everything from the imagery to the words you are using should match that emotional tone, while also clearly reflecting your purpose and driving traffic to your page, your website, or your podcast. If you are unsure about how a post fits your brand, pause before posting it, and give yourself time to think about it. This way, you get it right the first time. You never want to find yourself in a situation where you post content in a leap decision because you just want to get it out there, only to find yourself thinking of a much better way to say it later on and not being able to go fix it because it has already been put out. Taking your time and creating high-quality, well-branded content the first time ensures that your content spreads farther, makes a greater impact, and grows your podcast exactly the way you desired it would. Remember, you want to work smarter, not harder. Every post you make should reflect your distinct, stand-out brand; otherwise, it should not be posted.

CULTIVATING AN INVALUABLE AUDIENCE RELATIONSHIP

The relationship you build with your audience will help you stand apart from the crowd by making you memorable. Think about the last time you went and met a group of new people. Perhaps you went to a party, a meeting, or some other gathering and noticed that there were many new faces there. Out of all of the people you met that day, I bet one or two people stood out in particular. Why? Because in that time, there was a relationship built, even if it was only an acquaintanceship, and it made a lasting impression. Anyone who you did not get the chance to make any form of connection with, you have likely already forgotten about.

When your audience comes onto any social media platform, you want to be the one putting the energy into developing a relationship with them so that you are the one they remember. This relationship should not be a sleazy strategy you use for self-fulfillment, either. The relationship you build with your audience needs to be founded on passion, mutual interest, and a genuine desire to come together and connect over something you both find meaningful. Your number one focus should be on *real* relationships, not just fake or superficial relationships you create in an effort to grow your podcast.

UNDERSTAND THAT AS YOU CULTIVATE THESE RELATIONSHIPS, your audience will know right away if your "relationship-building tactics" are a sham you are using to grow your podcast. Everyone else is using these very same lame, surface-level tactics to build fake relationships with their audience so they can loosely back up the claim that they "care." Their potential audience already knows, however, they are not doing this because they desire real relationships, they are doing this because they desire a following and they need that audience to listen to their podcast in order to gain that following. It feels weak, greedy, and frustrating. Their potential audience feels used instead of connected with, and so they stop listening. Whether you realize it or not, every audience is growing increasingly more sensitive to fake relationship-building tactics that brands are using. They can smell the fake from a mile away, and they are steering clear of it. In fact, if you reflect on brands you have interacted with, you can likely recall ones that were alarmingly fake, too.

This is where we tie back into the reality that passion has to be the foundation of your podcast before anything else. Even if you want to make money, gain clout, or do anything else beyond following your passion, these desires must always be second to your desire to fulfill your passion. Otherwise, you will never have the energy to invest in doing the things that will actually make you grow. For example, making real relationships with your audience.

Creating a real relationship with your audience comes from being passionate enough to recognize repeat listeners and spend a few extra moments liking their comments, commenting back, and engaging with them in a genuine manner. Your real relationships are developed by caring about what your audience wants and creating more of it, and by genuinely receiving their feedback and using it to improve the quality of your show. At the core of your relationships should always be what you would offer to any relationship in your personal life, except that you are striving to offer it in a broader way. Be honest, trustworthy, and loyal to your following, and they will be open and loyal with you, too. Use listener recognition, contests, giveaways, shout outs, and daily attention as a way to give back to your followers. In return, they will passionately give back to you by sharing your podcast with everyone they know.

THE FOOLPROOF RECIPE FOR LONG TERM SUCCESS

WHEN YOU INITIALLY START YOUR PODCAST, IT CAN BE EASY TO get caught up in the beginning stages and forget about the fact that after you launch your podcast, you have to keep going in order to succeed. Yes, those early episodes and initial listeners are important, but after those first couple of months, you need to have a strategy to keep you consistent and motivate you to go after that long-term success. If you are not in it for the long-run, you will not receive all of the benefits that podcasting has to offer. Further, if you cannot picture yourself doing this for the long-run, you may not be pursuing your passion at all, and you may want to reconsider or adjust your podcast to ensure it matches your desires. If you are confident that this is what you want, maintain a long-term mindset, stay consistent, and use the greatest source of motivation most podcasters are sleeping on, which I will reveal to you in just a moment...

MAINTAINING A LONG-TERM MINDSET

A long-term mindset means that you have a mindset that is prepared to remain committed to your success for the long-term, even when you come up against adversity such as worldly events, life circumstances, or even your own lack of attention. Humans, in general, have an incredibly challenging time maintaining a long-term mindset because they want to be fulfilled by instant gratification. If that instant gratification is not fulfilled, they lose interest. Or, worse, that feeling of gratification is fulfilled by launching the podcast, but then it seems pointless afterward because it seems like they have already "fulfilled their desires." Of course, they likely wanted much more out of their podcast than just that, but their lack of long-term mindset leaves them feeling like they are "already done."

Creating a long-term mindset is key to creating longevity for your podcast. You can create it by developing a willingness to repeat the same process over and over, without seeing any significant or jaw-dropping results from your efforts. Instead, you will see small cumulative growth over time, and eventually, that will turn into significant results. You also need to be willing to motivate yourself to keep going, even when you feel challenged, bored, or distracted. Eliminate your desire to become obsessed with incredible results, and focus instead on connecting with your desire to do something you are passionate about and to have a long-term outlet to channel that passion through.

HOW YOU CAN STAY CONSISTENT

Consistency determines how successful your podcast will, or will not be. It is easy to maintain consistency at first because your podcast is exciting and new, so you are eager to record new episodes and get them up on your show. Over time, however, this excitement drops and you may find yourself less excited because the novelty has worn off. While your podcast does not require round the clock care, it is important that you learn to channel your excitement into a consistent routine so that as the novelty does begin to wear off, you find yourself still readily available to keep the show going.

Right from the start, develop a schedule that you can eagerly follow with your show. Your schedule should include when you will be recording your shows, when you will be editing them, and when you will be uploading them. In your schedule, aim to batch content so that you can record multiple shows at once, edit multiple shows at once, and upload multiple shows into your host at once. You should be able to schedule shows within your host platform so they do not go live to the public until a specific time and date, which ensures that your episodes are ready to go well in advance of their actual release date. The release date should be the only portion of your schedule that you advertise to your audience, though you can use small videos and clips of the "behind the scenes" parts of your schedule, including recording and editing, as a way to promote your podcast.

Aside from a schedule, a routine is excellent for your consistency, too. A routine defines what you do once you are planning and writing shows, in the recording studio, editing software, or at the uploading or promotional phases. Your routine defines what you do, when, and how each session goes, and it should be developed in a way that maximizes your efficiency while ensuring that the same things are completed each time. For example, during the planning and writing phase, your routine might include brainstorming your show, picking out the best parts of your brain storm, fitting them into a pre-made outline for how your show goes, and then writing the first draft. Then, you can edit your writing, read it over, test it out, and edit it once more. This type of routine ensures your show is always well-written, contains plenty of exciting content, and has the same flow in every episode.

You can increase your consistency, too, by increasing your confidence and expanding your capacity to stay motivated. The easiest way to do this is by writing down your small achievements every single day, whether it be completing a new episode, gaining more listeners, or receiving a nice comment from a listener. As you realize how much success you are creating with your show, you will find it easier to maintain confidence and keep going because you realize that the effort you are putting into your show is paying off. When you start to see how well-received you and your show are, it becomes easier to motivate yourself to keep going.

THE GREATEST SOURCE OF MOTIVATION THAT THE MAJORITY OF PODCASTERS SLEEP ON

There is a specific source of motivation that everyone can tap into that most podcasters are not taking advantage of. This source of motivation can explode your confidence, increase your desire to pursue your success, and stay focused on creating the podcast of your dreams. It is a source that virtually everyone experiences, too. That is: feedback from your audience.

So many podcasters are so focused on themselves and what they are doing that they forget to stop and listen to their audience. Rather than truly hearing their audience celebrating their efforts and praising their content, they stay focused on what is happening directly in front of them. That may be the latest course, book, trend, or to-do list that needs to get done. Whatever it is, it is taking their attention away from a powerful motivator that can give you the energy to keep going, while also making you feel entirely fulfilled for everything you have already achieved.

Every single day, stop and listen to the positive feedback from your audience. Let it resonate with you. Take it in. And, let it guide you for where to go next. Stick to a schedule and put out content, as this will keep everyone else on your schedule and spending time with you, too. Plus, a schedule will keep you consistent. The more you adhere to your own schedule, the more your listeners will too, and the bigger your podcast will grow. Don't just schedule your episodes, schedule all of the tasks that go into producing and marketing your episodes, too. Then, listen to all of the great feedback you are receiving and let it sink in deep, giving you the motivation you need to keep going.

HOW TO TURN YOUR HOBBY INTO INCOME

FINALLY, IF YOU ARE WONDERING HOW YOU CAN TURN YOUR podcast into an income, we are there! Creating an income stream from your podcast is easier than you think, and you can actually start this process as soon as you have the foundations of a community centered around your podcast. Once you have a steady audience listening to your content week in week out, you can start monetizing your show so you can earn money, too!

7 STREAMS OF INCOME

Let the seven streams of income theory sink into your mindset before you get started with any monetization strategies. The seven streams of income theory are that all millionaires have at least seven successful income streams, and those income streams are directly responsible for building their wealth. They start with building one source of wealth, master it, and then move on to the next one. Once they master that, they do it all over again until they have at least seven consistent income streams. Sure enough, it works every time.

This theory is important for your podcast because it helps remind you not to put your eggs in one basket. There are many opportunities you have for monetizing your show and earning cash from your podcast. You need to be willing to keep your mind open and search for as many different methods as possible, but it is important that you master each method before moving on to the next so that you build in a concise, simple manner. If you try to rush it, you might overwhelm yourself, fail miserably, and possibly sabotage your reputation in the process. Be patient, sure-footed, and consistent, and you will get results.

Seven excellent streams of income you can tap into with your podcast include: affiliate marketing, sponsorships, selling merch, monetizing your content, selling intellectual property, hosting events, content marketing, or receiving donations from listeners - easily done using Patreon or other subscription platforms.

HOW TO CONSTRUCT THE PERFECT EMAIL THAT WILL GET SPONSORS RUNNING YOUR WAY

The number one method for getting income through your podcast is through getting sponsors. Sponsors are individuals who pay you to create a podcast episode. More specifically, they pay you to talk about them throughout your podcast episode. A sponsor will generally ask you to talk about their business at the beginning, middle, and end of the show. At the beginning, it is often introduced by saying, "Today's show is sponsored by _____." And then quickly introducing the company. Then, halfway through the show, you can share another piece of information about the show, and at the end of the show, you can create a call to action for your sponsor.

Getting sponsors can be accomplished by first creating a consistent listenership. Then, you need to create the perfect email to pitch your show to potential sponsors so that they consider sponsoring your show. The perfect sponsorship email should be written in three parts: the introduction, the pitch, and the call to action.

Before you ever send a sponsorship request letter to a brand, you need to make contact with that brand, build a relationship with them, and increase your rapport. You should never make a sponsorship your first point of contact with a brand, as this guarantees you will experience extremely low success rates in your ability to receive sponsorships. Instead, warm them up using a letter that introduces who you are, thanks them for their product, and establishes a connection between yourself and the brand. Never talk about financial requests, samples of your ability, pictures of your stakeholders or users, need for their sponsorship, generic wording, or assumptions about who their target audience is.

After you have spent some time building rapport, either by complementing their products, thanking them for making excellent products, or by asking for tips on how to make better use of products, you can send a sponsorship letter.

Your sponsorship letter needs to include five key pieces of information: an introduction, the reason you got in touch, information about your audience, your sponsorship opportunities, and a mention of when you will follow up with them.

Your introduction should not be a long-winded explanation of who you are, what your podcast is about, what your mission and vision are, and everything else. Instead, it should be a brief 2-3 sentence summary of who you are and what your podcast is about.

Your reason for getting in touch should explain why you chose their specific company, *not* a request for financial sponsorship. Make it clear as to why this particular company was the best for you to use, what you appreciate about their brand, and why you thought the two of you should meet. Create commonalities here by identifying where your common goals align and why you think your audience would love their products or services.

Your information about your audience needs to include details on who your audience is and why you feel they would like the product you are requesting to be sponsored for. Never assume you know who the brand's target audience is, but do explain why you feel your audience is a part of their target audience. Never leave data about your audience out of the pitch, or you will be leaving money on the table.

Your sponsorship opportunity should explain how you plan on sponsoring those products so you can increase sales for that company. You should include three methods for how you will promote them in a way that your audience will love, and that will earn them higher sales through your show. Explain information about branding, sampling, product placements, or even contests you would run to promote their products.

Lastly, you need to let them know when you will follow up so they know when to hear back from you. This is important as it shows you are serious about working together, and it sets the intention that follow up will be sent off. This way, your sponsor does not think you are spamming their inbox, because you are actually just following up on a promise you made in a prior email when you email them again at a later date.

GETTING INCOME STREAMS THROUGH YOUR PODCAST

Aside from sponsors, you can make money through other streams with your podcast, too. Podcasters often make money through selling products or services and using their podcasts to advertise them, affiliate marketing, crowdfunding, virtual summits, events, and premium content. All of these different income streams should always be developed in a way that clearly fits your industry, and that fits perfectly with your podcast, and brand. Never advertise something that is irrelevant to your podcast. Even if you think you have the right audience, if it is irrelevant, it will turn out poor results. That is not why your audience comes to you. Further, they may start to judge you or resent you for making them feel like all you want to do is sell to them. In worst-case scenarios, it may confuse your audience and drive them away, and these hiccups could make getting into your next sponsorship or income stream method even more challenging.

When you do begin adding income streams through your podcast, make sure you take your time, thoughtfully develop each income stream, and introduce it in a positive and meaningful way. Especially with your first one, take time to create a grand opening around the introduction of this new income stream if it is a product or service you are creating and selling, and get your audience excited about it. Always give everyone time to get used to each new income stream being added to your show, as you want them to have an opportunity to become familiar with it, interact with it, and ultimately purchase before you move on to the next opportunity. If you pack too many on at once, you might overwhelm or confuse your audience. Be patient, be persistent, and be passionate about everything you do, and your audience will always happily accept your advancements.

CONCLUSION

Congratulations on completing *Podcasting Made Simple!* This podcasting book was designed to help you launch your dream podcast, have a blast doing it, and possibly earn some money if you wish to monetize your podcast. By now, you have everything you need to feel confident launching your very own podcast!

Podcasting may not be a brand new medium, but it is one that is certainly growing in popularity. As it does, there is still a window of opportunity for new podcasters to jump on board and make a killing off their shows. However, there is no telling how long that window will remain open, so you need to get started with launching your podcast *right now*. There is no more time to waste!

Before you leave this book, I want to make sure that you feel rock solid on the foundation you require in order to build the next viral podcast. It starts with having a clear vision and having a great amount of passion in that vision. Never pursue a podcast that you are not absolutely passionate about, because you will not have the energy that you need to get people interested, keep your show going, and work through the challenges you will face along the way. Your passion will bring a level of energy to your voice and approach that is unparalleled, and that cannot be faked.

Once you have a foundation of passion, you need to focus on the logistics. While passion, energy, and relationships are at the core of your success, you also need to have high-quality podcasting supplies to keep you going. Focus on getting the best microphone you can afford, get yourself somewhere nice and quiet where you can record your episodes, and learn how to produce your episodes using basic editing strategies. Don't forget your signature intro or outro, as they are an important part of building the emotion and making your show a memorable one!

With the logistics figured out, you can focus all of your energy into creating episodes, building relationships with your audience, and using efficient marketing strategies to get your episodes to your audience. Always, *always* choose efficient marketing strategies, as they allow you to work smarter not harder. The best way to use the most efficient marketing strategies available is to research trending marketing strategies and begin using them in your business. Then, pay close attention to what is working and what isn't, and ditch anything that is not moving significant engagement around your platforms. Focus only on that which is really driving traffic your way.

It may take some time to build momentum around your podcast, even if you chose an elaborate grand opening strategy, and that is okay. I encourage you to tap into that passion that got you here in the first place and to focus on nothing other than creating shows filled with that passionate energy. Once you have your shows consistently flowing, learn to pour that passion into fun and effective marketing strategies, and trust that one of them is going to hit it big and bring you an audience. If you have the budget, you can also use paid advertisements to increase your marketing efforts and bring the audience to you. Even without a budget, make sure you always execute attraction marketing strategies as they will help you stand out.

Before you ever publish anything, whether it is an episode or a piece of promotional material, make sure you always review it to ensure it has the right energy and invokes the right emotions. You want to inspire happiness, curiosity, inspiration, passion, and excitement in your audience as much as possible. The more you can generate positive, meaningful associations between your podcast and your audience, the more they will tune in and listen to everything you have to say. This is how you create an audience full of loyal listeners who listen to every episode you launch and share all your best episodes with their friends.

Of course, don't forget about the value of relationships, either. You need to nurture the relationships with your audience and with your network so that you can experience all of the support you need to build your circle and keep it growing. With your audience, focus on building a strong parasocial relationship by caring for them, showing gratitude for their presence, and inviting them to engage with you. Give more than you take, focus on building relationships, and look for every way possible to add joy to the lives of your audience. Learning how to be a giving persona will make all the difference in the joy you gain from your podcast, and the loyalty you gain from your listeners.

With your network, focus on building strong relationships and always look to connect people with opportunities that would best suit them, and watch how this results in you being connected with great opportunities, too. Be generous in your relationships, and you will receive everything you want and need out of them, plus so much more. Your passion podcast can bring a great deal of fulfillment and joy to your life, if you let it.

In the next book included within this bundle, you'll learn in depth how to grow your show to get the audience you desire.

Happy podcasting!

Daniel Larson

Podcast Marketing: How to Easily Grow Your Podcast Audience in the Thousands and Make a Lasting Impact With Your Brand

INTRODUCTION

So, you swing the mic glumly towards yourself and woefully think "here we go again." Then you realize: "This is not how it's meant to be." Indeed, it isn't. But this, coupled with fatigue, headaches, and general malaise means there's something seriously wrong.

You've been working like a dog, day and night, to get this podcast business going, and it feels like it's all come to nought. You go for a major check-up and everything's fine. The doc says that maybe you need a holiday. You tell him you don't have the energy for a holiday. The doctor laughs. You feel like giving him a resounding slap, but lack of energy helps you resist that.

If the thought of going before the mic fills you with dread, then this, with the above symptoms, means one thing –

podfading! It's fading momentum because you've been slugging away with little results. It's enough to make anyone want to give up. Many do. It is ubiquitous and strikes a podcaster usually around Episode 7 or so. It's at the time when your listenership seems to be dwindling by the day. You feel that the dream that you started with appears to be morphing into a nightmare and you feel that you're not cut out for this after all.

"The excitement is gone," you think as you morosely trudge out of your little studio that took such joy to assemble. "Wait! Not so fast, mister," says a voice inside your head, and if anyone should know what's going on, it's the voice inside your head. "What?" you say irritably to the floor. Your dog stares warily at you. After all, you've been snapping at the floor for a couple of days now. The floor, though, has remained resolutely silent. "Your dream, buddy, your dream! Are you going to give up this easily?"

A little spark begins to burn within you. You head for the computer and google Amazon, hoping to find some reading material on this condition. You were very lucky to find this very book whose introduction you are now reading. This is a remarkable step-by-step guide on podcast marketing and how to organically grow your listenership by the thousands!

I know exactly what's happening with this guy, and if he follows this guide faithfully, he'll soon be back inside his little studio, podcasting merrily away.

You see, I have worked with, and guided many podcasters and discover most of them pay no heed to marketing at all. This is a big mistake. I know what steps a podcaster should take to see the business booming. You'll notice that I often use the terms podcast and podcast business interchangeably. This is for two reasons. Firstly, the tough pill to swallow for most podcasters is that to actually see a significant and consistent uptrend in their listenership, you have to take the marketing side of it seriously. And to do this my friend, it's vital to view the podcast as somewhat a business - this means you are acting professionally and have a responsibility to hold yourself accountable for doing so. Having coached hundreds of podcasters, I can tell you now that a big difference between those who do well and those who podfade is this little shift in perspective. People who do well with their podcast, although it's still their absolute passion, treat it very seriously as if it were a business; they treat their guests with respect and continue to nurture their relationship after the show, send appropriate emails to their mailing list...the list goes on. But most importantly, they work and educate themselves on the best practices. They take consistent action with their podcast marketing which *of course* gets them better results. If you don't have this perspective you're far more likely to get complacent, become demotivated and watch your numbers dwindle.

Here's the thing. Your podcasting is a business, and as a business, you have to get involved in marketing to get your business to grow. That's fundamental to business progression. This is a point that does not seem to register on the excitement scale. What appears to be an inevitable sticking point is the one described above with the disgruntled podcaster, who thought that branding involved a hot iron and a cow. It does, but fortunately not here.

Hence, this book. I don't want to see any more podcasters falling victim to podfading, whiling away their time on some ghastly plateau. They fall prey to some dodgy blogs online, which very wrongly informs them that they are going to break the bank when it comes to marketing.

Organic growth means that you use all the tools (social media is a large part of this) that you have at your disposal and get thinking smartly about growth. Facebook, Instagram, and Twitter mean that you keep your money in the bank, not out of it.

You may well place some ads on Facebook, but you'll find all the info on that inside and this breaks no bank!

It also involves something very important. Probably the most important point to emerge from the book. That is, do you *really* know who's listening? You have got to get to know your audience backwards. Who are they? What are their likes and dislikes? What do they think of your podcast? What else would they like to see you have on your show? What are their spending habits? Leisure habits? What times do they normally listen? On what device do they listen? Where do they shop? What video games do they play? The list goes on and on and it's crucial that you have as much data as possible at your disposal. Demographic analysis is everything!

Triple-up on your engagement with your listeners. Find out what makes them tick and then give them what they want. In the end, it's not what *you* want. You can throw out ideas and think they're like the Dream Cruise liner docking outside your apartment. On the other hand, your audience could be turning off in droves. And a host of droves belting away is not a pretty sight. Listen to your audience. This is why you're in business. Otherwise, you'll be blabbing into the ether with not a single soul tuning in.

Podcasting is becoming a massive market. Witness the eagerness that Apple is giving to its podcasting efforts, as is Netflix and other streaming platforms. Everyone's getting in on the act. Do you know how many podcasts are being turned into TV series? It's huge.

Now, you can't just sit back and wait for the (branded) cash cow to start dropping money. As with most things in life, you have to work for it. Firstly, concentrate on your audience and build it, brick by brick, like they do with most skyscrapers. I have a friend who has just launched a YouTube channel and he has to religiously ensure he gets the viewers to "like and subscribe" so the algorithms calculate and reflect the audience numbers. This is the only way he's going to get big names on his show because the first thing that everyone asks is: "How many viewers do you have?", and he's got to prove it.

It's the same with podcasting. How many listeners do you have? How is that curve looking? Up or down? Now, you're already in a funk because of your declining, or stagnant, listenership, but now you know that there is something you can do about it. No, you're not going to place ads on billboards on the freeway because that will indeed break the bank. You are going to follow the guidelines presented here.

In the increasingly crowded podcast marketplace, have you figured out how you are going to stand out in the crowd? Also, how are you going to promote yourself? I feel like a stuck record (you know what that is, right?) here, sorry everyone, but that's the basis of what you are meant to be doing. This is the fundamental, basic point I have to stress.

This is how you go beyond your little studio and cross-pollinate your space. This is how you begin to monetize your business. It's how you'll grow like wildfire. You will get to the point where you look back at that glum person shuffling out of the studio and you won't recognize him at all. Were you really like that?

Maybe your podfading took a different turn and you just switched to something totally new while leaving your dream behind. You thought that maybe becoming a personal trainer at the gym is what you were meant to do, but you were never happy. That's because podcasting is what you were meant to do and that's why you spent so long getting started, making it a meticulous mission. Go back to where your heart is, friend, and get over the stumbling blocks.

Somewhere deep inside you knew it was going to be more than just your first love, talking into the mic. You thought you could get away with just doing that but then you realized you couldn't and so the conflict inside you began. "I can't do the other things," the old you said. "Yes, you can. Yes, you can," said the new voice inside. So just do it.

I know someone who once self-published a novel he'd written over several years. It was a rather good book too. So, he put the book on the platform and just left it there. He used to gaze at the book cover proudly. Then he forgot about it. Some two years later he found the book still there and the price, sadly, had decreased rather profoundly. If he had read up on all the jargon that came with the self-publishing thing, he would have realized that he had to market the book himself. The point is no one knew it was there. I told him to get to it, but he resignedly said, "It's just too much effort." The book continues to languish there.

I find that sad. That very much sums up what podfading can do for you. It also points you in the right direction of what marketing can accomplish. You will discover hidden joys with branding and see your dream recover and then you will take your business to places that it's never been before.

You've gazed rather wearily at the influencers that gather on YouTube and TikTok. Very often these people get paid by sponsors if they have a following of millions, which many of them do. Is that what you have to become to grow your business? No, sir. You want to be a podcaster, and that's what you will be. Becoming an influencer is for someone else. Not to say you can't bring one in as a guest. They can make great guests.

You've engaged with your audience and they feel that you're someone worth hanging onto, to discuss things with, to guide them, to inform them. It's a wonderfully joyous (and responsible) position to be in.

In this book, I will show you a clear podcast marketing framework you can use to consistently grow. You will stop guessing, save time and start feeling confident.

Who knows? That cruise liner may still dock outside your apartment. Wave at the people on board, and let it sail on. You? Get back inside. You've got work to do.

KNOWING YOUR TARGET AUDIENCE

"IF YOU ARE WORKING ON SOMETHING EXCITING YOU REALLY CARE about, you don't have to be pushed. The vision pulls you" – *Steve Jobs*

Crew: Captain Stephen Mark Ray, USN
ISS Location: Low Earth Orbit
Earth Date: 4 March 2021
Earth Time (GMT): 13:30
C1 FROM THE CAPTAIN'S LOG

Onboard the International Space Station, Earth remains a perfect, glowing orb. Its excellence astounds me. The fact we are actually here is riveting. I feel so in awe of the magnificence before me. It is perfect. It is life's aspirational endeavor encapsulated in one brief shining glorious moment. Forever.

What is everyone doing down there? Rushing about, forgetting about the glory above? Forgetting they, too, belong to the glory. It is above, below, surrounding and inside. They can tap into it anytime they want. But they've forgotten.

Except some. People who know the motivating power of a massive transformative purpose. Making the impossible possible, like us here on the ISS. Who would have thought?

Social movements, rapidly growing organizations and remarkable breakthroughs in science and technology have something in common – they're often byproducts of a deeply unifying purpose. There's a name for this breed of motivation. It's called massive transformative purpose, or MTP. I'd love to write more about the MTP right now, but I've not got time. But rest assured, my friend. By the end of my logs, you'll understand exactly how to make the impossible possible, with a massive transformative purpose. The more we organize around the massive transformative purpose, the harder we'll work. We know. Great people like you know. We are more dedicated and we solve big problems faster. Probably, and most importantly, the more fulfilled we'll feel about the work we do.

Research is done at the ISS that can't be done anywhere else. This scientific research benefits all on earth. This MTP work inspires us, that's why we do it. It inspires you too, even though you may not be aware of it. Your work, your passion, is just as important. Without you, there's no real reason for us to be up here. Think of that.

You've got your little studio up and running. This is your podcasting business and you're very proud of it. You have every reason to be so. Well done. You've figured out your shows for the week and you pat yourself on the back (slight contortion tactics needed here, so please be careful) that you've done a great job. Time to get the ablutions done and then record your podcast.

It's 10 am, so there's plenty of time. Your script is waiting for you on the table in the studio, you're going to get a lovely cup of steaming coffee and are set to have a great time with the topic you've chosen. It sounds like the perfect set-up. Your dream is coming true, and you're doing what you've always wanted to do.

But wait! It may be the perfect setting to do your podcast, but do you know who you are reaching? Is there an audience who's actually tuning in and, importantly, who exactly are they?

If you don't know, and be honest here, it can't just be your pals and Aunt Ruth, who you know are tuning in. You've got to have an audience! And you've got to know those people backwards and inside out, like you've known them all for years. You can then match that with your studio set-up, and, hey presto, you're starting (note, *starting*) on the road to discovery.

HOW DO YOU GET TO KNOW YOUR AUDIENCE?

With all the social media that's available, it's never been so easy to get to know an audience with data flying at you from all directions. You identify what's happening on the various platforms and who the responders are from their texts. You can accumulate so much information that it'll be coming out of your ears. You'll notice trends on the platforms, and you can identify with some. Do your podcasts reflect these trends that appear so vital to the people? So, you begin to build your database, which you will guard with your life as it is the most important asset you'll ever have.

From this base, you'll construct your business as to what the content of the shows will be and you'll know how to angle this content because you'll get to know your audience demographic intimately (male, female, ages, likes, dislikes, habits) and will be able to resonate with them immediately. You think I'm saying you need to change the main subject of your show to another related topic because that's what's more popular right now? Oh God no, I would never! There's no shortage of people interested in any sub-topic you can think of, and that's a fact. I simply mean that the better you know your audience, the better you can package your content to appeal to this particular demographic in a more tasteful way.

Physically, (if you can, pandemic wise) hang out where your audience hangs out and connect. Is your demographic correct? It more than likely is, and you've got to tell people what you do and find out from them what they would like to hear on your podcasts. Much more in the next chapter. If you're not a gregarious kind of person, become one. I jest, but at the same time, hiding behind a pillar and giggling isn't going to get you anywhere. I'm not saying you have to rush around demanding to know certain details. This is likely to get you punched or slapped, or both, so be gentle and caring about it. What I'm saying is be your normal self but be curious. In the course of things, you get to know people and an evening out can be full of surprises and great data-collecting.

When you're doubling up on this effort from home, get to your computer and put in the due hours going onto the various social media sites and getting to know who and what is trending. Get onto these sites yourself and become part of the trend. This way, people will get to know you, and you can drop in your post that you have a podcasting business and tell people what's on the next show. Whatever's trending will be a part of that show. This is not an overnight thing, so don't expect miraculous results immediately. However, you are most definitely on the right path. Know that, and it'll give you the confidence to carry on digging up data.

Knowledge is power, right? This database is both knowledge and power and will have a snowball effect with you adding to it. The people you meet on Instagram, Twitter, and Facebook, know other people on different platforms. They will tell their friends what a cool person they met, and so the ball rolls on. All this takes work and dedication. Sometimes you may feel that you're not achieving anything but give it time. At least you're starting to know who your audience is and not just dancing in the dark, as the saying goes.

THE IMPORTANCE OF KNOWING YOUR TARGET AUDIENCE

In the past, you've been acting like a shotgun and spraying away into the ether at who? You didn't know. All you knew was that you were talking about something very important to *you*, so people obviously would have tuned in because the topic was so critical. To *you*. Maybe not so much to the people you would like to be reaching. But how would you know if you don't know the people? You can't possibly set goals or determine the content and intended results if you don't know who you're speaking to. It's like introducing a new hairspray and advertising it to construction economists. It doesn't quite go, does it? As funny as that may seem, this is kind of like what podcasters are doing when their audience is a mystery.

You are going to get used to analytics and discovering what your audience is doing with your show. Are they clicking off? Why on earth would they do something like that? Was there any traffic generated? That should interest you, particularly as this will indicate whether you are growing or not. Knowing your audience will give you details of needs and hopes and you can address this not only on your podcast but on cross-plugs to social media platforms and possibly by email advertising and your website. There's much more on this coming up.

Remember, podcasting could be pulling in the older, moneyed, and educated listeners because of the very nature of the medium. It's not a visual medium, which is the starting point for many young people. In this instance, you could be faced with a complex dilemma. By becoming involved with your outreach, you will be getting the younger audience because they follow influencers and are more involved with social media. Not that moneyed and educated listeners aren't, but not to the extent of a younger crowd and also not for the reasons of that demographic. I wouldn't say that the corporate president of Global Finance and Futures heads straight home to TikTok, but he's obviously not adverse to Twitter and LinkedIn.

So, what do you do in this instance? You can't please everyone, and you will certainly not appeal to everyone. You must decide what market you want to reach – if it's the moneyed folk, get to know that audience. If it's the younger crowd, the same applies. It's just that you can't cast your net so wide that you think you'll grab (and please) everyone. You'll end up with no one. Make up your mind, choose a sector, and go for it.

One of my past clients had a podcast all about productivity, and helping people keep motivated and inspired. We'll call him Clive. There are so many shows like this out there and I had no problem with the topic. It's the angle in which he approached his marketing that dropped him in the vast, monotonous ocean of productivity 'gurus' wailing. That's not a pleasant scene to imagine, is it? If you asked someone who has a similar show who the show is for, their answer tends to be along the lines of:

"My show is for everyone, I don't like to put myself in a bracket. It's relatable and I want to help everyone. It's for anyone that will listen!"

The issue with this is it's too broad, the show doesn't speak to a specific target audience. It's for everyone. But think about it, when has something made for everyone been so attractive? We as humans love being part of a club or community. When you market your show in this way, you aren't speaking to a specific person who has specific needs. So when they come across your promotion it just sounds like fluff. It's noise, so they ignore it as once again, it's not speaking to them, it's speaking to everyone.

On the other hand, it's so satisfying when you find that perfect Youtube channel or podcast, TV show or even music that you feel is made perfectly for you. It's like an angel came from the sky and plonked it on your lap, just when you were thinking about something like this. Just as you were about to cave in and try that less-than-thrilling soap opera your neighbor keeps banging on about. Instead of the show being targeted at everyone, it should be specific. This way you know how to frame your promotion and content (both on the podcast and outside of it) to get the interest of that particular person.

Imagine you are at an archery contest and your target is everyone, that means everything. You don't really have a target at all, you don't know how far away the 'target' is, you don't know how much power you have to put behind your shot. You have no idea what material is best for your arrow. You have no clue how to approach reaching and hitting the target. Oh wait, that's because there is no target! But when you have an actual target, imagine the marketing efforts are the arrow. You now know where and how to position yourself to hit your target, you know what angle and how much force and power to put behind your arrow (your marketing efforts). You even know that there are better materials than others you can use, given how much (and how strong) wind is between you and the target. You're focused, you are far more likely to actually hit your target.

So back to podcasting, and the productivity podcast. After much discussion and analysing Clive's analytics, he decided he wanted to target university students who are struggling to stay productive and motivated whilst having the time of their life (so they say) at university. We positioned the podcast as the 'guide' for students in that particular situation.

Clive also decided that the marketing angle is going to be the fact that he wanted to help the students transition from being students to masters, and how is this accomplished? By sharing productivity hacks which will inspire these students to take the action needed to become a master and get top grades when they graduate.

When you have picked an ideal listener, you have a target audience. You now have a strong hook for your show. You can speak directly to the needs of those students and provide them the solution (listening to your show) they have been wanting.

After some more work, this was the refined hook for the show:

"Sharing productivity hacks so that you, the student, can become a master. Helping you stay inspired and motivated so you can graduate proudly and still have a blast at university!"

The best thing about this type of marketing is it can't be ignored, it's intentional and serves a specific purpose. There's no more *'guessing'* what will attract listeners. Anyone student in this situation who wants a productivity hack and is lacking in motivation will most definitely check out the show. It's not noise, it's relevant to them. It's exclusive!

It's like a birthday cake, it's much more attractive if it's got your name on it (and chocolate sprinkles).

TO GET BACK ON TRACK THEN, THE IMPORTANCE OF ANALYSIS and identification is vital for marketing strategies that are going to work. This is not necessarily conventional advertising per se, but any plans or promotions on-air or off-air that are going to drive listener growth.

You must sync your marketing strategies to your audience that is aligned to your podcast and if you are not a hundred percent aware of who that is, you are going to end up in a mess. We are talking about organic marketing growth. This is probably even more specific and targeted to a definite audience than traditional advertising and thus, audience identification is more crucial than ever.

IDENTIFYING YOUR TARGET AUDIENCE

Now that we know that you are not going to waste precious time, you must get into the particulars of your audience, and I mean the nitty-gritty which will help you to identify the perfect avatar. This perfect member of your audience will teach you everything that you need to know for on-the-spot identification of your target audience. We skimmed through the demographics earlier, but now it's time to dig deeper. We have to get into hopes and desires, as well as where this person lives, shops, eats, devours radio and TV (network or streaming?), what transport do they use, what social media platforms do they use, do they travel frequently, what problems do they have, what do they dislike? What do they like?

How are you going to get all this detail? You join the communities you can find that are most relevant to your chosen audience. The best place to start is Facebook groups. In nearly any niche, you can find plenty of Facebook groups with hundreds to thousands of members. You can also spend some time with social listening software, where you will gather an enormous amount of data on users of social media. You are going for information that you are not likely to get elsewhere. The best thing is to combine this with market research from sociologists which can be found online. You can go to www.survey-monkey.com or find other sites offering the same kind of information. This will cost you a little but will not break the bank and it's worth it. It's either this or doing your own survey, which is very time-consuming and patience-battering, so I would go for the former. This is very important as you're probably getting data your opposition may not have thought of, and it's defining who your avatar is. Go to www.hootsuite.com to get the lowdown on social media analytics as well. This, combined with your surveys, will give you a great lowdown on your audience. Any psychological analyses by marketers are vital. Use your ingenuity to wrap your head around what you find.

Is this not a little intrusive, you may ask, hooking onto subjects like temperament, sensitivity, and curiosity? Not really. Okay, it's deeper than just "What kind of soap do you prefer?", but then if you are going to get to the "real thing", the avatar supreme, then the sociological/psychological answers are what you need. This makes a person complete. It also gives the podcaster a magnificent eye-opener in what is going on in the minds of the audience. It will result in subjects that can be covered (generally) in the podcast, and because you now know it affects many audience members, you can be assured of good listenership. An avatar is the embodiment of your perfect listener. The right demographic completely and who fits everything that you've ever wanted in a listener. This listener would be empathetic and will always find time for clever, fun engagement. This avatar should be a fundamental element of your brand strategy (much more on this is coming up) and a key element of your marketing. This is "someone" who anyone in your business can turn to when they are in search of the correct demographic for your show.

Here's an example I made, to help one of my clients who ran a home security podcast.

I'd like you to meet Robert. He is 40 years old and owns a single-family home in a large city in the United States. Robert has two children, a stay-at-home wife, and owns two vehicles. He purchased his new home two years ago and some of his neighbours have experienced some sort of security breach. Robert uses Facebook, although he is not overly attached to the platform. His favorite genre of music is rock, although he is very much partial to the classic mainstream hits that were prevalent when he was growing up in the 90s. Although Robert is a middle-class worker and doesn't have lots of money to throw around, he is looking for tips on how to secure his home without having to buy an experienced monitored system, though he might buy one in the future.

This is by no means set in stone once created, you should update it whenever you gather more data or feel that certain parts become outdated. Roll with the times! And yes, *it is okay* to change your opinion or stance when presented with new information.

THE A-Z OF ANALYTICS

You've got to get used to hearing the word because it's going to get bandied about rather a lot. It follows on from what we've been talking about, the profiles of the audience members. Now you can get the total number of members that have turned into a specific episode, how many have clicked out, and much more. Everything about audience members is essential knowledge, but analytics is what gives marketers the reason to use the podcast business to advertise, or for the podcaster to get top profile guests onto the show. You'll get to know if your downloads are on the rise, what episodes are the most popular, and so on. Without analytics, you wouldn't have a clue. You can now make strategic decisions and apply them.

The most common analytics provider is Google (Google Analytics), and this is used for online measuring virtually everywhere. Other providers are Apple, Spotify, and the host that you use. There is a bit of a problem with podcasting analytics now in that they are not fully standardized, and this can cause a bit of a headache when trying to get a complete picture. However, IAB certification promises a very accurate analysis. The name of the program which will become your best friend is Captivate.fm and this will give all the details that are required in a friendly-to-find way via a dashboard. If you want to know how podcast downloads are counted, you will find all the details here.

To gauge your download success will also depend on what your idea of "success" is. It could be that you want to know if you've risen from 10 to 80? Or it could be that you've begun to shoot for the stars and need to be in the thousands. Whatever your idea of success, I hope that those figures have started to rise. Don't forget, though, the rationale behind the real success story is what changes have been made to ensure you have begun to know your audience so well it's like breathing. True success, the lasting kind, does not happen overnight. It takes time to build that community that you're after and even longer to ensure that you keep that ever-so precious audience.

Okay, back to the dashboard. Those analytics! Captivate.fm will bring together analytics from multiple sources which save you from hunting around. It will let you know how many subscribers and non-subscribers have tuned in. Your goal, naturally, is to convert those non-subscribers into subscribers! It's much harder to get this done as opposed to, say, YouTube, where you can like and subscribe online while the video is playing. Podcasters usually don't charge for a subscription but having a *definite number* who want to be a part of your community can be valued not in monetary terms, but loyal listenership. You can thus prove to topflight guests, booking agents, and potential sponsors, how many signed-up members you have. This is very important!

HOW TO MEASURE AUDIENCE ENGAGEMENT WITH PODCAST ANALYTICS

Unique Listeners are very important, and this is how Captivate.fm describes them: "A Unique Listener is defined by the IAB as a listener with the same IP address and the same device within a certain timeframe. It's 100% anonymous and is a great way of estimating how many individual people your show is reaching." Unique Listeners are used to measure true audience size, so obviously, this is something critical and, as said, also can be used as a bargaining chip.

Stats can be used to note the number of downloads as well as the popularity of the show and a particular episode. Keep a beady eye on this! This is a true representation of how your shows are doing. With Captivate, you can also go to a specific episode and get a complete dashboard of stats, including trends, web player analytics, demographics, and downloads. In case you forgot how a particular guest fared, or how your topic was received, this handy tool gives you all the info in one fell swoop!

If you want to see what episode is trending, you'll be able to find out just by logging into Captivate. The analytics tool gives you so much information about everything you can think of and your hosting would suffer without it. For instance, you've thought of a great sponsor who thinks this could fly but needs to know the numbers. Luckily, thanks to your old pal Captivate, you have the numbers. The sponsor, though, is still a bit worried about the demographic and their motivation. Well, prove it to him via all the reams of data you have on your audience through your work via Social Streams and the surveys that you've scoured through, that you know your audience intimately and that this sponsor would be perfect. Chances are that he will be mightily impressed with your work. Once you've done your homework, you'll get that well-earned confidence. Knowing your audience means you're hitting the mark. It's a bullseye, buddy.

If your episode ratings continue to go up, you know that you're really onto a good thing and you've proved that you can sustain your growth. But be careful. I can see you going uh-oh, what's coming up now?

Something big.

You've seen the movie. A rapidly rising star is off to rehab. It seems that everyone's off to rehab. It's sort of like a rite of passage. But *not* for you. Get that? You're made for better things.

Burnout is a common condition for podcasters due to the stress of growing listenership and keeping the channel high on the ratings. Sometimes, this is when podcasters fall away. It's rather alarming to realize how ubiquitous this is among the podcaster fraternity.

However, and you must be very grounded to do this, you could talk about what stress you face and how debilitating burnout can be. Maybe add in a guest who has been through the same stuff. This could make for an incredibly great show. Rising podcast star and Riza Miller talk about how stress can get you, especially when you're riding high and bring you down with a thud! Also, discuss what you can do about it (what you're doing now is a good start) and overcoming it. People will love you for being open and honest, and having the same fears and tribulations just like they do.

HOW TO USE STATS AND SURVEYS

How do you produce the kind of show that's your dream to do? If you've been following the analytics details you will know how to optimize the stats you've been presented with and know what things you've got to change. It's been an *annus horribilis* of a decade so far and people want something that's going to set them alight with curiosity and desire. You've been through all those research sociology stats (okay, not yet, but you will) so you know what gets the people going, what their fears are, what they worry about, what their ambitions are. If everyone's fleeing the ship because your content is not hitting the desired mark, you have to go back to the drawing board and adjust your marketing, content and production plans. At what point are people fleeing? After 10 ? After one minute?

Seeing as you will become *au fait* with all this detail, you will be able to tell at a glance. If they're leaving after one minute, sometimes very drastic overhauling is needed here.

You are going to come up with a show that will have people glued to their devices. Speaking of which, you'll find out what the devices are from the analytics and you'll know just how many are tuned in to what device. When you find this out, you can find out which platform to drive traffic to.

Analyse which of your past shows has done well and dissect the info to find out why. What was the topic for that show? What do the peaks and valleys show at varying points of the podcast? You can align the analytics of the show and see what was happening during the high spikes and downward turns.

If you start to see a trend in people tending to drop off when you stray too far away from the topic of your show, we can assume your audience is mainly coming to listen to you discuss the title of the show. I see this too often with some of my clients, you have a podcaster who is passion driven - they know what they want the title of their show to be but they also like being "natural and letting the conversations flow". This is great of course, but the only issue is that you can get side-tracked and end up on an entirely different topic, where many listeners will switch off. Keep people's attention in mind. Don't make your show longer than it needs to be. You want to have a fine balance of your personality and off-cuff conversation, with relevance to your title. Now don't get me wrong, I'm sure when Joe Rogan does an episode on how martial arts changed his life but starts talking about his top 3 snack cakes halfway through, there are still tens of thousands of people eagerly anticipating which cake takes the top spot (how can it not be Twinkies?). However, as a less established podcaster, while you are *still building the relationship with your audience*, unfortunately you don't have the liberty to talk about anything in the world and have them continue listening. You can't have your (snack) cake and eat it.

If your audience wants to get their daily dose of a topic that you promise to deliver, stick to it. If in post production you realise you've gone off topic, cut it to where you come back on track. Don't feel like you have to get to that hour mark just for the sake of it. What's the point? You would be wasting time and energy as no one's listening that far ahead...

You analyse your analytics and realise that there is a trend that halfway through your one hour show, listeners start dropping like flies. This once again can tell you the attention span of the people who are watching your show. You have to remember that listening to podcasts is a habitual act. They could be listening to your show on the way to work, washing the dishes, at the gym. The point is, a lot of podcast listeners almost have a cue as to when they will listen to your show. And there you have it, another reason to create an avatar! To guide you into creating episodes that are best suited to the people on the other end's listening habits. If a good 70% of your listeners tend to listen to your show for 30 minutes but the show is an hour long, maybe they go on a walk which takes around 30 minutes. Although they might want to finish your show, they don't. They carry on with different activities and forget to revisit the rest of the show (life happens). This would be an indicator that you should split up your show into two parts, which has multiple benefits:

1. Increase the perceived value of your show. When you finish listening to a podcast entirely, you perceive the value of what you're listening to very high! It's a subconscious thing that happens. Compare it to if you made it halfway through a podcast and clocked out. You never went back and finished that episode, did you? It's the difference between getting upset that a movie is finishing and not realising 120 minutes has gone by, compared to looking at your watch 30 minutes in, wondering when it will end.

2. Increased retention time for your show which will increase the organic ranking of your podcast on your platform. Directories use retention time as a way to rank how relevant your podcast is to keywords related to your title. (More on SEO later). The algorithm highly values shows as it keeps your audience engaged for a longer period of time. 80-90% retention time is far better compared to 40-50%. Not all hosts have this feature, but Spotify does. Although you may not get the most accurate data if you have only a few listeners on Spotify, it's still better than nothing, and gives you a rough idea of when people are dropping off.

3. Increased engagement on your podcast with your audience. People will listen to your call to action, do you know why? Because they are actually listening to the entire show so they actually get to a point where they hear your call to action. This increases your audience base if you're building a community outside of the podcast i.e. Facebook group. This also means you can get them to subscribe, rate and review your show. Again this is only possible with 80% engagement or more. So if you're wondering why people aren't engaging with your show, it's because they clocked out long before they could listen to you giving your call to action.

4. Increased content and interest for your show. You are able to provide more content for you listeners to indulge with, by splitting your show into two parts you're leaving them at a cliffhanger, leaving them longing for the part 2. This also means you become less stressed as you haven't got a busy uploading schedule, things are nicely spaced.

You'll soon learn what not to tackle or what to do again and what you were doing/saying during the high and low moments. Yup, even though the show was trending, and it was a magnificent piece of work even if you do say so yourself, there are times when it could have been better.

How are you doing so far, friend?

Hopefully, biting your nails in the anticipation of the next chapter! It's going to be good. If you can't get listeners after what you've read on these pages, go drive a bus. Only joking - you should only go and do that if you can't get more listeners after reading all of the book.

~

CHAPTER TAKEAWAYS

- How to get to know your audience. If you don't know who you are going out to, there's not much point. Even worse, do you know if there's anyone out there listening to your show? If it's only cousin Gus, things are looking pretty bad. Get to know your audience. You know the kind of person you want? Go after them.
- What should you know about your audience? You should know about their likes and dislikes, their hopes and dreams, where they stay – in fact, as much as you can. You know what you want in an audience and there are many ways that you can get to know how to attract them and to enable them to resonate and relate to you and your content.
- The importance of social media analytics. These will give you the who, where, why and not of who's listening, how many are listening, where they are listening, what your best show was, is your show

trending? Oh, and so much more. This can't be over-emphasised enough.

- Who are your Unique Listeners? They are used to measure true audience size and this, in turn, is gained from your analytics. This is vital information to have on hand when pursuing would-be sponsors and guests.

- What do you need to prove to be able to book top-flight guests? You need to know the number of people you are reaching, and who it is that you're reaching to convince people to part with their money or time.

- How to construct a great show. You need your head to be working in its true ingenious style. You know what you are the most informed about and love to talk about these topics. Also, get ideas from listeners and guests.

CALL TO ACTION

CREATE YOUR TARGET AVATAR, AND DON'T CUT CORNERS! USE our dear friend Robert from a few pages back as a template.

BONUS #1

If you're reading this as a paperback, visit this link to access your bonuses: https://daniel-larson.com/pmbonus

GROWING YOUR COMMUNITY ORGANICALLY AND LEVERAGING IT

"MAKE YOUR LIFE A MASTERPIECE; IMAGINE NO LIMITATIONS ON what you can be, have or do." – Brian Tracy

Crew: Captain Stephen Mark Ray, USN
ISS Location: Low Earth Orbit
Earth Date: 10 March 2021
Earth Time (GMT): 15:30
C2 FROM THE CAPTAIN'S LOG

It's at this particular time, I've noted that the sun's rays crash in through my portal. This is when I love to write. Since the last entry, our research continues apace. The radiant orb below continues to float. We are busy, we are motivated, we love what we're doing.

We are deeply driven by Massive Transformative Purpose (MTP), like certain people on earth. We know you're busy discovering it.

How do we know? We just do. Call it a Passion Performance that rebounds through space and time. Some people have been attuned to this vibration for a long time, probably since birth. One of them is Elon Musk, to whom we owe so much. One of his SpaceX's crafts has just delivered a ton of supplies and research material to us. We find it natural that Elon is aligned so closely to space. He is driven by the belief that humans must become multi-planetary species. Making this reality is his purpose. SpaceX's MTP to revolutionize space technology and enable people to live on another planet creates a shared aspirational purpose within the organization. His Tesla cars are computers on wheels. That this man is one of the world's richest men is no coincidence, although his mission, I feel, means much more than that. SpaceX's MTP is – huge and aspirational; focused; unique to the company; aimed at radical transformation and forward-looking.

It's focused on creating a different future. It engages people's hearts and minds to work together. If you're thinking like this, then MTP is part of your life and your future. The only difference is that we're up here, and you're down there.

HANGING OUT WHERE THE AUDIENCE IS

Hey friend, how ya doin'? Feel revitalized and ready to go?

You need to do something for me first off. This is a night exercise. It's got to be as cloudless as possible. I want you to lean out your window or go outside and gaze up into the sky. I know in NYC, LA, London and the other big guys, the sky isn't going to be as clear as in the country but gaze up anyway. Count the stars you can see. Think of those stars as listeners to your podcast. Isn't that great? You've lost track even before you've turned your head. If you could have just a handful of what you see...

Well, you can. And you've already been through the starter pack in Chapter One, so you know what to do. In this chapter, we're going to go deeper into the engagement of your listeners. It's a kind of "were you really listening in Chapter One?". If the info in this chapter sounds foreign, it is advised that you read that chapter again. Don't grumble and go back to that snapping at the floor. We've been through that. Right, you've closed your mouth and widened your eyes. That's the spirit.

Ready for adventure? Off you go on Mission Engage and Grow!

Your audience is very much present online and on myriad social media platforms and you most definitely will connect with them there. Where do you start? Where to go to find maximum win-through? You suddenly feel overwhelmed, and all the while retreating into the safety of your little studio, falling over the dog, who's given up on you, and landing up in your well-known chair in front of the mic. You quickly buckle yourself in, airplane style (you thought that was rather a cute touch back then) and fold your arms across your chest. "I can't do it," you say through clenched teeth.

You can, and you will. If you want to grow your podcast you will. If you don't, well, stay where you are, and I'll spray anti-cobweb spray over you so at least the spiders don't get to you. How else are you going into the heads of people that are hopefully going to be your audience? And importantly, how are they going to get into yours?

A great tip here would be to get a guest – this could be a friend who's very knowledgeable in a specific area and has an active social media following or at least a strong presence on social media. You'll be able to leverage off his social media once he has made it known that he's going to be discussing this topic with you, and in so doing you make a start on social media. We'll be going through these topics in a lot more detail throughout the book, but this is to get you thinking about it. You could plug your website, too, during the show. Yes, you've got to have a website, and although some companies have made it very easy for you to build one, if this is not your thing, pay some bucks and get it done properly. Once you have a thrilling website (as opposed to a boring website that proclaims it's been done quickly by an amateur), you will attract lots of visitors. Hanging out where your audience is, is knowing where they are active the most on social media. Check your Twitter feeds, Facebook, Instagram, Spotify and find out who's saying what. You've got to start adding your voice here and add some controversial elements too. This is a great way to get people to react. Remember, nothing happens overnight. Start off using Twitter with a hashtag so people can start following you. You are going to have really interesting topics on your podcast…talk about them.

SENSE OF COMMUNITY

Your audience is more likely to want to connect with you as you become well-known to them and they start to take you into their confidence. I suspect that many will turn up as guests, and that's great. There is a sense of community here, and that's important to have for your podcast. You have become the voice of the community. You get inside their heads and speak about things they are really into, their hopes and desires and what's happening generally in their lives. There's a sense of belonging here. It's great for you, and great for them. You can leverage a lot out of this intimacy.

All the time, you've figured out so much about your audience, you could write a book on them. I know I've asked a lot here, especially the helping out bits, but if you want to go from zero to hero quickly, this is one sure-fire way of going about it. There are many top-class community platforms online that can be used to network and discuss topics, which in turn lead back to your podcast. You starting to notice how everything links together? These platforms could provide potential new listeners and guests. The main thing is that you have begun to converse and interact with your potential audience.

THE TOOLS (IN BRIEF)

So, one of the social media platforms you're going to connect with friends and talk about your show is, firstly, Instagram. This could be your primary tool for marketing your show and staying connected. The visual nature of the medium could be great for connecting with pics from night-outs and so on, and for publicizing guests that are going to be on the show.

Twitter is a great platform for quick, easy connections. Start a hashtag for your show, and your persona, and let that be the driving force for people to connect with you, and vice-versa. You can also tweet photos in real-time during your recording, which are great memorabilia for you and the community.

You can create music that can reflect your podcasting business. If you feel that you can't do this, get someone to do it for you. There's a lot of creatives around and a lot without work since the pandemic. Music, as we know, is an intensely emotional thing and a tie-in with you could work wonders. Don't forget copyright laws! If it's not your composition, you need rights for using music. Check out www.prsformusic.com and find out about royalties.

To get moving, and bear in mind this is an interim measure, you can place ads on Facebook and Instagram. This won't break the bank, and at least it's a start to letting people know you exist while you grow your audience. There's a whole chapter on social media coming up. This is just to whet your appetite.

BUILDING YOUR OWN COMMUNITY

All podcasters face a common problem – that of acquiring listeners and making it sustainable. You'll usually find podcasters leaping from one thing to the other in a manic fashion trying to accomplish everything in one go. Wrong. You'll end up accomplishing nothing. Problem is, they don't know who or what they want. They start getting the wrong crowd. Things don't happen like they should on these podcasts, and it's no wonder. Most people don't have a reliable way to effectively grow their podcast.

This is why you need...a Facebook group. Okay, it doesn't have to be on Facebook, the platform will depend on your demographic. Bottom line is, it's important for you to have a safe place where you can engage with your audience, outside of your show. You can get similar outcomes on other platforms and still create a sense of community on Instagram and Twitter, but I say Facebook is the best platform for having a group community. I mean for starters, you can actually make a group. Unlike a Facebook page, your reach isn't limited with a group. The primary reason for this is because Facebook pages are made for running ads. For those of you reading who have tried promoting with a Facebook page, you know just how small your reach is. You might have 150+ followers but it will only reach 15-20 people max. What a calamity.

What dictates your reach within your Facebook group is whether the post gets good engagement or not. The more engagement you get on your post, the more members will see it. The more engagement you have in general, the more the group will be pushed out to people outside of it, attracting new members on autopilot. It's really as simple as that.

Of course, having a group also means you have a level playing field where your community can engage with each other, start conversation and provide you feedback on your latest episodes..

With a group you can also promote your latest episodes to the people that care the most. Another bonus is the sense of exclusivity. Think about it. There is a much different feeling if you are following Beyonce on instagram compared to being in a group with her, where you know she will probably see your post. It's a much more intimate feeling. What most people forget about as well, is that a group is a way to carry on building your brand, spreading your message and furthering your podcast message. You're probably thinking that this sounds too good to be true, and that I'm actually an undercover Facebook agent. One of these statements is true, the other is false. Yep, you guessed it! This is all a bit too good to be true, because there is one flaw with Facebook groups. There's no clear strategy on how to grow one from scratch. It's all good talking about how more engagement = more members, but how do you do this if you had little to no members in the first place? Podcasters gasp for air as they try everything to grow the number of members in this group. The result is normally a poor quality group. What do I mean by this, you ask?

Many podcast groups aren't filled with listeners who are interested in the podcast content, but rather with family and friends. And although this isn't a bad thing per say, it's not what I would call a high quality group, for reasons I would hope are obvious. So what you need is a clear path to follow. Or should I say...a cycle, yes. Over time, you will come to love this cycle, because it will bring you an engaged audience. Ah, the promised land!

You need to understand this cycle inside out. This strategy has seen one of my clients (who runs a history podcast) grow their group from scratch to 150 in just under a month. This translated to a download increase of 1000+ the following month! And this is at the smaller scales. I call it the Growth and Hibernation Cycle. It may even sound a bit odd to you because this is a bear thing, isn't it? Yes, it is. It's also a podcaster thing and it can reap rich rewards.

GROWTH AND HIBERNATION CYCLE

At first glance, it may appear incredibly simple. You work. You rest. That's a Biblical principle, isn't it? It is, indeed and it's there for a reason, albeit slightly different to ours. The point of the exercise is not just growing your listener base, but growing the particular *kind* of listener base you want for your business. It is for this reason you're better than the rest, standing out from the crowd and being recognized by the very people you want to connect with (think target avatar). You're not being a snob by saying you don't want just any old listener. You want a sussed, with-it kind of person. This is the kind of person who would love to interact on a visceral level, and this is the kind of person you will get if you follow the steps in the growth and Hibernation Phase. We'll call these listeners superfans. You will get great debates going, some controversial points being flung out and the kind who will work wonderfully with the kind of guests you are choosing.

The cycle is tried and tested and is reproducible (meaning it can be repeated over and over again and still get great results), it converts well and helps you filter podcast listeners and non-podcast listeners.

THE GROWTH PHASE

These are characteristics of the four steps to growth:

Group Identification Phase: Here you identify and join Facebook groups that you know could be a part of your audience. Look to find the three biggest and most active groups within your niche. The optimal amount of posts in a growing group is 3-5 posts per day, that's the sweet spot. Check the average number of posts and join those groups that have this. Anything less, you shouldn't waste your time on.

Active Phase: 7-9 days. You become an active member of the groups, liking, commenting and sharing. This is valuable content that is related to the niche, but not directly related to your podcast. This will solidify you in the group. People will start seeing you as a responsible, nice and active person, and you will come to realise just how vital this is for conversion to listeners later.

Listener Identification Phase: In your three active groups you start asking specific questions relating to your show. For instance, would they listen to a fun show about history with a twist? This would help identify who is interested in quirky themes as well as your "normal" servings. This could place you in front of your competition. You still need to go through the initial 7-9 active phase for higher conversions, people need the like and know-how of you, you need to provide actual value beforehand (hence why the active phase is VITAL and should not be skipped over!). In marketing, this is what we call 'inbound marketing', providing free valuable content to potential customers/listeners to gain interest.

What then would be the indirect approach?

Well to keep things simple, you can ask questions that gage the interest levels of people. So, for example, if you were in a history niche you could add a comedic twist to it. You can ask a question that can filter out the people who may like your show to find your perfect listener. Here are three examples with explanations as to why they are important.

1. Comment down below is one the funniest things/inventions that has happened in history – this is great as you are filtering out those who have no knowledge or interest in the subject, and those who do, meaning they are interested in the fun and quirky as well in-depth stuff. They have gone out of their way to stay educated, and if they comment that means they're connecting with people who are engaged and willing to be active. It shows they have a passion for the topic.

2. "Omg, I recently came across a well-known show called Horrible Histories. It's so funny." Tell them to like if they agree. This is great as you are commenting on a famous show, which has relevance to your podcast's show about historical events with a comedic twist to it. You are filtering in people who are willing to engage in contrast to liking a post that has a lower barrier to entry (it's much easier to go through with the call to action). Meanwhile, you know that people who liked it are future candidates (guests) and

potential listeners. You are speaking to your target audience who has an interest in your podcast's topic.

3. I have recently started listening to some audiobooks and podcasts, wow right? So much value! Anyways, I was wondering if anyone has heard of any good/funny history podcasts? I would love to check them out.

I hope by this point you get the basic gist of these questions, it's a way to not get spotted by the group admin warrior, while at the same time setting bait for your target audience to like, comment or show any form of interest. This way you aren't directly doing self-promotion. So no rules are being broken, you are just starting up a conversation that your target audience will be involved with.

You are helping the group by driving interactions, and of course, this works best if you are already active in the group, so the admin people are far less likely to see your posts as a threat as you're a key member. Trust me, I know my group (*Podcast Marketing Made Simple*). It now has over 2 500 members, and it's very active. I am far more likely to be generous to the main contributors to the group as they bring so much value and with that said if they were to run a promo, once in a blue moon I would let it fly as a way to say 'thank you'. My point is that you are a higher level asset to the group so, even if they think it's a promo, you are less likely to be kicked out. It's human nature, they like and appreciate you for keeping the group alive and kicking.

Inbox Phase: Whoever likes and comments on your posts, you need to make sure you engage with them first within the group. It should be a fun interaction and you should always end with an open-ended question to keep the conversation following. This is important because you will be reaching out to those people you have engaged with on your posts, and are about to send a personalized message (PM) to. Remember the guy I said gained over 1000 new listeners in a month from the Growth and Hibernation Cycle? Well this is the *exact* message I wrote up as a template for him to send to people on Facebook he'd interacted with in these groups.

This is a hook, a way of getting those potential listeners in. I have since given it to multiple other clients who have had great success from it, so I feel it's worth using. Now I'm giving it to you, my dear. This is how it goes:

"Hello, I'd like to start by saying sorry for the private message and intrusion, I know how annoying they can be. So, I'll get straight to the point, I saw you left a (...) on my recent post about (...) in the (...) Facebook group.

I am the researcher, writer, presenter and editor of "Dickheads of History", a podcast which focuses on all of those individuals in history who are glorified and famed in one way, shape or form and as a result of this, the listeners are shown another side to them that they may never have heard, outing these individuals for the dickheads they are.

Anyway, I recently started a Facebook group called (...) for the listeners of the podcast so that 1) the listeners of the podcast can have their say on what happens on the episodes and have their input of who the next Dickhead of History is 2) allow the audience to interact with interesting facts, polls and questions where participants of the group's voice can be heard and finally 3) create general podcasting discussion as both creators and listeners can help each other grow as individuals. I would love to add you to the community and think you would be of great value.

Regardless of your answer, I hope you have an amazing day filled with happiness and prosperity."

Isn't that great? Sure it is. It's the kind of letter I would treasure.

By posting the kind of material mentioned in the Active Phase, people will get to know you and won't take offence at a PM. People could easily do, but if it's a name they know and trust, you'd be welcomed.

THE HIBERNATION PHASE

On your side, this is where you shut down, bear-like, and go inwards. A lot of meditation techniques will have this as their basis of growth, and I know many people have said it has done wonders for them. Our Hibernation Phase is somewhat different, although inherently alike in that it is a Growth Phase, just a different Growth Phase to the one before. That was a physically hyperactive phase in drawing in the people you would like as listeners and guests. The right people. That is a very intense phase. Hence the need for the Hibernation Phase, which is all about nurturing and cementing your online community. More on effective ways to build a strong online community later.

Many people in different businesses use the Growth Phase permanently and then wonder why they burn out and disappear. You can't keep up a Growth Phase permanently, especially in the podcast industry, as you and your podcasts will suffer. You will more likely even forget what you started to do. This is why this phase is so vital. You need recuperation physically and mentally. You need to withdraw and focus your intentions on what you have learned and the people you have gathered together that like the way you think. This Hibernation Phase is so important, it puzzles me that more people don't know about it and practice it fervently.

The point is that you know about it now. If you don't practice these two phases with all the vigor you have, you have only yourself to blame.

Once you have added 20 people to your group, you should go into the hibernation stage. This is where you stop reaching out to new people completely and just enjoy the interaction among people you have become involved with. You want to get to know the new members and begin forming deep and meaningful relationships with them.

If you are at ease (you're hibernating, remember!), you won't feel stressed and pressured about shows that have to go out, guests that have to be contacted, and so on. You peacefully welcome people that want to be with you in your podcaster's world. Keep on being a valuable member to the three groups you joined, but you can tone down the amount of time and energy you spend in each of these virtual hangouts. Just don't disappear off the face of the Earth, as then when you come back to 'harvest' more leads from these groups, it will seem like you are only being part of these communities to gain something.

You will find that it is the *quality*, not the *quantity* of listeners that matter in this exercise, so out of all the people you embrace into your group, if only half prove to be worthwhile, so be it. These are the people that you nurture.

How long should this Hibernation Phase continue? It's really up to you, but I have found that 15-20 days is normally a good period. I wouldn't go on much longer because you still want to keep your community growing, and for that to happen you need to keep gaining momentum and pushing forward. After 15-20 days that should have been enough time to have 3-5 conversations with each member of your community. You can personalise this strategy and the specifics of it to your needs as you grow more familiar with it.

Also, it's worth saying that later on, we will cover exactly how to be sure you have a high-quality group and how you can manage quality control. Now, you can launch yourself back into business.

BE THE BEST LISTENER EVER

As I just mentioned, it's crucial for you to have at least 3-5 conversations with people in your audience. But why? Simple, you need to start building trust. Who's going to become a loyal listener of your podcast - the person who you spoke to once, joined your group and never heard from you again, or the person who joined the group and a few weeks later, feels like they know you? Hopefully both, but the second one has a higher conversion rate than the first. The best way to do this is by having casual conversations about the topic of your show, but also mixing in conversation about life in general. You can start your 2-5th conversations with openers like: "___ how was your weekend?" or "How's (insert project or event they mentioned) going?" You want your audience to feel like they know you. By doing this, you begin to occupy more space in their minds so that when it comes to engaging with your content, and listening to your show, the law of reciprocation works its magic. The great thing about having these conversations is that you get to learn more about your target audience, their needs, wants, triggers and all that juicy stuff we talked about in chapter one. Hell, you might even get to find out which soap they prefer after all! This means you can produce content that is better suited to them, which in turn brings you more success. It also means that if and when you have a guest on, you can conduct a wonderful interview your audience will love as you know what type of questions they want to know the answer to. This all takes time so make sure to be patient and considerate.

Also, show you are a great giver. It's not all about you. It's about your audience. The people you've nurtured within your community. Without them, you wouldn't have a show! Being a good listener is not easy. You also want to get your point of view over. All the time. Just don't go on and on and break in when others are talking. Breathing space is what people need for succour and growth. If needs be, keep your mouth shut and let the people speak.

Are you listening, friend? To your community? You have enough time to organize your feelings and hopes for your business. You have to realize that the quality of being able to listen carefully is the most vital part of networking. If you go to network at a function and spend all the time talking about yourself, people will quickly give you a wide berth. You've learned how to be a vital part of your community and part of that was just being there. A reliable, honest person that people could rely on. If you're also known as a great listener then people will welcome you. Most people are the exact opposite and by their very nature prove they're only interested in themselves, not you, by talking about themselves all the time. You will become a very valued person and revered in the community. If you wait until all have had their say, you can follow up with some comment later, but you have demonstrated to whoever has been talking to you that you're curious and interested in what they have to say. Thus, you make the other party feel very special.

BEGIN MONETIZING AND REINVESTING

You are demonstrating that you are a willing and valuable member of the community. Keep on showing that you are making a difference, and people will naturally want to be around you. People will also help you to survive and ensure your podcast business goes from strength to strength. See how the one hand helps the other!

You will come to understand, now you have engaged and built trust with your listeners, that this is the time that you can begin to monetize from the business. You can make money through physical products, affiliate marketing and promotions. Let's look at them.

Affiliate Marketing, or performance marketing, is where you can earn money by referring people to companies and they purchase a product that you have recommended. You can find affiliate programs – popular products and services are bound to have a program – at Amazon and elsewhere, but my bet is Buzzsprout, which has just added an affiliate marketplace.

You can go for sponsorships (here's where you need decent listener figures) and ads. When they are targeted at a specific area only, like where you and your listeners hang out, they're you could do a cross-plug among your many other efforts. You advertise certain places in the area and you get free group cocktail hours, for instance, when you could hold a community meeting, or whatever. So, no one pays any money and each score. Speaking gigs are also great. It's only natural that you would get offered these gigs, being a podcaster!

Test out paid ads on social media. These won't break the bank and they could work well for you. Merchandising is another money-spinner. These days, "merch" is everywhere. There are tie-ins for virtually everything.

Once you start rolling, friend, you will find opportunities for making money will present themselves like it's Christmas every day. We are being brief in this section because, purely, this is not the aim of the book. Just be sure any money you make from your podcast be sure to reinvest in your business, your brand!

IS YOUR PODCAST POWERFUL ENOUGH?

Still not seeing the engagement from your audience that you need so badly?

Just keep at it. When you eat, sleep, breathe podcasting, you will carry on building until you get that coveted prize!

Here are some added tips:

- Schedule your social media activity for when your audience is most active. By scanning the platforms, you will know this easily enough. Sometimes, though, the simplest of things go whizzing over our heads.
- Social media thrives on engagement, and did you know that the Instagram algorithm gives priority to posts that are packing them in, so you could get maximum exposure here. And so, you add to listenership. Day by day, this is your mission – and your delight. Ensure this becomes a daily activity. If you are posting items that hit home for your would-be audience, it's guaranteed they will tune into your show.
- A sure-fire way of getting people to hook into your posts is by running a competition. This is a favorite with any audience. Get a great prize and do some cross-plugging on your show. Follow this up with a plethora of posts across all social media platforms, and hey presto! You have a winner.

Incidentally, there's much more on social media coming up.

11 POINTS TO GET READY FOR BLAST-OFF.

You will know what to post if you know your audience. And, even if you don't know them inside out just yet, you should be well on your way to doing so. Remember, earlier we spoke about having an avatar. This is a graphical representation of your most faithful and intuitive listener. Your avatar will help you, embodying the nature of what your perfect listener is.

Facebook groups are just fantastic! Remember, we touched on this earlier. This should be your #1 go-to when you're trying to increase your numbers. You can engage with would-be, and existing, audience members here. This is a tremendous way of drawing in people and promoting your business without using an in-your-face approach. This is all about learning and sharing, that's what makes Facebook groups so popular. It would be well worth your while in creating one and turning it into a busy meeting spot.

It's easy creating a group. Facebook will take you through the steps. Tip: You have an option of closed or open groups. Always choose a closed group – this adds to the mystique of the group, as well as security and your safety. There's a whole lot of nuts out there, and you need to keep them that way – OUT.

Here are 11 Facebook group engagement tactics to keep in mind:

1. Always welcome new members to your group. Not only is this polite, but it also adds a warmth to the welcome that is not normally found on social media. Don't forget to converse with the new member to make that person feel welcome. Protip: Ask an ice breaker question within the welcome post – Like would you rather… What do you think… make it something fun and clever that your audience will find easy to engage with. How to structure your welcome post, Welcome to…(Name of community), where we.. (Message of your show). To get you fully initiated within the community, answer this following question…(Icebreaker)

2. The visual power of attraction. Create a video that will resonate with all the members and don't let it stagnate there. Change it regularly to keep this hook fresh. Get your members to send in their videos. Your imagination and creativity are vital here. You can add a thumbnail pic too. Get those juices flowing!

3. You must have a poll, survey or quiz going. This is a great way to get to know members and this also adds to your engagement mission. The easiest way to get a poll running is to focus on a trending topic and get your members to add their opinions on that topic. Always add a GIF on Facebook. It's a feature that is available on the platform. They're great fun and can be added here or anywhere in this section. What you should do is ask members to respond with their poll or

quiz answer and add a GIF as well. This way, you all can have a whole lot of fun, and get a great bonding session going. You can also run a GIF competition. You can call it the GREAT GIF-OFF! This could turn into a big number, so prepare for the deluge. Others have tried this, and it works every time! Among the benefits of GIFs are increased engagement among your members (and yourself), more traffic to your Facebook group, stronger relationships because it's a shared experience and an increased sense of community. You can also crown someone the GIF champion.

4. Ask questions of the group. Make sure they are mostly related to your podcast topic. People are in the group because of the content you offer and because of your show. See that your group and the community you have built are in line with your message. Your community is an extension of your show so things need to stay in theme, not always but a good 85% of the time. You are building your brand, always have this in mind. The message of what you are trying to achieve with your podcast and your community, need to be the driving force of the content, as it's the thing that keeps people's attention, builds anticipation and interest.

5. Post the most ingenious or the funniest photos you've ever seen! This is a great way for the group to comment on each other's pictures. Keep in mind the

likes and dislikes of your group and you must make it a rule that no one posts an offensive picture. They've got to be clever and fun.

6. It has been proven that the content that works best with groups is Edu-tainment. A mix of both elements has been shown to have great pulling power. Make sure they're quality posts, as this will up the algorithms as well, in turn giving you more status!

7. Post at the right time. SEOpressor shows you which times are the best and worst, so go with the experts and consider your data on your target avatar. However, once you have enough members in your group to see some trends, you can use your data via group insights on the Facebook group. Lock in your posting schedule with Facebook, so your timing will always be correct. Facebook will take you through the steps.

8. If you are considering going live, make use of StreamYard. If you've watched any of the myriad presentations on YouTube where people have made use of StreamYard, you know how effective it can be. Many have used the platform for special presentations where they have several guests on the show and the faces of the people are in squares on the screen. They make it very easy to bring people in and out, while the host of the show stays constant, controlling the show from his podcaster studio. It's free too. This platform is well worth a look in.

9. Ask your members to turn on "notifications". This way, nobody misses out on anything that is happening in the group. You can mention at the end of this post that this is the only way you can be first in line for new competitions, GIFs, or vital info about the show. You could also add a little rider at the end of your show: "I hope you angels enjoyed the show! Don't forget to learn about our fab mystery guest on the next show, exclusively on our Facebook group. So, leave the "Notifications" on, people, and be the first to know!"

10. Like, Comment and Respond! This is a given, peeps, as you want to come over as warm, friendly, curious and forthcoming – which you are, just don't forget to say it. Leave open-ended questions to get the activity going in the group. People want to be part of something that is buzzing and active, so they'll willingly join in. And so, the engagement grows.

11. The power of Facebook Group Insights. This is a great way to measure levels of engagement within the group. By looking into the top contributors of your group you have a list of your superfans. You can use this insight to your favor by encouraging and acknowledging your top contributors. You can do this by simply sending them a friendly message saying you appreciate them and their engagement. People love to be recognised. Hey, hope you enjoyed the chapter. There's a lot in it, but don't feel overwhelmed!

How do you eat the elephant? Slowly….

CHAPTER TAKEAWAYS

- Get to know your audience. You have in mind a certain type of audience. This kind of audience (sussed and fun) will be the best audience for you to interact with. You know what they like because it's what you like. You have to ensure you filter out the people who are not suitable.
- Get to know the Growth Phase and Hibernation Phase. This is vital for you to understand and implement. When you're starting you ensure you start to grow with your brand in mind, so you start growing your audience. Then comes a period of hibernation where you consolidate all you have achieved in your Growth Phase.
- Be the best listener while networking. People don't realise how hard it is to listen. They'd much rather be talking. You show a generous side of your nature when you listen. It shows that you have an interest in whoever is speaking to you. People like that. They gravitate towards people like that.
- How to make money and reinvest in the business is naturally an essential part of any business strategy and there are ways of making money while podcasting.

You're not going to be an instant millionaire or anything, but you can earn a decent living. Ensure you reinvest in your business.

- Let your avatar show the way. An avatar is the embodiment of the ideal member of your audience. So you will turn to your avatar, who you can think of as your 3D hologram in your mind because that person is the ideal. You've identified people who fit the personality through your avatar.

- Create a Facebook group for great returns. It is here where you will start interacting with your ideal group. 3-5 posts a day in the group is compulsory to get the algorithm working in your favor and bringing in more of the same people. You will ask many open-ended questions to get the narrative going and to ensure that you are interacting with the right people.

CALL TO ACTION

CREATE YOUR GROUP AND PLAN 5 QUESTIONS YOU CAN USE TO set bait in the 3 large communities to attract potential listeners.

CRAFTING YOUR MESSAGE THROUGH BRANDING

"It's not whether you get knocked down. It's whether you get up." – Vince Lombardi

Crew: Captain Jeffrey Wight, USN
ISS Location: Low Earth Orbit
Earth Date: 16 March 2021
Earth Time (GMT): 15:45
C3 FROM THE CAPTAIN'S LOG

We had a pretty hectic day today, things here and there had to be fixed. We were involved in ongoing microgravity research. Did the routine exercise where a supply ship docks, and we unload and send the ship on its way back to the motherland. We're always very careful with the routine stuff as you can get careless with that. We have no room to be careless at all. It's only when I write my entries into the log that I am reminded why we are here at all. What will it be like in 20 years, 30 years from now? Will we have ships whizzing by on the way to Mars? Further even?

Back to the here and now. One of the robotics seems to have a problem. Urgent call. Inspection. Quite easy to solve, really, and nothing to do with Mr Hibbs, what we call the one robot. There's an overlock in the system. In about five minutes, it's solved. I think about what they're calling MTP on earth. The Motivating Power of a Massive Transformative Purpose. I think about how it's reshaping and remoulding the minds that are attuned to it. Or maybe, how MTP is changing because of these marvellous minds. I think about that a lot on the station. MTPs as they know, and now you do, are not representative of what's possible today. They're aspirational and focused on creating a different future. We've done that already, and they're busy doing it on earth.

This aspirational element is what ignites passion in individuals and groups. It's what engages people's hearts and minds to work together to realize their goal. Not in the least bit different to what you're doing. Don't scoff. I know we're on the ISS, you're in your studio. Are our minds different? We may seem miles apart, and indeed physically we are, but the spark that aligns us is very much alive.

Do you know that in 2014, Salim Ismail published "Exponential Organizations" with Mike Malone and Yuri van Geest? The book analyzed the 100 fastest-growing organizations and synthesized their key traits. They discovered that every single company on the list had a massive transformative purpose.

But that doesn't surprise you.

When I say, "We're on the same wavelength," you know exactly what I mean.

IT'S BRANDING TIME, SO BRING ON THE COW AND THE HOT IRON!

Oh, come on, no diving under the bed in fear and trembling.

I told you it's not that kind of branding, although it makes a good illustration of what branding is.

So, branding and podcasting. People don't generally think of the two together. In business, branding is one of the most (if not the most) active ingredients of business success. When people talk of a company, they mention the company name: "Oh, did you know that Amazon has so many books they could fill two of their giant warehouses?" What they don't mention is the logo or what that does to their recognition of the brand name. Although branding is not merely a logo, it forms part of the story, which is in itself the branding. So, branding is the story that is behind the business and the logo. Sorry to repeat myself, but it's that important to understand. Movies do this very well. They brand a movie so you really want to see it. Take a movie like "Alien". The tagline is, "In space, no-one can hear you scream". You wouldn't think much of just "Alien", but the tagline triggers an emotional response that sets you quickly on the road to the ticket office.

EMOTIONAL ATTACHMENT

"So, podcasting and emotional attachment?" you say curiously. "I didn't think anyone could form an emotional attachment to a podcast!"

Oh, absolutely they can. Especially podcasts! They should strike to the very heart of the subject. If the podcasts are the correct theme, contain the correct delivery, the attachment will be there without saying (pun intended). So, while your business may be known as "Joe's Pods," which is as quickly forgettable as possible, what your business is all about could override that because of the brand attachment you've already formed. This is branding. Just get someone to help you with the name.

Today, I saw an ad that claimed the History Channel was "the highest-ranked factual TV entertainment brand". I don't know whether that's true or not, but it immediately rises in stature, having told you that the channel is part of an "entertainment brand". It's a huge thing involving all the senses. Immediately there's an emotional attachment, and this has the strongest impact on brand loyalty. It's not just your podcast that we're talking about when it comes to branding. It's podcasting in general. You could be "the giant of the podcasting brand" and that story works its way into your heart. The brand is the genre if you will, and you are a part of that genre.

197

Products that have consumer-brand relationships will always sell more. It's part of brand loyalty, which has a strident love-loyalty at its core and will, therefore, be much more popular. So, when I say that a brand is more than a logo, what I am saying is that the logo should represent the story behind the name and the reputation of the company.

If you want to develop a strong brand relationship, concentrate on the emotional aspects that are intrinsic in the story, which is the ethos of the company. This all may sound a little complex, and warm and fuzzy to boot, but be that as it may, that's what branding is all about, and we'll be taking a thorough look at it so you won't have to quiver in your boots all day. Okay, friend?

Also, it's very important for your podcasting business.

TWO STUDIES THAT PINPOINT THE WAY

We're going to look at two studies which demonstrate branding most succinctly – the one is entitled The influence of Brand Trust, Brand Familiarity and Brand Experience on Brand Attachment – a case of consumers in Gauteng, South Africa, and we'll look at that first. The authors were Elizabeth Chinomon and Eugine Maziriri. We're not academics, so rest easy, friend. The importance of the study is how it backs up everything I'm saying about branding.

The results of the study showed "that brand trust, brand familiarity and brand experience positively influence brand attachment in a significant and direct way. It showed that brand managers for companies in the Gauteng province ought to concentrate on strategies that enhance the brand experience because it is likely to yield the desired brand attachment." The company is naturally after increased market share and profitability and the study notes that brand management applied correctly is the only way of doing this. Celebrity endorsement of the brand merely added to its customer attachment, loyalty and love. The authors found with this endorsement that there was heightened brand awareness, brand recall and brand loyalty. The study found that when the products in question in the branding study were not available for customers, there was acute regret and sorrow, like mourning. This is part of brand dynamics that you will seek in podcasting. No need to reason why. They found that brand trust could reduce consumer uncertainty "because the consumer not only knows that the brand can be worth trusting, but also they think that the dependable, safe and honest consumption scenario is the most important link of brand trust."

The study noted that "customers tend to personify a favored brand and thus build a close affiliation with it. Brand attachment is a critical construct in describing the strength of the bond connecting customers to a brand because it should affect behavior that fosters brand profitability and consumer lifetime value." The study found that brand familiarity could be improved by making sure that the consumers know that the brand exists, and this can be done through promotions and advertising."

So what does this mean to you, dear podcaster? Your listeners need to be aware of your message, what you stand for and where they fit into the brand. Your show must be inviting to your target audience, and by you inviting them in they feel like they are part and parcel of your show. Your beliefs align and they stand for your message, this in conjunction with the community you're building starts to build a strong sense of belonging and soon after, attachment.

THE OTHER STUDY WAS ENTITLED "THE ROLE OF EMOTIONAL aspects in younger consumer-brand relationships" by US-based Jiyoung Hwang and Jay Kandampully. The study aimed to investigate the role of three emotional factors – self-concept connection, emotional attachment, and brand love in the context of younger consumer luxury brand relationships.

The study explained: "Theoretically, this study expands the scope of brand research by investigating unexplored but important roles of emotional aspects for enhanced brand relationship quality. The implications are meaningful given that the market for luxury brands does not solely depend on a single consumer segment and thus it is critical for marketers to know who their customers are, where to find them and know the key factors that drive their behavior". Once again...target avatars, people! It goes on to say: "Material possession attachment supports the idea that people may use objects to narrate aspects of themselves, especially with self-identifying possessions that reflect who they are or how they are socially connected to others. A brand, however, is a *perception* rather than a material possession..."

In conclusion, the study found that emotional attachment has the strongest impact on brand loyalty, followed by self-concept connection and brand love. So, branding is so much more than you thought it was. If you want to go over those points a few times, that would be terrific. It would certainly cement the knowledge that branding can take you places you never thought of, and garner listeners who you thought you never would.

BEHAVING EMOTIVELY

As a podcaster, you behave more emotively than you would care to admit. The studies we have looked at have shown that emotion is strength, which is probably not what you were told in the locker room at school. Discard what you were told in the locker room at school. *"Do you hear what I'm saying?"* is a great tagline for you and will sum up what you are attempting to do with podcasting, your brand.

In business, though, and that means you, Mr Podcaster, it's a whole new ball game. If you can condense what you and your business are all about in a couple of words and they have a poignant, direct emotive connotation, you're well on your way to describing what your brand is. Many companies find the idea of a brand extremely difficult to wrap their heads around. It's the emotive thing. They're meant to be thinking about profit margins, and they have nothing to do with emotion, right? Wrong. They have everything to do with them.

Branding reflects a clear-cut story. Is that what your podcasting business does? What is your story? Who do you serve? Is it enriching your community? That's your story. Can't get more clear-cut than that.

HOW TO BRAND YOUR BUSINESS

1. What your brand says about you is that you're living up to your promise to your listeners.So, are you being honest? Are your listeners hearing what you promised they'd hear? Don't forget, that's part of your brand – "Do you hear what I'm saying?" – means that you *should* be hearing what I'm saying. You could be *missing out if you don't hear what I'm saying.* What I'm saying could probably change your life. It means everything to you – and me. This is branding at its best. It is called

the truth brand. Take Jeff Bezos, for example. When he first started with Amazon, he said he was going to build an "everything" store. He worked for many years and then built a brand around it. Your show is different to others because of your honesty and clarity. You have become a Unique Voice!

2. Brand identity clarifies and forces focus. Does your business tell people who you are? Do they believe in your story? Do they believe they will be missing out if they don't listen to you? Have you proved that? You could be saying the most amazing things. Sure, they're great stories. But are they a part of your brand? People are not stupid. They will discard you if you are a great storyteller but tell untruths.

3. Moving past the mundane. With companies that have a great brand, there's something about doing business with them that means something exciting just happened, although you may not be able to put it into words. You can't explain it, it's just "there". You can feel it in your gut, and it's telling you that this experience will always be here whenever you want to feel good, cherished and exalted. Also, would-be sponsors would be more inclined to favor you because you have a trusted listener base. Someone in the podcast sphere may have more listeners but an unsavory listener base. The sponsor will always choose you!

4. A powerful brand strategy is built on emotions. "Can you feel it? Can you feel it?" went the amazing Michael

Jackson song. He never said what there was to feel, and you discovered that there wasn't anything to feel, but you still felt it. It's everywhere but nowhere you can see or touch. And it's very real. It's called emotions and they can build a bridge of gold between, say, you and the listener. We all want to be rational, but we are emotional. When you deny this, and you're in branding, it's like you're denying yourself. Nothing's going to come of that.

5. A well-defined brand will guide advertising and marketing. Have your story in place. Know what you are and aren't. This will define you and your advertising and marketing will reflect that. We realise that our past marketing efforts haven't been effective because our branding has not been strongly and clearly defined. There's no clear brand strategy or emotional trigger, hence the subsequent disastrous effect. Put in the effort to understand your emotions and their emotions and things will start going right. "Right" being, people will start engaging with your brand on social media, spread awareness through word of mouth and share your episodes.

6. A strong brand aligns and engages employees. When you have a well-defined brand and a clear internal communication strategy, people like working for you. It's the same with listeners, they like listening to you. People are just happy being aligned to something good and honest and truthful. Let's face it, there's so much

dishonesty and awfulness in the world, having a safety bubble from all that means the world to your employees and your listeners. Having a shared direction for workers and listeners means a pleasant, comfortable environment. Even though you may be working on your own now, you never know when you'll need helpers, so take heed!

7. A strong brand builds financial value for your company. All the branding bru-ha-ha means one thing – financial value. If your company has a powerful brand story that invites your listeners into the narrative, it reflects on your marketing or sponsor push and your great workforce. Ask Mark Cuban or Mr Wonderful. They'll tell you the same thing. Take Nike for example. "Just Do It." I'm sure you've seen this slogan before. Nike uses this to invite their audience into the narrative by challenging them to face their adversities and...just do it. This attitude then becomes what people associate with the brand, creating that revered sense of belonging.

PRACTICAL WAYS ON HOW TO BRAND (OR RE-BRAND) YOUR PODCAST

1. Complete your brand strategy. Do a detailed plan of what you're trying to achieve, and how to achieve it.

This comprises Brand Heart – (purpose, mission, vision, values), Brand Messaging – (brand voice, messaging, tagline, value proposition, brand messaging pillars), Brand Identity – (logo, color, typography, and so on).

2. What is your current brand messaging? You need to tweak your current brand messaging if your goals have changed with the times. Your messaging needs to speak directly to your target audience, so be extremely specific. Make sure your messaging also invites your listeners into your brand's narrative. You can do this by painting a picture of what you're trying to achieve, showing them the finish line, and where you're taking them. Doing this successfully will trigger emotions and if your message aligns with them, they will have no choice but to want in on the narrative.

3. Know your "face". Whatever your face is, is it the face you are comfortable with representing your brand? Are your listeners happy with it? Do you feel proud whenever you look at this face? If not, you must change it to align it with your current thinking on brand imaging. Your face could be a sound bite you play at the intro and the end of your podcast. Is the mood correct for this? Are your listeners happy with it? Do a poll and find out!

4. Identify your competition. Do you know who your competitors are? Much like finding out who your listeners are, it's also vital to know your competitors.

You may have a Unique Voice, but what about your branding? How does your brand compare? Are they a much-of-a-muchness? Is this an opportunity to blow everyone away with branding that is both breathtaking and believable? Don't miss out on this chance. You need to be unique. If every other podcast in your niche has the same message and mission it's hard for you to stand out and build those loyal listeners.

BRANDING YOUR PODCAST – RISING ABOVE THE CROWD

1. Make sure your podcast is soundly designed – that is, you have given listeners a podcast that is free from pops and clicks and mouth noises. If you're going out live, obviously editing will not be possible. Have a run-through before you go live and iron out any problems that will detract from the main podcaster and the phone-ins.
2. There are many programs that you can use to help you in this quest. Go to iZotope RX or Waves Restoration Bundle, or many others. Just Google your request, and you'll have a bundle at your disposal.
3. Think of audio segments that you can use during the show that can enhance what you're saying and define your brand. You can find many free audio clips that

you can use and there's a host to choose from. You can Google "Sound design for podcasts" and find people who will choose music bites for you that you can weave in and out of your podcast. Also, go to "Sound bites for podcasters" where you will find 35 000 different tracks you can use for free.

4. Your podcast must have a beginning, a middle and end, and you can sound design this to tell listeners where they are. In other words, you don't have to state it. This is a mark of a professional, which is what your podcast should always sound like.

5. You can segment episodes with games, music, news of interest, and so on. Just ensure it's an interesting listen. Give people something to expect and start to look forward to - maybe it's wondering what your song of the week will be, or maybe it's your one minute freestyle rap at the end of each show. You just want to make sure that no one gets bored and thinks "When is this going to end?". Nothing worse than that. Remember your brand and ensure it's not tarnished in any way. Enhance it!

6. Make sure after you've posted your podcast that you use tweeting and Facebook to reach out and engage with your listeners. This makes it a completely immersive experience that envelops your audience. Don't forget to check the good old emails as many people prefer more lengthy conversations and will use this platform. Reply to every mail. Facebook is great

for this purpose, and you can post pictures of yourself and any guests in the studio.

7. Make it as real as you can. Be open and honest, and share your struggles, hopes and desires. This will strike a chord with your audience, who are more than likely jumping over the same hurdles. If someone asks a question you don't know the answer to, be honest, but try and point them in the direction of where they are likely to get the right answer.

8. A solid position statement is needed. This is part of your brand identity. This statement solidifies whatever you stand for and what you hope to achieve. In your audio segments, in your comments, in your podcasts, this position statement has to be your grounding. It's what you stand for, where you come from and what your ultimate desires are. Your tagline also grounds this. I have suggested "Do you hear what I'm saying?", which means if you didn't you have missed out and you'll have to find out. Your position statement must be aspirational at all times. Take your audience along with you. Make them long for the ride.

When I said that you must "rise above the crowd", I mean this with every fiber of my being. Do you know there are hundreds of thousands of podcasts that are active? And more are going live every day. What is going to make you stand out? It's what

I've been saying, and more. You have a unique voice in that you have identified and are targeting your audience. But do you know how many others are doing this too? How on earth do you stand out from those that are already standing out? By reaching out and engaging with your listeners in sync with your podcast! By having a map for the aspirational journey. Not everyone will have your vision or your empathy or your understanding. These are special qualities and you're going to be developing them and using them more and more. That's why everyone's not cut out to be a therapist or a psychologist. So many are in those positions but don't have enough empathy to cover my thumb. That's why after the first visit, the patient disappears. The move-overs in this area are huge.

It's the same as what you are doing. You must have empathy and understanding in abundance. You have been engaging with your listeners and you are learning to know what makes them tick. This is the best thing you can ever do.

CREATIVE IDEAS FOR YOUR PODCAST

Ensure your shows retain your brand elements. You must try and involve listeners on your podcast as much as you can. Guests can also include musicians, influencers, family members, friends, and whoever you think may add relevant depth to your podcast.

Choose questions you will be asking and tell people you have chosen as guests to check them out on Facebook. This will make listeners excited and feel they have a dominant role to play in the show. This should be a consistent and ongoing practice and should make everyone long to be a guest! It's also a good idea to have a guest host an episode. This makes their involvement even more substantial and will up the excitement level!

Your main themes for the show should naturally be your story, and this is how you stamp your personality and brand firmly on the show. But by involving listeners as an integral part of the show, you add to your brand and you build your audience. Everyone wants to be on air. It's like people love seeing their photos as part of a post online and giving direct quotes from them on-air as well as on social media, makes them feel so valuable. Protip: involve your audience more and more!

Once your audience starts believing in you, they will take your recommendations seriously. So, when you talk about a movie, or a play, a book, a restaurant or a holiday destination, people will check them out. That's what I meant earlier on in this book when I spoke about the podcaster becoming an influencer. It's a natural progression, not an all-out viral-quality depiction of you doing a workout session or whatever. It's called building trust, which is part of your brand.

A must is to start using a hashtag, and you can read the posts using that hashtag. You have a wonderful medium at your disposal – podcasting – and you can let others know what people are finding funny, interesting or disturbing. This has a snowball effect, and you will grow your base even more. You can also feature an artist, movie or show and "spotlight" them, as to giving in-depth info on the director, the theme, and what made the musician write a certain song.

Ask yourself these questions when you are considering the above point:

1. How does this segment fit my show?
2. How can I position this show to make it different from others who are doing the same thing on their podcasts? Looking at the relevant podcasts that already exist, what do I wish was around, but isn't? Is there a certain topic within this niche that is underserved? If not, how can I come at a different angle to everyone else?
3. What system can I have in place to ensure my audience is always at the centre of these segments? For example, you can always have your audience pick the last 3 questions by asking in your Facebook group or doing a poll. This way you are actively involving your community.

In all the elements discussed above, the listener experience is the most important of all. Some podcasters make the mistake of trying to push home a point that is not in the best interests of, or applicable to, their audience. This is when the interests of the self-override the interests of the listeners. Just because you think this is a vital element to discuss doesn't mean your audience thinks so too. If you've thrown the idea out and you get a negative response, drop it. Immediately. Don't try and make your audience like something they're not into. Big mistake, and switch-off time! Your brand is increasing audience engagement, and telling them things that are new, wonderful and pertinent, and upping their value, participation and *anticipation*.

~

HOW TO IMPROVE THE SOUND OF YOUR VOICE

You've listened to many voices, probably more intently than most people because you aim to be the best podcaster there is, and, of course, that's all about your voice. You've identified that the best voice of all is the "trailer voice" – that's the voice you hear on forthcoming attractions for movies. It's deep, resonant, exciting and thrilling. Wow! That very voice has sold the movie for you already.

Can you get the same kind of voice for your podcasts? You've listened to your recorded voice. How does it sound to you? You say, "Not too bad, but still not right."

Do you know that 38% of people perceive what your personality is from your voice? It's essential, then, that you need the absolute right sounding voice. Can people hear you, then? If your voice is too high or thin? This shows a lack of confidence, which is the last thing you need. Your tone will deliver exactly the kind of message you want people to hear.

Most people, when they first land up behind a mic, are tense, and their voices are tight and lifted. Before you record, you must do some voice exercises to get that voice lower and relaxed. Take a deep breath and start humming. Go lower and lower with your humming until you've reached the lowest it will go and hold it for as long as you can. This will stretch your vocal cords, and your voice will automatically sound a lot deeper. Try this for at least 10 minutes before you start your podcast. Practice this daily, even if you are not doing a podcast that day.

You can relax your throat muscles by yawning while inhaling breath and then breathing out slowly with a sigh. Place a finger on the Adam's apple when you practice this. It will drop as the throat relaxes and expands. You can also run your tongue over your teeth with your mouth closed to lift tension in the larynx. The best you can do for the lowering of the voice, and all the professionals recommend this, is to hum. And then some.

IMPROVE YOUR SHOW

We're not going to spend too long on this point. Suffice to say that your show must sound professional. There's nothing worse than listening to crackling and hissing! It must be crystal clear or it's no good! Keep control of your show with a script or notes, but don't use a word-for-word method. You want your show to sound as natural as possible and you're going to have to be flexible. By keeping the show "natural" doesn't mean it drifts off all over the place and ends up not meaning much to anyone, *it just means the show is conversational and flows.* You must control the show. Be authoritative with guests who won't stop talking. Be firm, say that's a good point which will be expanded upon in a show to come. With the non-stop talker, also be firm. "That's a great point, Roseanne. What do listeners think about that? Go to our group on Facebook and have your say!"

So, your brand remains intact. That's your VIP – Very Important Point. We've come a long way, friend. Well done.

It just keeps on getting better!

CHAPTER TAKEAWAYS

- Emotional attachment defines your brand; without it, there is no brand – merely a name, tagline and logo.
- Studies have shown brand trust, brand familiarity and brand experience positively influence brand attachment.

- Emotional factors link together to form brand unity, especially, but not limited to, the younger demographic – self-concept connection, emotional attachment and brand love.
- How to brand your business – are you living up to what your brand espouses and the aspirational aspects it purports? Don't offer a country when there's only a village to be had.
- Your message and mission must invite your listeners into your narrative. When you're able to communicate your values and the purpose of your show, you attract your ideal listeners, you create a sense of belonging within your community and you create emotional familiarity which creates lifelong loyal listeners.
- A well-defined brand will guide advertising and marketing which will reflect the brand and provide many opportunities.
- Creative ideas for your podcast – involve listeners for your show, which is wonderful for your brand and builds your audience.

CALL TO ACTION

KNOWING WHAT YOU KNOW NOW, ANALYSE YOUR SHOW AND ASK yourself:

1. Is it unique?
2. Is it specific enough?

3. Does it stand for something that your target audience can get behind?
4. Does the message you're sending invite listeners into the narrative?

If the answer to any of these questions wasn't a convincing yes…you know what to do.

SCALING THROUGH GUESTING AND MUTUALISTIC RELATIONSHIPS

"FAILURE WILL NEVER OVERTAKE ME IF MY DETERMINATION TO Succeed Is Strong Enough." – Og Mandino

Crew: Captain Jeffrey Wight, USN
ISS Location: Low Earth Orbit
Earth Date: 07 April 2021
Earth Time (GMT): 13:50
C4 FROM THE CAPTAIN'S LOG

Sometimes, I get into the log early. It's not that I want to get it over and done with. I love getting to the log. It's one of a few of my favorite things, as Julie Andrews used to sing in that song. Wow, bet if someone had suggested an ISS back then, they would have thought we were mad. I know we should be more ISS-specific in the log, but Houston doesn't mind. It keeps us in touch with ourselves. They know what I mean. I reminisced a lot today about Earth and looking down, I fall in love with the old planet all over again.

The ship is behaving splendidly today. We have some new crew members arriving tomorrow and we're all pretty excited about that. We are a tight, bonded crew, which is how it should be on any ship. But you'll find this with MTP – the Motivating Power of a Massive Transformative Purpose – which is a feature of this Log, and rightly so.

They're getting into this big time on Earth, and this warms my heart. We've been talking about guys like Elon Musk and Salem Ismail, and what they are doing is truly transformational. They are leading with views that are huge, aspirational, unique, and forward-looking. These are the guys of tomorrow who, with MTP, have inspired whole communities and evangelists to form around them.

They are focused on creating a different future. It sometimes may appear to be a bit wild, but we know anything's possible. Who knew that a rocket that blasted you into space could come back and land on exactly the same spot it took off from?

All over the media on Earth big people are talking about big things. I get my wife to record TED talks so I can watch them when I get back. She knows exactly what to record on what program. There are a lot of giants on Earth and they're saying some incredible stuff.

We passed over Ohio just now. Give or take the odd country. I know that's where you are and I know you have a Unique Voice. My daughter says she listens to you and you're great. I'll give you a listen-in when I'm back on terra firma.

"HEY, OLD FRIEND, WHADDAYA SAY, OLD FRIEND...HOW MANY are like us? Damn few!"

I'm sure that Stephen Sondheim wouldn't mind us borrowing that lyric from *Merrily We Roll Along*, one of the great musicals he wrote. It says it all, about us. You and me, friends. I'm teaching you all sorts of stuff and you're lapping it up. Come the day, you'll probably teach me!

Anyway, we're now onto the subject of networking and the very important part it plays in the growth of your podcast business. I can see you smiling because you love this stuff. Good on ya. Okay, so we've spoken at length about networking. However, that was with your listeners and building your audience base. This is with companies and guests who can build your podcasting business. As we started this segment, so we continue. The power of relationships will never cease to amaze you. Without it, you're not going to get very far.

THE POWER OF RELATIONSHIPS

Guests on your show, as we've said before, are vital. They add to the entertainment value, draw listeners, and make for a fun-filled hour or so. But we're going to go beyond that and see how they can draw publicity that will hook listeners, for sure, but also see sponsors and potential advertisers perk up and target your show.

Speaking of guests, though, you never know when you're going to get someone with a massive following, who will simultaneously bring listeners by the number to your show. The point here is that you never know when you are going to meet this guest who will work wonders for your show. He or she could be just around the corner, so you'd better work on your befriending skills. Even if you bump into someone, start talking and something good may come of it. You could be introduced by a friend, and all of a sudden you're a guest on their show and they're a guest on your show. Reciprocity is the name of the game among friendly podcasters. You will have audience numbers by the score, and more, and listeners have more to listen to. Tip: Gracious, friendly podcasters have more to gain by sharing than by being uncaring.

You can kiss opportunities goodbye if you are uncaring, or selfish. "What's mine is mine. I'm not sharing with anyone," you say, greedily, with a touch of paranoia. Well, good night and good luck, friend. Thank goodness my friend isn't like that at all. Sometimes I've got to hold him back from being too friendly! In this business, who you know is everything. That's the point of networking. Every chance you get, network!

HOW TO INVITE SOMEONE TO YOUR SHOW

One thing you must realise is that great guests, or influencers, are not **always** going to ask you to be on your show. Most times, you must pitch your show to them on a "cold call" basis. Better brush up on your pitching skills! Getting a guest to come on your show can mean rejection after rejection. That's hardly fun except if you have a masochistic personality, but normally you tend to lose hope and think it will never happen!

You must research, write emails, get contact numbers, send the mail off and wait. You can follow the mail off with a call, but most time, you'll never get through. You must change your mindset here and see it as something that's going to take up a lot of your time, but hopefully will bear fruit in the future. You can't do this on speed dial. You can't rush around like a lunatic and shriek at the guest (or the agent) that if they don't appear you'll die! This would be hysterical if it weren't true and sad. The gent I know who tried this tactic is no longer in the business. The guest and/or agent couldn't have cared less.

There are three words you must remember: patience, patience, and patience.

MISTAKES WHEN PITCHING

Okay. You're going to be using email a lot. This is the way to contact your guest. The pitch is where most podcasters come apart. A poorly worded pitch with grammar and spelling mistakes is not going to do the trick. Get a writer (they're all looking for work, so they'll jump at a couple of dollars) and get him to show you how to do it. Use that as a template.

You should be using empathy in your emails. This may sound odd, but not to me. I've spoken about empathy before. I can't talk about it often enough. Why should the guest you're after appear on your show? Research what topics this guest loves talking about. Get a different angle on that topic – this will surprise the guest and make him or her curious and interested. Find out how you can enhance that topic so it becomes much more than just what the guest has been talking about. Will your audience stand to benefit from the words you're putting in the guest's mouth? These are important points...especially getting a new angle and could well land you the guest. How do you know that the guest won't snatch your ideas and use them on another show? You don't. But if the person does, that guest wasn't worth it. You're honest. You're looking for honesty in your guests too. This will pay off in the end, believe me, friend!

The pitch should include three legs – the topic, the theme of the podcast, the emotive value for the audience. Make sure the legs are aligned. Also, is this all in sync with your branding? Don't change your branding to suit your guests. That kind of desperation is a huge no-no. Your main priority is to serve your audience, they come first and by having a guest that aligns with your brand it provides great value for your audience. Doing this consistently is what helps you build deep trust with them. This podcast may not be right for the intended guest and give him the right to politely decline. Say in your mail that if this isn't a fit, you won't take this any further. If it is a fit, though, ask if you can continue chatting and fix a time and date.

Another tip when writing pitches – keep it short and sweet. Use the hook in the first or second paragraph and bullet points are good. Many podcasters make the mistake of writing novels on the pitch. Where they were from, how the idea first came to them when they were having a bath at age six, and so on. In all likelihood, it will get deleted before you can yawn.

WHY YOU SHOULD STOP CHASING BIG NAMES

The truth is, getting a big name guest unfortunately often doesn't give the after effects you'd expect. I saw a post in a podcasting group the other day where someone was venting their frustration that after hosting a guest who was an influencer with over a million followers, they only got another 200 or so downloads on that episode, and there didn't seem to be much of an influx in the episodes after. Of course, this indicates that that small percentage of the guest's audience that did tune in, only listened to that episode. It might be that that particular guest just shares the same story every time they get a feature. In which case, you should do your research on their previous podcast features and outline things that haven't been asked yet, that might interest some of their audience on a deeper level. With that said, if their audience aren't podcast listeners at all, don't bother! They're not going to be interested enough to take 20-40 minutes of their time out to listen. The point is, getting big names as guests as a method of growing your reach is not the be all and end all. Instead, you will find that you expand your audience by featuring as a guest on other shows too. This way, you can find podcasters with audiences very similar to yours rather than taking chances on big names actually having followers relevant to your show. You are then gaining exposure in front of the very kind of people you desire.

Additionally, there are more opportunities that may come from this. For example, you feature as a guest on another podcast and you really click. They then pass you on to another guest that they've previously connected with, because they believe you two would be a good fit as well. It's the stuff of dreams! The amazing thing about guesting on other podcasts is you never know what new opportunities might open up. The guest might love what you do and want to collaborate with you on a profit generating project as they like you so much.

If you do decide to chase a big name (or any name for that matter), then ensure a good fit by a simple quality check:

1. Check how many podcasts they have previously been on. If they have been on a lot, have a quick listen and figure out the main talking points. Evaluate your questions and think about things you believe were missed or weren't spoken about enough within the show. This way you can make sure your show isn't a repetition of the rest.
2. Have a look if they have a track record of promoting things they have featured in.
3. Ask your audience if they are actually interested in the guest- give a brief bio of the guest and what you wish to discuss and get your audience to have an input on the direction the episode goes in. The more you know your audience, the easier this is.

PODTOURING

Have you heard of podtouring? Unlike the Growth and Hibernation Cycle, there's no ambiguity over the meaning here. Podtouring is exactly what you're imagining in your head right now. Your mic is held proudly in the air as you cruise through the streets in your (pod)tour bus, elegantly stopping at the most revered places for various guest features. People dash out of their houses and into the street to catch a glimpse of you and the renowned bus, after hearing of your adventures when you featured on their favorite podcast earlier in the week.

Okay, it's not really like that. Perhaps it could be, but you suggest we start small and work our way up, and I wholeheartedly agree with you. Podtouring is essentially when you go through a period of break from uploading your own episodes, and instead dedicate the time and energy to guesting on as many podcasts as possible.

This has remarkable benefits for exposure, which we discussed just before, in the last section. That was speaking in terms of individual guest features though, so you can imagine how much that kind of growth obtained from guesting on a show with a similar audience can multiply when you're guesting on...around 3 shows a week. 3 shows a week for a few weeks is highly impressive; aim for this, but don't beat yourself up if it ends up being a bit lower than that. To summarise, podtouring allows you to reach new audiences who are both relevant to your niche and already avid podcast listeners, leverage the trust built between other podcasters and their audiences (and return the favour, of course), and drive traffic to your show from multiple sources. You can reap these benefits even from one guest feature, they are simply amplified by doing many in a short period of time - a podtour.

Quality check for guesting on other shows:

1. Read the reviews and make sure you have a well rounded understanding of the show and how it aligns with your brand.
2. Check their social media. Do they do good job of engaging with their audience consistently? Do they do an amazing job at promoting guests?
3. Are the show notes of high quality?
4. Finally, make sure to listen to the show you want to go on, this is a great way to get a feel for the host (this is a no brainer).

HOW TO FIND YOUR POWERFUL STORY

"The human species thinks in metaphors and learns through stories." - Mary Catherine

You need to realise that when you are opting in to go on these shows and be a guest you need to have an attractive story that you love to share and will resonate with their audience. Stories are powerful because they provide a deep level of under-standing to the lesson, as well as a deeper connection to the main character in the story. It's the easiest way to build a connection with a new audience. See this as your shortcut into the hearts of these new sets of ears. They don't know it yet but they will be so invested in you and your story they'll want to hear more from you.

Well that's great, but how can you tell your story and what makes for a good story? No need to panic friend.

YOUR STORY NEEDS TO BE SPECIFIC, YOU NEED TO KNOW EXACTLY what you are going to say and why that piece of information is actually valuable to the audience. You need to provide insights and allow the audience into your world. Be vulnerable, be yourself, be genuine. People are attracted to originality and by being vulnerable, you make yourself much more relatable. What should your story be about, you ask? Come on, think a little harder...I know you've got the answer deep inside you. Think back to the branding chapter, think back to your message and values.

So think back to chapter 3 on branding: about what your brand represents, your mission and the powerful message you want the world to know. Tell and share with the audience your mission origin story. Oh you don't have one? Nonsense. You do, just think back. When did this mission start meaning so much to you? Maybe you had a rude awakening when you saw a person of ethnic minority experiencing discrimination, and realised you weren't doing enough to spread social justice. You felt not only guilty but responsible, and so you began taking actionable steps to spread awareness about racial discrimination, amongst a teen demographic in America (see what we did there? We are being specific about our message, not broad). Then, you lead on to explain what you are currently doing and paint a picture for what you want the future to look like once you're done with your podcast. Now that's a powerful story. People who have been in a similar position to you will want to join your cause and be part of your narrative, be part of what you stand for. They will share your message. They are now part of your brand and they don't even know it. This is the *best* type of marketing.

I know, I know, your peaceful meditation podcast comes from an awakening that wasn't nearly as extreme as the racism story! How on earth are you going to plug your values into the template I just created to deliver an equally powerful story? Your story doesn't have to be as explosive or sensitive, not all podcasts are on such topics. Maybe you started to realise as you got into your twenties that so many of your friends and family deal with some form of anxiety, and everyone around you seems to be stressed. When you discovered meditation it changed your life, but as you advocated for it, the taboo surrounding it and the associations a lot of people had (that spiritual, voodoo bunch of baloney) became evident to you. Rather than deciding to retreat and practice meditation as a private part of your daily routine, hearing the common misled opinions on it actually strengthened your desire to set things straight, and hopefully inspire young adults in similar situations to explore meditation as a viable treatment to help with stress relief and anxiety.

Even if you just read the above and felt dissociated because you don't think your story can have the same galvanizing power, you just need more time to think and reflect. If you are struggling to find your story then ask yourself, why did you start your podcast? Scratch your head and have a really deep think. If you have something that you are passionate about, you have a story to tell. And of course you have an area you're *extremely* passionate about - you're a podcaster!

A GOOD RELATIONSHIP BETWEEN YOU AND YOUR GUEST

The importance of the relationship between you and your guest is vital. People pick up on all sorts of nuances in verbal exchanges. One exchange I listened to demonstrated the obvious – the podcaster and guest hated each other's guts! Well, maybe not so harshly, but there was no connection there at all. It makes for an uncomfortable listening **experience** and people will switch off. Never force the issue. Don't need the guest so bad that you're willing to sacrifice listeners with his *or her* presence.

Use your head. If you don't click, you'll notice. Don't push it. He or she is not the beginning and end of your world, so go looking for someone else. When you find the right guest and there's an instant connection, go for it. The dialogue in your show will flow, everything will feel comfortable and natural, and what's more, your audience will love the feeling! You can invite the guest for a return visit and enhance what already has been built.

EVANGELIST ANGELS

This may sound like a new TV show. In any event, it sure caught your eye, didn't it? It goes like this – you have a guest on your show who had such a good time, that they are now spreading the word about you and your show. They want to come back onto your show, which is terrific. You must be doing something good because they're carrying on like you're the best thing since sliced bread. This is what is known as an "evangelist angel" and the words say it all. Spreading the word and acting like an angel, with your best interests at heart.

Nurturing your guest is, thus, one of the most important deeds you can ever do. Especially if that guest has "pull". To get this person onto your show in the first place was a coup for you, but it's since gotten even better. He loves the way you conduct your show… "it's like being in front of an orchestra", he says. He is just blown away by your style and your professionalism. You'd better believe that he will keep coming back. Not only that, but he has gone and spread the word on every social media platform that he uses and has huge followings on all of them. So many people now know about you and your show, it's amazing! He has become a feature of your show and you two feed off each other like it's the most natural thing. A connection between people is a natural thing. It's either there or it isn't. You can't make it happen, so when it does, make the most of it.

Use the news (that's a good saying) on your URL, which has now grown into a fully-fledged website, post blogs and pics of your guest and has excerpts from your shows. Your fans and his fans will gravitate naturally, and excitedly, to this site. It's all about building your business, don't forget. This is a great way to build it. Our angel also knows of sponsors who would be interested in your business. That's what angels do. They point the way to bigger and better outcomes.

How often does an angel come along? Who knows? I don't think very often. Now, maybe if I knew that famous angel call, I could use it to get 'em flying over! Most importantly, make sure you're ready for a visit from one. Are your pitches great? Angels study these very carefully, you know...

NURTURE YOUR WAY THROUGH PODCASTING

Running your podcast is your life. Its mission needs to be nurtured if it is to grow, much like watering a plant. If you tend to the plant, you'll have a great plant to show off. The same thing goes with your relationships for business, or your guests and influencers on the show. You can have long-lasting and nurtured relationships, just ensure it's not a one-sided thing. In business (where you are) many are out to take you for a ride. They are two-a-penny, and you must be on your toes to safeguard yourself and your guest.

Your basic character is to nurture people anyway, so you have a major plus here. You get many people who are just out for the money, and to hell with the people. Not good. You will attract great people because of your nature, and you will find that these guests are much like you. Part of your upbringing has been to be kind and courteous, so you will go out of your way to make your guests feel at home.

Like the angel, the guests will be attracted to you and your business because of this and the vibe you spread. This is a great way to get your business to grow organically.

YOU ARE FEATURING EVERYWHERE

You are networking, so you should be everywhere. Whether you do this online or offline, or a mixture of both, this is the time when you should be the most visible. "Shouldn't I be spending time on my scripts and themes, or whatever?" you say, aghast that I should be dragging you out of your studio. Not at the moment. You'll have plenty of time for this. Now, we're thinking of building a business, and we are network-ing. Without the business, there won't be any scripts or themes. I'm sorry if I sound firm and a bit grumpy, friend, but you keep on forgetting that you are running a business. Got it?

We need you in top form, with ideas and associations coming out of your ears. Seeing as you don't have a budget that stretches from here to eternity, we need to try and do as much organically as possible.

NETWORKING ON THE INTERNET

The best part of the whole networking deal here is to get a well-known podcast entertainment site (like Good House-keeping/Entertainment) to review your podcast and, hope-fully, to rave about it. They are an excellent site to get your podcast known by the right people, who in turn, will tell everyone else about your genius.

You can also get onto a hit site like www.podchaser.com which broadcasts podcasts. It's like radio, except its podcasting. Podchaser has a huge listenership that features new podcasts daily. There are categories like business, comedy, music, audio drama, true crime, society, news, technology, sports and much more. The shows have reviews and are rated by a star system. You can turn your podcast into a major hit by being on this site. And many other sites like it. The Internet is littered with so many sites like it. It's like your networking opportunity has never been so enormous. You will never think of your podcasting job as just being the podcast, end of story, ever again. It's a full-time job, and joyously so. Just looking at the various podcasts I have come across while trawling the Internet, I could spend day and night just listening.

BUILD CONNECTIONS

It's not as difficult as you first thought. It takes time and effort. It's your business!

Start conversations online and begin reading blogs. React to those blogs and tell the writer (there is more than often an email address at the bottom of the blog) how much you enjoyed the blog. You can also find articles on various sites that allow you to comment, which you absolutely must do, and this very often becomes a two-way street.

This is how you build up connections (networking!) and get your name known. Don't just copy and paste emails to a data list you've conjured up and then sit back and wait for the mail to come flooding in. It doesn't happen. While we're on the subject of data lists, be careful with those. You sometimes spend a fortune buying a list only to find that the list is unusable. It's probably about 12 years old, has never been updated and you have a deluge of returned emails popping up in your inbox continually. That is not a smart way of going about things. When you build a database, you must do it yourself, step by step, the hard way. This is gleaned from all the networked candidates along the way, from your Facebook group, from being hosted by a service online, from the queries that come your way after a podcast. Sure, it takes time. But at least you know that the list is completely valid and usable. For instance, do you run a sports broadcast? Go to your local sports team, speak to the coach, and get some great contacts from this visit. You also will feature a player or two as guests. They get their name mentioned on-air, and you have found a whole batch of new listeners. This hasn't cost you a cent and you've gained some valuable names for your database. It's the same with any genre. If you run a historical podcast, get to your museum or school and find out how your podcast can help get funds in, or whatever. This is where you become an active part of that community, and in no time at all, everyone knows about you. This is the kind of network that you can start building up right away. Podcasters often forget to first start small, within their local communities.

SURROUND YOURSELF IN A GOOD ENVIRONMENT

This is all about immersing yourself with like-minded people, who will help you in your quest, and carry you on their shoulders when the need arises. You will reciprocate. This involves podcast networks, mastermind groups and communities. I have touched on this before, but it's worth repeating here, in greater detail. There is an advertising model which works well if you have a large audience but not so much if your base is small. Focus on the non-advertising model which is the one that brings you more connections and grows your base. This is a great networking strategy that will add your show to the playlist of other shows in your genre.

Communities such as Facebook Groups (and your group which you started or will start) where you are surrounded with like-minded folk, can make all the difference to motivation and mindset as well as offering the potential for great networking opportunities. I have a Facebook group called *Podcast Marketing Made Simple*. Joining a group makes you feel immediately at home, which is important, especially in the early stages, for the building of self-esteem. It is an incredible basic support and knowledge-support resource and is vital for your health and growth. Ensure that you give as much as you get and become a valuable member, offering support and succour. Podcasters are creatives too, and as such need reassurance and support in many areas.

Somebody had a loose wire somewhere on her sound desk. See if you can help, being quite a tech person yourself. Other than problems (there's always problems) you'll find many valuable connections to spread the word on your show and will know other contacts that can provide great guests. Podcast Masterminds are private groups that normally consist of anywhere up to 10 people. Everyone is on their podcasting journey, but the group is small enough for you all to bond and become very close. This is the benefit of this group as opposed to the very large groups which by their nature can't offer the same kind of deep emotional support. You can talk to anyone about anything podcast-related, and it doesn't matter what stage of the journey you're on. You can motivate each other for your shows and hold each other accountable to complete the goals that you have set for yourselves.

You don't need to feel ashamed to admit being lonely, as podcasting can be a very solitary affair. As a member of any group, you will get the support you need to find new friends and supporters. In the mastermind group, specifically, this comes as a given, whose ethos is to help support and grow the members. The most important move will be to join any group that is aligned to your genre and is one you feel comfortable in.

LIVE EVENTS

Live events are also an opportunity to meet people, network, and hopefully get some guests to appear. These have been thin on the ground thanks to the pandemic, but things are opening again slowly, and events are coming! Buzzsprout has a list of forthcoming podcasting conferences, always a great place to network. Many of these are still virtual, but I suspect that as the year moves along and things begin to open up, they will become in-person. There's a host of top-class expos. You can find out about them on Buzzsprout.

You never thought there'd be such an amazing world outside your little (or not so little anymore) studio, did you, friend? Stick around though. Your world's going to get even bigger!

P.S: I meant to tell you I am enjoying all this too. It's been my life for so long, the pleasure I get in sharing it is immensely enjoyable!

CHAPTER TAKEAWAYS

- In this business, who you know is everything. That's the point of networking. Every chance you get, you should network!
- How to invite someone to your show.
- Pitch with perfection. Your networking is going to fall flat when your pitch is banal and boring and only serves for people to give you a wide berth.
- A website page can do your networking for you while you're out and about doing the Facebook group conversing thing and the myriad other things that you're involved with.
- Why you should stop chasing big names, and start featuring on as many other relevant podcasts as you can, to gain more listeners.

- How to find your powerful story (yes, everyone's got one) and share it effectively to resonate with other audiences.
- Evangelist Angels can work wonders for adding to your base by spreading the word and the love about your show.
- Build connections! Start open-ended conversations on your various devices (use a hashtag!) and get those connections spreading the word.

CALL TO ACTION

Start crafting your shareable story and note down 3 podcasts you think could be a good fit for you to feature on (and maybe vice versa).

BONUS #2

GROWING WITH SOCIAL MEDIA
AND BEING A CONTENT CREATOR

"We Generate Fears While We Sit. We Overcome Them By Action." – Dr Henry Link

Crew: Captain Michael Ork, USN
ISS Location: Low Earth Orbit
Earth Date: 4 May 2021
Earth Time (GMT): 13:30
C5 FROM THE CAPTAIN'S LOG

May the 4th be with you! I'm the new Captain on board and would like to give you my first impressions. I felt the love when I floated in here. We're a disparate group superficially, but very bonded and together on a different level. This is the level that counts, the research, the analysis, the things that will benefit us all. I felt that too when I arrived. The seriousness, the urgency of our mission, though tempered, was still there, and I locked right into that. My teammates welcomed me like I was one of their own and the guys that came with me. It was like one big family.

I think back to my time on earth and what I was doing when I wasn't involved with NASA. I was involved with groups that were getting MTP, or Massive transformative Purposes, going, and I remember giving a TED talk on it. I was a bit nervous because it's so important I didn't want to screw it up, but then once I got going, I was fine. I told them about how motivated we all were, even bringing in an organization like TED, who gets people to spread the word. Like evangelists. Someone asked me what made MTP different to other kinds of endeavors that are also spreading the word of the future, about radical breakthroughs for mankind. I told them what an MTP is not – just a company's mission statement, technology-specific or narrowly focused, representative of what is possible today, motivated only by profits, just a big goal. I told them what it must be – driven by a purpose to create transformative impact, prioritize big thinking, rapid growth strategies and organizational agility, all having substantial payoffs in the long term. It must have a shared purpose of passion, to galvanize a community. It must draw people who want mission-driven work and remain completely motivated, it must create a positive feedback loop by channeling intrinsic motivation towards a shared purpose.

Incidentally, young man, my predecessor, Jeffrey White, gave me a recording you'd made as a podcast that his daughter listens to. I must say I was quite amazed at what you were talking about. I found it could fit in quite neatly in the MTP loop. Well done, son. Keep at it!

ANSWER THIS QUESTION – WHICH OF YOUR HANDS IS MOST important? "Both of them," you say. "Right," I say, "Which one do you use the most?" "The left one," you say. "Okay, then, concentrate on making your left hand stronger. Don't forget the right, naturally, but make the left your priority."

I see you looking at me as if I've just stepped off the alien ship. "Trust me," I say. "I know what I'm talking about."

It's an allegory, of course, and you should know that friend. What I'm trying to portray is this – in this chapter on social media, which is uber important, that you should focus on what part of social media is vital for your listeners and, therefore, to you. You don't forget the rest of social media, but it's so vast, it's almost like the universe itself, if you try and cover it all at once, you'll probably end up in a black hole. Or so far into Deep Space, you'll never find your way out.

You're still giving me a funny look, so I continue hastily (before I lose you), with podcasting we've been talking a lot about social media and you may be here, there, and everywhere. It takes some time to digest, so don't fret. It's simple. Your audience, you've discovered, is most active, say, on Facebook. Don't, therefore, plough all your efforts into Instagram, which is not their hangout. Okay, you get it, even though you personally love Instagram. You're not giving it up, or anything else on social media, it's just for the moment, so you don't become overwhelmed. Too many people try to do everything at once and end up doing nothing at all. We're saying, then, spend 90% of your time on Facebook, where your audience is, as you get going with podcasting. As your audience grows and becomes more stable, (over monthly 3-5000 listeners), then you can start expanding into other sectors of social media.

MULTICHANNEL MARKETING APPROACH WITH SOCIAL MEDIA

Multichannel marketing is the interaction with customers using a mix of indirect and direct communication channels – websites, retail stores, social media, mail order catalogs, direct mail, email, mobile, etc. preferably to buy your product or service – using the channel of their choice. In the most simplistic terms, multichannel marketing is all about choice using multiple sources and options available.

For the book, we will not be focusing on retail stores, so our definition of multichannel marketing will only focus on the multiple platforms of social media. The point of examining multichannel marketing is to make you aware of what is available when you come to do this exercise, and how involved it is. The definition we would use in this instance is The use of multiple social media platforms to expand the awareness of your podcast. The aim is to reach as many potential listeners as possible. A great example of this is Airbnb. Airbnb uses multichannel marketing to attract and retain its clients. The company placates a plethora of user-generated content to boost its social media presence (on Facebook, Twitter, and Instagram) to up its brand awareness on channels popular with its users.

There are many examples of multichannel marketing, with many using the retail space as its center of brand experience, and the many arms of social media radiating outwards from this hub. Big names like Apple and Starbucks use this to maximum effect. As said, your focus will be purely on the social media experience. Multichannel marketing is all about choice – customers have a smorgasbord of options available to them. You, as the marketer (podcaster), must realize that this whole exercise is only effective for you if done correctly. You must know what triggers your listeners.

1. Your message must be highly targeted. If there is irrelevant copy (writing), it's going to fall flat and have no value. Your listener is simply going to tune into another podcast.
2. With the array of choice, a campaign is choreographed across several channels. You must get to know each channel thoroughly.
3. Poor optimization of channels. You have to pinpoint which channel offers the best response.

Remember, this is indispensable – but it's also complex and time-consuming. You don't have all the time in the world to execute this grand marketing plan. You're a podcaster firstly and a marketer secondly. Your podcast has to be right before you can market it. I have personally known quite a few that have dropped off the podcasting hemisphere – taking on too much when they should have taken their growth step-by-step and laid a steadfast grounding before going any further and becoming a victim of burnout. It's so tempting, I know, to leap in and make use of all that social media has to offer but follow our advice and take it easy! It won't give you the desired results while your podcast is going through the Growth Phase. The last thing this book wants to do is baffle you and over-whelm you. This all is simply to make you aware that this awaits you when you are ready to do it.

THE IMPORTANCE OF SINGLE-CHANNEL MARKETING

This is what you need at this stage of the game. Single-channel marketing at this point works the best and yields the most effective results quickly. Single-channel marketing focuses on one platform to engage with its target audience. The aim is to put your maximum effort into this one channel to ensure you reap the rewards of tremendous growth. Use this channel until you get to the point where you are confident enough to move onto the multichannel approach.

Most importantly, your content has begun to reap results, so you know that your content creation is spot on. You should be able to finish this section with a deeper understanding of why you should focus on one channel to start with and you can figure out which channel will give you the results you require.

PLATFORM ELIMINATION PROCESS

You will be able to work this out by using our Platform Elimination Process (PEP).

Choosing the Right Social Media Platform for Your Business:

1. Identify who your audience is. The first step is to identify who your audience is.
2. Define what your goals are for that audience.
3. Find your audience.

The preceding chapters have gone over in detail the identification of your audience, your goals and how to find that audience. Just from those exercises alone, you would have discovered how time-consuming they are. You have spent a major amount of time writing blogs, emails, answering texts, approaching would-be guests for the show, recording the show and marketing it.

If you are not clear on any of the three goals above, you should review those chapters and find out how to identify and discover your base. Chapter 2 specifically goes into depths about how to know your listeners. Use this knowledge in choosing which channel to hone in on.

TESTING PERIOD

If you are still unsure, I recommend that you go through an intense two-week period of testing. This is called "listeners' pinpoint location".

How this works is thus:

1. Pick a date that you want to begin testing.
2. Create an account (not page) for TikTok, Instagram and Facebook.
3. Create content for each platform before testing.
4. Pick a date to start testing. The only criteria here is that the date is one where during the following two weeks, you'll be able to keep up the testing.
5. Record a shout-out for the podcast and post on your chosen channels.

The aim of the testing period is to give a certain social media platform/type of content a real effort, for enough time to get a worthwhile gage of how your audience reacts to it. From this, you can start to figure out where the sweet spot is between what content you enjoy making, and what your audience resonates with (and where they are most active). Some of my clients were already active on all 3 or 4 social media platforms. When we tried to figure out which platform most of their time and energy should be dedicated to, I asked them one question: "Which platform are you currently getting the most amount of engagement on?" Voilà.

You may not have enough time to go through the testing period, and that's totally fine. You're a busy podcaster! The alternative is to find three shows that you class as similar to yours in demographic, so even though your show is about productivity hacks for students, another podcast where the demographic is students will work, even if it's not geared towards productivity. Of course, these shows must also be doing relatively well in your eyes. Follow them on every platform they use, and observe. You will see what content is working well with that demographic.

If you are focused on just the one channel that has shown the greatest response, you won't feel overwhelmed. Easy does it, friend. You don't want to get involved at this stage with a huge amount of content creation. You feel you have to better yourself with each post, and that will start to weigh down on you. This is what a lot of podcasters struggle with because they're trying to do too much at once. This often results in a situation where they end up doing way too little, from being overwhelmed and unorganised. To be honest, some are just like this from the start, blissfully unaware of how much they should be posting. They post infrequently, believing it's enough to keep the attention of their audience. In either of these situations, the bottom line is they aren't active enough on social media, meaning they fail to keep the interest of their audience and can't build a buzz around their show.

Thankfully, in this chapter I will outline how to resolve both. I want you to feel confident knowing that every minute you spend marketing your podcast on social media isn't a waste of time, but rather will lead to tangible podcast growth. Content creation for marketing should be like your blog - short, simple, to the point. Emphasize your exciting bits – like the guests you have got coming up, trending projects in the news that you have commented on, and which team you're rooting for if you involve sports. You get the idea, though. Don't ramble.

BENEFITS OF USING ONE CHANNEL

1. You grow your audience much quicker. Because you are focused on a single entity, your efforts are concentrated laser-beam-like, on that one channel. You have more time to spend on that one channel. Other than your podcast, you sleep, dream, and eat that channel. If you have multiple channels, your focus is everywhere, and find yourself being nowhere (at this stage).
2. You won't become overwhelmed by constantly conversing with audiences on multiple channels.

Simplify and become confident with one channel at first.

3. You won't become burdened with multiple content creations.

4. You find yourself relaxed and enjoying your show.

5. You feel more connected to a concentrated group of people.

6. Increased traffic to your group because your engaged audience knows the place they can rely on finding and engaging with you.

7. Give a clear call to action. Believe it or not, people don't like choices. They spend so much time mulling everything over that they end up doing nothing. Say: "If you'd like to know more, then head to my Facebook Group – 'Call to action: Podcast Community' or whatever you chose to call your Group. The conversion rate for the call to action will be significantly higher compared to "Hey, guys, if you want more content, follow me on social media," while proceeding to name all your social media handles. It's too much for people. Many people suffer from paralysis by analysis and will not follow through with action if it's not clear, direct, and simple.

8. You have your active listeners in one place.

9. Once you're at a stage where you're feeling more comfortable and have a handle on all that's going on, you can pivot more quickly to new platforms.

10. This is a matter of quality over quantity. You are able to build far deeper, more meaningful relationships, when you are focused, meaning you can build more superfans who love what you do. You give them the time of day and are able to better show appreciation for their support. This isn't always possible when your attention is divided.

Think about these new-fangled influencers that we mentioned before (and remind yourself you don't have to be like one to succeed in social media growth). They just focus on blowing up on one platform. Then, *once they are known* they begin to expand their reach to other platforms, knowing that people will follow them onto these new pastures. Most of the time, these influencers growing online is their top priority. They spend countless hours each day devoted to that one channel. Most clients I work with have many other obligations and responsibilities on top of the current hours they put into their podcast; family, friends and work. So, think of these influencers who have all the time in the world to focus on one channel and get really good at it. They didn't start by trying to get big on all of them. So, what are the chances that you will grow rapidly when you *don't* have all the time in the world? Is going an inch deep on different platforms really the best use of your precious time? Wouldn't it make sense (and make life easier) to follow an already proven model for growth and engagement by going 6 feet deep in one platform?

By using a single channel, you can make sure any of your listeners in that channel, once they are in, are captured. Because my friend, your content is perfectly suited for them, and the quality of your content isn't half assed. It's out of this world. This is how you get amazing results.

This entire idea of single channel marketing is thinking long term and doing what is sustainable. You have busy lives with family, friends, work and many more responsibilities that you need to attend to. Podcasting is a long game. You need to be patient and do things that will allow you to maintain a high standard over a long period of time, instead of going all in, burning yourself out, and getting poor results.

$$\sim$$

FREQUENT, ENGAGING CONTENT

When you first started, you may never have realized (most podcasters I know didn't) that you would have to write content other than your show. It comes as quite a rude awakening to discover that you have to, indeed, be a content creator on social media as well as podcaster supreme! If by now the reasons why this is a necessary part of podcast marketing aren't clear...well, everyone spends an absurd amount of time on social media these days. You can use this to your superior advantage and make people become so obsessed with yours, that they helplessly fall in love with your podcast. Creating content for your social media in order to draw people in and direct them to your podcast is called content marketing. I do suppose this whole chapter could just as well be called *Content Marketing*.

Remember how you squirmed about and grumbled when I told you about writing blogs? Yup, I can see you blushing slightly. Now you love it. You've discovered a passion for it. So, what's different, then, about writing for social media? Is your website not social media? Of course it is. Social media is any digital tool to quickly create and share content with the public – and, specifically, your listeners. There's really only three types of content you can and will make. The three E's are educate, entertain and encourage. When you think about it, your podcast will also have the purpose of one of these E's. So, any kind of content tends to fit into one of these categories. Of course, you should focus on creating the type of content that aligns with your podcast. Are you an entertainer, an educator, or an encourager? You don't have to rigidly stick to one of these categories only, but this is just something to bear in mind when creating. Using the purpose as a guideline will help you to make your content valuable every time. It'll also help when you're stuck.

You have to consistently engage with your audience, and that means most of the time. People are looking at their devices all the time. There's nothing worse than some stale old content that's been around for two weeks. People want change, they need to find refreshing new content. You should change it daily, at the least. Don't do too much, either, as you'll find yourself worrying about it all the time and then you'll be heading for the burnout pit.

Your audience can also get demanding. Don't succumb to their whims about wanting to see new content every 10 minutes or so because they find you addictive! You think, if I don't reply right now, I'm going to lose this listener. You won't. They like your content, and they love your podcast, so they'll stick around for more. That's a good place to be. You're not going to leave them hanging for days, then they may well move on, but the following day is just fine.

Pacing yourself is a very powerful thing to do. Not many people know how to pace themselves. It takes the right amount of discipline to pace yourself. It's rather like placing boundaries. People loathe doing that because they don't want to upset anyone. Tough if they get upset, and you've had the right to place those boundaries. Even if they holler that they're your most devoted fans, stick to your guns. Calling at 3 am is just not on. Neither is harassing you or your guests. If boundaries are called for, place them.

Okay, back to writing!

I've gone through multichannel marketing and single-channel marketing and you should be au fait with the when and hows of those.

Let's concentrate more now on content.

BECOMING A DAILY CONTENT CREATOR

How do you integrate great content daily into your life and stay consistent?

Are you aware that sometimes the greatest content comes from whatever happens during your day? I know you don't think of yourself as a content creator, but you are! You probably don't even realize it, but daily events are what happens to everyone and there are hassles in daily life. What are you thinking, how are you behaving? When this or that happened, how did you react? Why did you react in a certain way?

Listeners (and readers) want to know this because they can relate to it. Can you give this a lot of thought? The two greatest points on which to build are aspirational and relational...and if you can combine the two, you'll have something that everyone will want to listen to. The relational part of the podcast as a blog or podcast is the trigger that people can find a home in. Create a home (group) and everyone will flock. You are saying, "Yes, I understand, because it happens to me all the time." Add some humor to that (along with some insight) and people will love you. The greatest stand-up comedians use this as a basic part of their routine. Sometimes for their whole routine. People go mad. They love it. That's what you must do as well. People will go mad. They'll love you as well.

So, you became a content creator. Did you not know you were only already? It's just perhaps you weren't using all that valuable information that was staring at you in the face every day of your life.

Today's digital user is very online savvy and very particular about what they see and when they see it. If your writing is not inspired, you will lose followers. Even if your podcast is great, your writing could let you down. You must take from the inspiration given you for your podcast and put it into writing. It's as simple as that. You need people (your audience) to envelop what you're saying with your brand. The two are symbiotic. Don't forget your brand whatever you do. The emotive escapade that was embarked upon when the listener first encountered you, must be continued throughout your podcasts and your content creation for social media. This is your brand talking, and it's your brand pulling people in.

Creating content is key to an integral strategy. That has to be like musical notes on a page, and when played together forms a symphony. Let that take you on your journey. See your strategy combines your wisdom, wit, and wordplay. Combine those into a fascinating scenario that will drench your listeners with delight, like a moment that has arrived and left you shattered and breathless. This is what your audience wants to read. They want to feel moved beyond speech, pun intended. If you can manage to achieve this, you will be a content creator like no other. Even if you get to a tiny bit of this, you will be rewarded with an increase in listenership. People are so tired of the mundane, which is what a lot of writers in social media are, and their writing as limp as a listless cloth, that they are despairing of ever coming across true treasure. Let them find that in your writing. Write, and consistently, as if your life depended on it. Then you will truly see results.

If you have a block, and most of us do from time to time, spy on the competitors and see what they are up to. That might just spark something in you that will lead to a great guest, great copy, and great ratings.

CREATING A POSITIVE ECOSYSTEM

Before we really get knees deep into this chapter with specific social media strategies, I need to tell you how to really ensure that your social media and podcast grow together, with an indisputable positive correlation. A problem a lot of my clients faced when it came to actually growing their podcast with social media is that although they are growing their social media accounts, their podcast downloads don't seem to follow suit. They might have family, friends and other followers who come along, follow them and join their group. But somehow, they aren't actually falling helplessly in love with the show. This is a big issue! If you are currently in a position where you are all over the place with your social media strategy and find yourself unable to drive traffic to your podcast, you need to create a positive ecosystem. At the moment you just have...well, just an ecosystem. First hibernation, now ecosystems? It appears podcasters have a lot more in common with nature than we first thought. Don't think I don't see that smirk on your face.

This is the best way to ensure that the two entities (social media and podcast) grow in tandem, feeding into one another. It's what I like to call a self fulfilling growth strategy. Or, a positive ecosystem. This strategy works best with a Facebook group, but the underlying principles work well across all the main platforms. We will investigate each one of these platforms in great detail in just a moment. Hold your horses, friend.

You need a Facebook group or your social media that is able to filter podcast listeners from non podcast listeners. You need to be able to create incentive for those people who are part of your group/social media to listen to your podcast, and you also need your listeners to take your call to action and join your group, so you have them captured and can retarget them once they are a follower of part of the group. This is what is called a positive ecosystem. Your social media and podcast are working together in perfect synchronicity to grow each other and creating a loop where podcast growth and social engagement is quite literally the only outcome.

Of course, a positive ecosystem is best effective when you're doing everything right, like ensuring both the quality of your community and the engagement level within it is high. Let's not forget the podcast actually has to be good too, otherwise it's no wonder that people aren't transferring from your socials to your show. However, there is actually a single under-lying principle of a positive ecosystem that we haven't discussed in enough detail, and it can be applied across all platforms. It is our good old companion FOMO. In marketing FOMO is used as a way to get a reader, customer or in our case, listener engaged and actually taking a call to action. It works so well as it plays on the fear of missing out which we as humans just can't escape. So by showing your listener what they are missing out on, they are more likely to actually follow through with your call to action. Rather than telling them what they will gain, tell them what they will lose if they don't. This is a legitimate psychological trick supported by plenty of research, notably a study called *On the Psychology of Loss Aversion: Possession, Valence, and Reversals of the Endowment Effect.*. The subject of the study was loss aversion itself; the human tendency to prefer avoiding losses over gaining something equivalent. For example, humans would rather ensure they retain a thousand dollars, over gaining a thousand dollars, in the sense that a loss of $1000 is more painful than the gain of $1000 is joyful.

Anyway...for the community and podcast to grow in tandem, there needs to be a sense of missing out by not being in both places. You need to make the listener/follower/group member feel like they have an ice cream cone in their hand, with no ice cream. Tantalising! This is most effectively done by using calls to action.

The call to action in your podcast should be given at the start of the episode, to ensure your listeners actually hear it. And just in case you've forgotten the other 17 times I've said, the call to action needs to be specific, clear and singular. It must direct traffic to your main channel. You need to tell them what they are missing out on by not being part of your online communities. Remember all the stuff we covered in chapter 2 regarding engagement tactics? Think giveaways, polls, shoutouts, bonus content, valuable resources and so on. Maybe it's that you get your audience to pick the ice breaking questions between you and a guest. Or even have a shoutout section, briefly putting a spotlight on a member of your community who is doing something awesome. People need to be given a reason to join. Come forth o mighty steed, challenge your listeners into action!

Following on from the above point, you need to create a sense of FOMO within your community and make those on your social media feel as though they are missing out by not listening to your podcast. Talk about specific topics covered in the recent episode and create discussion in the community around those topics. By creating discussion around those topics you get a better understanding of who is actually listening to your show, so you have a good gage of the quality of your social media, whilst at the same time enticing those who do follow but don't listen, to listen and find out. They don't like that they aren't in the loop of what the community is talking about. Of course, you want to make this accessible for them so that they are able to easily listen to your show and get in on the action. Including timestamps work particularly well for this because it makes the statement more real in people's heads as it provides an accurate reference point. This is a great way to spike curiosity and build interest around the topic. "What did you think of me and ___'s contrasting opinions on how to enter a flow state whilst in a noisy place? This was at around the 08:33 mark in my recent episode (insert episode name) which you can find a link to below." This is great as you invite those in your community who haven't seen the show to become part of the conversation. They will either listen to the entire episode (jackpot), or, if they are busy but still want to get involved due to FOMO, listen to a juicy part of the episode and have a short but sweet experience of your show, because you've provided them an easy way into your podcasting world. Look at you, you clever marketing expert!

You're doing them a favor which they will appreciate, but also doing yourself a favour by getting that listener onboard and invested in your brand, even if it's just a little bit. That's how it all starts, anyway.

Right, the part you've been waiting for. Or dreading. Let's tackle the parts in social media where you'll be casting your focus, at first anyway. These are your big three. Forget about the rest in the social media universe for now and focus on 'the big three'.

A DEEP DIVE INTO THE BIG THREE

In most cases, a target audience can be found on these big three – Facebook, Instagram and TikTok. These are the ones I can witness from experience that were the most satisfying, and also, although there are others (Twitter is hot on the heels of these three, and for some audiences will be the most important one), I don't want to bombard you with all the intricacies of those platforms. You have enough on your plate as it is.

INSTAGRAM

Instagram is a social media platform that uses photo and video sharing via its mobile app. You can take, edit, and publish visual content for your followers to interact with through likes, comments, and shares. Instagram is very different to the other platforms in that it's jazzier and funkier, but used correctly, you'll stand out among the crowd. Being a visual platform, ensure that your visuals are going to make an impact.

This platform is now officially the most used social media platform for business. Hootsuite says that some 76% of businesses in the US are making use of Instagram. More businesses and consumers are adding to the busy traffic program daily. It seems that this is the favorite place for brands to connect with their audience. Agencies rush to get their copy and visuals onto the platform, and with the audience it draws, there's that reason why. You can be less formal with your audience, and that's part of the attraction. You can engage with them by using questions, polls, music, and style.

The harsh truth about Instagram is that as of their recent update, they have made it clear that you have to be committed now more than ever to grow successfully (this is generally the same across all the major platforms). The platform is here to stay and they want it to be the absolute all-in-one hub for creators. This of course means that the platform wants you to use all of the features they offer. This means you'll be using stories, reels, livestreams and IGTV week to week. Instagram is rewarding those who are constantly delivering content and engaging on the platform. What's the matter, friend? You look scared. I know it's a lot of work. This is why we have the single channel strategy so you can give this a proper go and actually see growth. Besides, although posting short videos, long videos, images and interactive content multiple times per week seems daunting, you can obtain a lot of this content directly from your podcast episodes. Phew! You breathe a sigh of relief. Let's get into the actual strategy and carve you a nice clear path.

PICK 3-5 COLORS YOU LIKE AND BELIEVE GO WELL TOGETHER. Where possible, your content will be based around these colors. It's likely you've already got at least a couple attached

to your brand, so don't spend too long on this. If you want to get some inspiration, visit Pinterest or as I always say, have a look at what your peers are doing on the platform. I've read debates on whether having a cohesive feed and a clear aesthetic on Instagram is as important as it used to be, but it's important for your brand to be emotionally familiar and an aspect of how this is achieved is through visuals. Your followers will associate a certain aesthetic with you and your brand and then each time they see those easily recognisable colors, they'll stop scrolling because they know it's you. Plus, people are always going to be slightly more likely to follow a page that looks nice.

I recently attended an Instagram masterclass and a big talking point was posting frequency and schedule. I obtained what I guess we could refer to as the magic formula. It goes as follows:

- 3-5 posts per week
- 4-7 reels (short form videos) per week
- Stories daily
- IGTV (long form videos) once per week
- Livestream once per week

You're probably gasping for air right now, and I can't say I blame you. That posting schedule is not realistic for everyone, so don't panic. Remember that this is the magic formula for Instagram growth. The key is to create a schedule that you can commit to, that is as close to this as possible. If you can post either a reel or regular post once per day, an IGTV video once per week and go live every fortnight, you're still going to be doing pretty well. That sounds a lot more manageable, doesn't it? With daily stories too (which will be easy to maintain), you'll be in the money! Now let's see how you can hit each of these targets.

THROUGH ALL THE DIFFERENT DIRECTIONS INSTAGRAM HAS taken over the years, regular posts have always been there, and always will be. Firstly, remember what the purpose is. You are educating, entertaining, or encouraging. You have your target avatar down to a tee. You know what they fear, what they find funny, relatable and interesting. Bear this in mind and create content surrounding this. If you're educating, you can whip up some brief how to's, or top threes and so forth. Once a week it can be a discussion post regarding a topic on your recent episode. The actual image can be text dominant, and you'll make it eye candy by using your primary colors and a nice font, which can be done easily on Canva. People can engage in the comments, so keep this in mind and ask a question at the end of some posts or say something that people can get involved with and give their opinion on. Post at what time your target audience is most active on the platform, silly. Once a week the post can be a more personal photo that is more about you and less about *them*. If you're doing this in propor- tion to the other posts, it'll have a good effect on your brand

and parasocial relationship with your audience. Just make sure it's aesthetically pleasing as possible otherwise many will scroll past it.

Instagram reels are a relatively new feature that was added to the platform to compete with the soaring popularity of TikTok. Reels are short form videos designed to be catchy. As you can imagine, the platform has been heavily pushing this content and rewarding people who are using the feature. Similar to TikTok, the videos only gain traction if they capture the viewer in the first couple of seconds, so there's no time to waste. The point here is that your video has to be clever. With just one look, you'll be able to tell exactly what could have been said in 100 words is now a video with some copy on it. However, Instagram has a different demographic to TikTok, so not all videos that blow up on TikTok have the same effect as reels. The difference is that it's more important for reels to be aesthetically pleasing than TikToks, so keep to your general aesthetic that I mentioned before.

Along with keeping the aesthetic in mind, another way of ensuring your reel is actually watched is through text. Many people scroll with the sound muted and unmute when they see something worthwhile. So it would be prudent to use text to sum up what the video is about or get across any necessary information, as they might miss it in your voiceover or audio. Doing this will increase your chances of people watching.

So with reels more than any other form of content on Instagram, users who are seeing your content and brand for the first time are unlikely to give you the time of day and watch your reel all the way through unless it's made with them in mind. You have to bear in mind that people are watching from a selfish point of view (until they are already followers of yours) so instead of "my morning routine", you need to think more "morning routine to help you feel less stressed during the day". And like always, this should be tailored to your target audience - you know what their problems and fears are, so create with them and this in mind. On the flipside, for those entertaining...you know what they find relatable, and you know what makes them roll on the floor laughing. Or should I say ROFL? If you catch a case of reeler's block, then search hashtags related to your brand and have a browse with your pen and paper next to you. You should always include hashtags in your reels, as they have a direct correlation with exposure. Even if you don't actively search up hashtags to see certain types content (or follow them, as this is also a feature of Instagram), Instagram knows what kind of hashtags are most associated with the content you enjoy and use this data to create your explore page (the page where you see personalised content from accounts you don't already follow).

Instagram Stories is an amazing feature. You can post something, and it will "disappear" within 24 hours (although you can choose to archive and highlight later). What's the point of this, you may say, aghast? Well, there's FOMO, you see, and for those not in the know, it's 'Fear of Missing Out', so fans will make this a stop on their journey. Instagram stories are presented as a slideshow, so not only do you have to be quick and concentrate firmly on what's being presented, but you also have to make haste in case it vanishes before your very eyes! There are tools and features galore inside the Stories that make the target of posting on them at least once a day easy. You can share music directly from Spotify, create polls, ask questions and users can answer directly from the story, which is splendid for engagement. You can be clever and actually post a question asking people to ask you questions, and then either answer them on stories or even go live and answer them all there. You can set rating bars and subject your meal, outfit, recent episode or just anything to the judgement of your followers. Scary, huh? Not surprisingly, you need a hashtag to go with your stories so people can find you.

IGTV allows you to share videos longer than one minute (if it's less than 60 seconds it can go as a regular post). As a podcaster, this is a great way to promote your podcast directly by sharing an enticing snippet of an episode 3-5 minutes in length. If you record your podcasts visually and upload them to Youtube, then this is perfect. If not, it's unlikely many people will want to watch a 4 minute Audiogram so you'll have to take a different approach. Think of three topics recently covered within your podcast. Run a poll on your Story asking your audience to decide which of the three topics you should discuss on your IGTV. This way you are actively engaging them and finding out what they want to see, so these people are far more likely to tune in. You can talk about that topic within an episode for a few minutes in brief (but still providing value) but then drive traffic to that episode at the end with a simple call to action, telling people you go into much greater detail there. You can use live streams for a very similar purpose, just make sure to use them at least once every 2 weeks so you're in Instagram's good books for using all of their features. However, if you are ever in a situation that can only be shared live and your audience would enjoy it, do it on the spot!

With mobile use and video sharing at its core, it's easy to see why it has become such a favorite with such a huge cross-section of people. Rumor has it that Instagram is going to implement SEO on the platform. So, start thinking about the way you write your captions, that will not only help you rank if SEO does get implemented but that also invites your audience into your world, rather than "this is what i have for breakfast", "here are the top 3 must have snacks for a healthy breakfast, are you a breakfast person or not?" You heard about the saying kills two birds with one stone? Well this actually kills three birds with one stone, one you're educating, two you are engaging your audience and three you are optimizing for SEO. SEO would also apply to what's in your bio, so consider this too. Have a short sentence in your bio relating to your MTP and message, to be an absolute beacon for when the right people visit your profile.

You can engage with other accounts. This may seem obvious and a reiteration of what I've been saying throughout the book (my friend puts his hands over his ears whenever I say it, he knows the saying so well), but Instagram works on relation-ships, so it's perfect for your needs. The more that you engage with other people's content, the more yours will be high-lighted and prioritized.

Use all the network info learned before this chapter and you can cross-plug with similar accounts and grow by following and messaging followers of similar accounts. It's worth mentioning that you do need to ensure your account is set to public rather than private otherwise the app won't be able to push out your content to anyone who isn't already following you. Oh, and don't use third-party apps to automatically do any of this as Instagram has recently cracked down on this process. Ensure to do everything manually.

Top three hacks:

- Do something that involves people featuring you in posts and reposts of their own. The usual way of doing this is by using a shareable give-away. Here, you can say that to enter the giveaway, they need to post your post and tag you, or share a hugely followed episode of their story and tag you. Tie this in with a great incentive (the give-away) and you'll have masses taking part. (More listeners!).
- Get people to send your posts via DM to people and 'save' them. Instagram has recently changed its algorithm so that 'saves' and 'shares' are more valued

than 'likes' and 'comments'. So, if you can boost the number of shares (either by DM or re-posting) and saves you can get, you will be working the algorithm in your favor.

- Use the archive feature to hide any posts from your profile that are outdated (were time specific and no longer have any purpose on display) or don't fit with the aesthetic so that your profile looks as attractive as possible to the onlooker. And save other people's posts you like so you can look back at them for inspiration later.

TIP: Instagram works on relationships. Build them slowly, carefully, lovingly. These are the ones that last.

TIKTOK

TikTok is for making and sharing short videos. They are tall (not square like on Snapchat or Instagram) and you scroll through them easily. Are all the videos about funny people dancing silly, or is there more to it? Look, there's a lot of people dancing silly and doing other silly things, and acquiring huge followings in the process, but, yes, there's a lot more to it.

Using TikTok is a great way to show another side of your brand (a very important point) and build a niche community (your listeners). With the right strategy, you can use TikTok to grow your business. What you have to realize is that this platform has content creators and brand managers just like you looking in. Are they doing the same thing as you...? Looking at how to grow their audience? You betcha. And why not use the most popular platform to hit the social media scene in decades? Do you want to reach millions of people? Of course you do. Well, you're at the right place. It's known as a 'fun platform' – and is your brand not fun, among many other things? Is fun not emotive? Could you make this work for you? You think you're being very clever by thinking these things, and indeed you are. But so are hundreds, if not thousands, of businesspeople. How can I grow my business? How can I engage with the viewers? By the time you've thought about this for a while, you'll have figured out the answer. Is your brand about tight-lipped, savoir-faire people doing business at your favorite retail store (which is almost going bust) on the High Street? Could their hearts be reached by TikTok? Well, that's touch-and-go, but probably no.

You've got to understand the platform before playing on it. And by that I mean, let the wacky, outgoing part of your personality dictate what you are going to do with the platform. What I'm saying is, yes, most definitely, use this for business, and do it properly, then you'll have backed a winner. What I'm also saying is that let the real fun part of your brand shine through, and the audience will take to you. Here, you can experiment with video and drive people to your site. That's clever thinking. Brand managers with no vision will diss the platform out of hand as 'not for us' and move onto…. where? Print ads?

The main point here is to upload consistently so you have a barrage of new videos hitting the people all the time. What you have to do most of all is respect the platform. Let the platform guide you, shape you and present you as you would like to be seen by thousands of faithful viewers. You have to be ready to do that, and it doesn't happen overnight. Uploading two to three times per day is optimal but as a podcaster, it might be hard to keep this up. So once again, find the uploading schedule that works for you and aim for uploading at least daily. Again, you need to be committed now more than ever if you really want to grow. The same way that you batch record your content for your podcast you should also batch create content for your social media platform ahead of time. Try to follow only accounts that are related to your niche or an account that is posting content similar to what you like, and is doing so successfully. Stand on the shoulders of TikTok giants (figuratively) and let them lead you to magic land. You want to be inspired by the right people, and keep an eye out for what is and isn't working for them. You can be sure to check through their old videos to find out when exactly they started to blow up I.e. their first 50-100k plus viewed video and then reverse engineer the content to find out how you can do the same.

Let your whacky, "other side" of your personality come through in all you do, in all the videos you make. And if you want to be clever here, present something everyone might not get but will love. This is you at your creative best. You'll have to think about this a lot, but if your humor verges on The Far Side, you won't have to think too long. And, all the while, building your brand, engaging with the audience. TikTok is a process of trial and error. Let's have more of the trial and less of the error. Spend a few weeks just watching the platform, and then make your move. If you move too quick, your video will get lost in the TikTok black hole, never to surface again. You want your video to catch fire and be pushed out to a mass of people. It's relatively common for a good TikTok video to get over 100, 000 views. Not be sneezed at!

BREAKING DOWN THE ALGORITHM

When you first get into TikTok you have a massive boost in terms of your reach on the platform. But why would they do such a thing? TikTok is a place for both consumers and creators and they want both of these parties to be massively engaged on the platform for them to continue to grow. So as a way to reward someone who is just starting off using TikTok, they actually give you a bit of a advantage showing your content to more people, and with this initial boost it's awesome for you as you will see huge growth in numbers, This is TikTok's sly way of getting creators hooked on the platform. Okay, maybe we should look at it from a more positive light.

It's TikTok's way of encouraging the content creator to produce more content on their platform. Think about it, it sucks when you put in so much time and energy into your project to share it on Facebook or Instagram and have a small reach where barely anyone sees what you are creating. In a way, TikTok has figured out how to solve this problem for many creators with this initial boost.

How can you take advantage of this to ensure you get maximum exposure for your podcast? Well the solution is quite simple. Start your content creation journey with a banger! If you have already started and are thinking "But Daniel, I wish I knew this earlier - I've had my TikTok for a long time now so my content isn't going to be boosted." Don't worry, I still have you covered - most successful TikTok accounts don't know what they were doing to start with. The first video is not the be all and end all, it's just an added bonus if you haven't started yet. And even if you read over this chapter and feel a new account might be necessary, then go for it. I'm here to support you.

With a lot of other platforms, your existing followers play a large role in whether or not your content gets seen by non-follower accounts. That's not quite the same with TikTok. When you post on the platform, within the first hour, TikTok will only show your content to existing followers of the account. This is a testing phase. During the testing phase the app is trying to figure out if your content is good and if they should push it to more people. They have an internal tracker which tracks these metrics (we will discuss more about the tracking metrics later and how they rank your content), letting the algorithm know what to do with the content depending on your results. Now after the testing phase is over and done with, your content will start being featured on the 'for you' page. This is the holy grail. Similar to the explore page on Instagram, the for you page is where TikTok provides its users with content tailored to them and their specific needs, based on past behaviour on the app. However, rather than being a separate page, it's actually a whole feed and is what's shown by default when you go on the app. The second feed shows videos from the accounts you follow. Once your video makes it to the for you page, your content will be shown to a couple hundred people, then a couple thousand. Viewership only reaches the four digit mark if the internal tracker decides your video is good enough to move to the next level. This cycle keeps repeating with bigger audiences each time. Until the point where your content stops receiving good engagement, the TikTok algorithm will keep pushing your video up in the ranks until it's getting seen by 10,000 people, then 100,000 then a million. You're probably wondering how this internal tracker decides the content is pushing to the next level. Here are the two main metrics:

Retention time: This is essentially how long viewers watch your video for. You can have 2 videos each of 30 seconds in length. The average point in the video where people click off is 15 seconds on one, but 30 seconds (the full length) on the other. TikTok's aim is to have people stay on the platform for as long as possible. Which video will rank higher? And which video are you likely to push to more people? The one with a 100% retention time of course, but it's a combination of metrics they use in order to fully rank your video. So hold your horses friend, don't think you can make a five second video and it'll blow up making you an overnight success. It's a combination of all of the metrics that will determine that.

User engagement rate: You can check how many views your video has, and then simply match up the engagement on that particular video. Are people liking, commenting and sharing? How much engagement is there in proportion to the amount of views? You can use this engagement rate to give you a broad understanding on whether or not the video is likely to do well or not. A good engagement rate is 10% I.e if 100 people view your video and 10 of them like, comment or engage in any way, that is a good sign. Gosh, I feel exhausted. Who knew when I started writing this podcast marketing book that I would have to do so much complex math?

I hope you're following along and not getting lost too much in the numbers. With that said, the higher your engagement rate the better. If you have a 25% engagement rate, I think it's fair to say you've done something immaculate.

TAKING ADVANTAGE OF THE ALGORITHM

So now that you understand how the algorithm works, let's look at two ways you can ensure you pass the metric tests, get engagement and increase retention time whilst getting your content in front of all the right people to grow a following.

Then later we will go into the video formula you should use. It's a super simple three step process, don't worry.

Open loops: This refers to creating video series to keep people engaged.

An open loop is a way for you to open a narrative for a concept that you would like to elaborate on in future videos. It's a way to leave people on a cliffhanger so they are left wanting more and to see the rest!

Creating short videos that are linked to one another means your audience is able to get invested and actually start looking forward to your future videos. It might be a challenge in which you keep increasing the level, or you're attempting to play as many theme tunes as possible in 30 seconds on your piano/guitar/triangle. Step by step guides, cooking hacks, shocking facts, the list goes on further than you can imagine. Maybe you're explaining a certain concept you recently discussed within your podcast. If you had a mediation podcast, maybe you could try out different breathing techniques, and provide your feedback on them. This is great as it invites your audience in but it's also related to your podcast theme.

Although TikTok is amazing due to the insane amount of reach you can get from them, a lot of people are notorious one hit wonders. And that is not you, my friend. By creating video series, you keep your audience coming back for more and more. Don't expect to blow up instantly, just be patient with the process and trust that by the law of averages one video will go viral. Of course when one video goes viral, you can rest assured that a good number of those who viewed the video will go back to indulge and catch up on the entire series! Video series are an awesome way to ensure you have recurring viewers who will eventually be converted into recurring listeners, when you create your positive ecosystem between your podcast and TikTok.

Another great way to create an open loop, is by actually having your community take part on what the next video should be about. This is a great way to get them actually interacting with your post. How? Simply let your audience know the top comment with the most amount of likes will be the subject of your next video. Like we have previously discussed, this results in them being more likely to actually show up and engage more with your next one as they feel like they have contributed.

Full stack: Make sure everything from caption, music, and video content aligns with the topic of discussion because TikTok uses this to decide who to place your video in front of. By having a video theme, it makes it easier for the algorithm to index your content, which increases the chances your video will be shown to the right people in the masses.

A colossal part of what makes TikTok a force to be reckoned with is the algorithm's ability to actually provide its users the content they most resonate with. It makes sense right? If you want your users to stay on your platform, make sure they actually see the content they most prefer consuming. TikTok uses everything from caption, music choice and topic to hashtags and keywords to index your content. These categorisation metrics deliver content to the right people. A video being full stack means your captions, music, topic, tags and keywords follow a synchronized structure. I know this might seem obvious but you want everything to be related to the topic of the video. Doing this will make it much easier for TikTok to categorize your content!

I'll use the mediation example. This is how you can ensure the content is 'full stack:

- Caption/keywords: Wim Hof breathing exercise
- Tags: Mediation, breathing exercise, stress relief, calmness, mindfulness
- Audio: Ambient calming meditation sounds

Do this successfully and you've significantly increased your chances of being seen by the right people!

3 PART STRUCTURE

Create strong hooks at the start of your videos by making a promise to grab the viewer's attention. This is how you can get good average retention time. By giving a promise of what they will learn, discover or even laugh at in the video, you invite them into the narrative by telling them what they should expect from the video.They need to watch the entire video to get the promised thing.

You must hook the viewer within the first couple of seconds. What makes a good hook:

- Grabs attention, shocking fact
- Instantly builds curiosity
- Speaks to a specific target audience, and specific problem

"I am about to show you a simple 7 second exercise that you can use in public to reduce your anxiety." This is enticing for anyone who is looking to reduce their anxiety, so as the host of a meditation podcast, it speaks to your target audience and tells them exactly what you will give them. Consider them retained.

At the end of your video, give a call to action. Maybe alternate between asking them to share your content and going to check out your podcast where you talk further on this topic.

3 step magic formula:

- Hook, grab attention, get them interested and invested in the three part story.

- Get straight to the point, give them what they came for, have the video cut so their time isn't wasted. If it can be said in 2 sentences, don't write a monologue.
- Leave them at a cliffhanger so they want to see the following videos.

If you create a one off video which isn't part of a series you can still use the same structure but rather than leaving them with a cliffhanger, you can give them the final pay off such as delivering on your hook, or giving them a call to action.

As a podcaster it's hard to make a highly valued piece of short content, as you are so used to producing the opposite. This is a new skill which you need to practice. Try out new things, figure out what your hook for the video will be and how exactly it ties into your brand and your podcast. At the end of the day, you're not trying to be an influencer so don't get wrapped up in joining in on trends if they don't relate back to your show. You're trying to increase your brand awareness, you are trying to grow so you have more of your target audience invested in your show. The end goal is always to drive traffic to your podcast and get people listening to the amazing stories you have to share. You're doing amazing, take a 5 minute breather. I know it's a deep dive but it's important for you as a creator to have all the tools needed to become successful on these platforms. And these tools are what I am giving you!

People will begin to follow you and start to take an interest in your profile and, naturally, your podcast. You have a magic formula here. Just work it properly.

If you consistently share niche products creatively, your perfect audience will find it and engage with it. Isn't that just exactly what you want?

As you grow on this platform, you can direct people to your website. Gosh, my website isn't great after watching my stuff on TikTok. Yeah? Well, change it immediately. You don't want The Night of the Living Dead, but you don't want The Best Ugly Cryer either. You want it to be fun, clever, creative. You want to leave people breathless again. You can do it!

Take a look at what Jacqueline Jax from Ava Live Radio's essentials to blowing up on TikTok are:

· Be active. Hyperactive is even better. TikTok loves energy.

· Collaborate with former Crown users.

· Initiate challenges to get instant fame.

· Show your skills via auditions.

· Come up with your niche. Consistency is important. Find your niche early and stick to it.

· Become a 'funny storyteller. Everyone loves to laugh.

· Share your video on other social platforms and link your TikTok on Instagram.

· Comment on other people's videos.

This doesn't necessarily all apply to you. It's a basic formula. You don't need to be hyper to succeed. The many themes on the platform include quick-cooking hacks, life hacks, how many theme tunes to play in one minute, how many characters can you be in 30 seconds…and so on. The possibilities are endless. And you let your video and music do the talking.

Be reassured! You don't have to go leaping all over the place with a funny face. That does nothing for you and your brand. And it's not you! But you do have to be clever, as I've said, and that is most definitely you!

Top 3 hacks:

· Abuse trends. TikTok has several trending themes at any given time. Study them and make videos for them. You become an expert at doing videos and it's also a sure-fire way of getting exposure out there!

· Go live at least once a week when you hit a thousand followers. TikTok users spend a vast amount of time on the platform. It's easy to engage with them. Don't miss out on the opportunity!

· Use hashtags. This puts you on the radar if you're taking part in a trend and will work with the algorithms for putting your video on the 'for you' page. Hashtags are vital for this platform. Whether you take part in a challenge or get your followers to create a challenge using a tailored hashtag, this will work very well for you. This all plays into the categorization metric! It is about telling TikTok who they should put your content in front of rather than trying to be discovered by users looking/searching for your hashtags.

TIP: You are as versatile as your podcasts. Prove it on TikTok!

FACEBOOK

This is probably the most balanced platform out there. Everyone knows this platform. It's been around for a long time (since 2004!) and is very popular with the late 20s and upwards. Over the last few years, it has seen a large decrease among the younger demographic, but it remains the one with the largest range of audience. Among the older generations, it remains a firm favorite. It is not only balanced in wider demographics but also its range of content. Both TikTok, Instagram and Twitter content is usable on Facebook. Whatever you can think (or not) about what people may post, you'll find it on Facebook.

With Facebook, you may assume that it's all about your podcast's Facebook page. Rather, it's about your podcasting page's Facebook group. I could write a book on why a group is better than a page, but to put it succinctly – Facebook now has a different feed for groups than it does for regular friend and page posts. People will scroll through the main feed often aimlessly, whereas when they switch to the groups feed, they are expecting your content, and they find it, on your group and others. Also, a page interacts with the audience. A group allows both page and the audience to interact with one another through targeted groups. This creates a sense of community which is vital for your show. There is also the opportunity to create brand awareness. There's more to why page reach is horrendous compared to group reach that we discuss in the next chapter regarding paid ads.

Facebook groups can be used for a wide array of purposes, but some common ones for businesses include networking needs, building customer relationships, and developing brand ambassadors. People usually include Facebook among their group of platforms, because of its steady and known reach that it has. There's no second-guessing here. Facebook is spot on when you have a certain target audience who lives on Facebook. You have many that are very faithful to the platform and brand. Hell or high water wouldn't move them, and no one tries to. They are great audiences to reach for targeted campaigns.

There are three types of groups to which you can belong on Facebook. You want it to be a closed group, so people can be invited to it, keeping the spam and troublemakers out. Being a secret group is unnecessary because no one will be able to access it. An open group is also opening the group to the potential for random visitors to dilute the quality of the group. Facebook algorithms work in your favor the more active a group is. This means that Facebook will extend the group to the correct people and bring in interested people if there are at least 3-5 posts in there every day. You will find that group members are far more direct and targeted because you all share a common interest. That's a given. You don't have to put out feelers and hope that you may touch on someone who shares your aims and ambitions.

The group's the thing wherein you'll find the business of the king! This is slightly altered from 'Hamlet', but has the same meaning, so I'm sure William S. will give us the nod.

The business of the king is why the group was started in the first place. You're the king, and I'm sure you'll be delighted at that. So, you gather your subjects around you who are thankful to have found a home they can trust, a leader they have faith in and topics that are pertinent to everyone belonging in there. It's a great place to be in, your group. You need to treasure and nurture it. It will stand you in good stead in the years to come. Your group needs, as I've said, around 3-5 posts a day. To begin with, you will need to take this task on yourself. Nobody else will be posting and you need to be putting the copy out there to emphasize your aims and ambitions and also to lay a grounding, a foundation, that's firm and secure.

Once the group grows and starts contributing to the posts, you can relax on the number of posts you put out. The type of content that you'll find on Facebook is a lot more varied than on other platforms, which could make it more difficult to know what to post. You may need to research to find out what works best, and what doesn't work at all. You'll find the stuff that 'doesn't work at all' is small. Somewhere, someone on Facebook will find that interesting. But then, that audience who wants to find out how chickens can lay blue eggs is not the ones you want or need. Because you will need to post more frequently than on other platforms, you will be doing different kinds of posts throughout the day.

You can get into polls, questions, and random facts in your search - the easy to make Instagram story content can serve for standalone posts in your Facebook group. You can create a branded image that you use every day with different texts and images. You can have the tip of the day, song of the day, and so on. These are very popular on Facebook. Your aim, I might add, is not just to have a good time (which you will) but to find those lone waifs wandering around in search of a home, a place of safety and succor which you can provide. All they want is to know about podcasts and who can abide by them in their interests. Viola! Another member is found. Such searches can unearth a good treasure. Facebook can provide you with an "all sorts" kind of mixture, among which you may well find hidden gems. Video content is especially good for engagement, and Facebook is very much in favor of this because it keeps people on their pages longer.

The bottom line is that the content you will post to Facebook is a combination of everything we've mentioned regarding Instagram and TikTok, and you'll have to use your knowledge on your target audience, and a trial and error process to find the sweet spot for engagement. It sounds overwhelming, but actually it's better; you have the choice to focus on the type of content you find easier to create, or enjoy more. Well, you should give each type a fair go, but you can start with your favorites.

Top 3 hacks:

- Create questions for why someone would want to join the group. This is a vital part of audience research. Don't make them too demanding. Asking for an email is a good way of building your audience and a route to monetization – but you need to make this optional. Make this the last question, so they are not put off by the ask, but ideally offer a gift via email.
- Following on from the organic growth strategy outlined in earlier chapters, apply these strategies to your Facebook group and see the results.
- Stand on the shoulders of giants. Learn what makes a good group by joining similar ones and being an active member.

TIP: If you want to understand what social media wants from you and why they do certain things, like creating algorithms the way they do, watch *The Social Dilemma*. A great movie!

Finally, remember the importance of engaging with this group. Don't just post, engage conversationally with every comment.

CHAPTER TAKEAWAYS

- How single-channel marketing should be your focus right now, before moving onto bigger and tougher things.
- Create an account for TikTok, Instagram and Facebook – and how these platforms will play a vital role for your podcasting.
- Why you should go through an intense 2-week testing period and how you will grow your audience much faster.
- How not to fall into the trap of being overwhelmed and finding it difficult to move on.
- Become a frequent and engaging content podcaster. Consistency is what you must be about.
- How to succeed on each of three major platforms (although not at the same time) – Instagram, TikTok and Facebook.

CALL TO ACTION

CHOOSE WHICH PLATFORM IS MOST RELEVANT TO YOUR PODCAST and niche, and create a realistic posting schedule you can stick to.

BONUS #3

CRAFTING KILLER ADS THAT CONVERT

"SECURITY IS MOSTLY A SUPERSTITION. LIFE IS EITHER A DARING Adventure Or Nothing." – Life Quote by Helen Keller

Crew: Captain Michael Ork, USN
ISS Location: Low Earth Orbit
Earth Date: 5 June 2021
Earth Time (GMT): 13:30
C6 FROM THE CAPTAIN'S LOG

A funny thought occurred to me today. I would love to bring members of the Flat Earth Society on board so they can look at the beautiful sight of the perfectly orbited Earth. I chuckled. Bit of an odd thought, that society. Never thought of them before.

The ship was a hive of activity today. Bit of a breakthrough in the research department. Probably wouldn't mean much to most of you folk, but to us, it's quite a step. And for the future of mankind, it's going to mean a lot. This is the start of the research, so it may take many years to develop something significant. I can't say much more because it's classified. Just know that this will have far-reaching effects.

Much like what I was involved with on earth – MTP – Massive Transformative Purposes. You'll have read quite a bit about it in the log, and the people to whom MTP means everything. MTP is involved in the now for the future. Like that old saying "keep your feet on the ground and reach for the stars". Don't think that ever had more meaning than it does now. Look at SpaceX. Can you track the mind of Elon Musk? Interplanetary mission is not just an outward desire for him. It's an inward motivation. When people are aligned on purpose, it creates a positive feedback loop by channeling intrinsic motivation towards a shared goal.

Did you know, like a north star, an MTP keeps all efforts focused and aligned, which helps organizations grow cohesively? As the organization evolves and scales, the MTP provides stability for employees as they transition into new territory. That's quite a mouthful, but when you examine it, it's not that difficult to understand. Just as space is perfect, so is the vision of MTP. Is it that some people are to the manor born, as it were? I guess so. There's something inside that cannot be denied, and that's the ambition and passion that is inherently part of the person. Like, what we're doing up here. And my MTP friends down there. We're always reaching for the stars.

Just like you, friend. I know you're reading this. Take heart and keep your mission firmly in your mind and heart.

You're going to go places. I just know it.

YOU'RE ALL DRESSED AND READY TO GO, FRIEND. WOW, THIS IS the first time I've ever seen you so eager to get moving. What's that? Oh, you're still having a little trouble wrapping your head around the social media thing. It will come to you. You're new to much of this, so don't worry. Go over Chapter 5 again and again and that spark will light up!

This chapter will be much easier for you. This is about how you can use paid advertisements if you want to start quickly, achieving optimal success when weighing up cost, time, and long-term success of conversions. You will also learn the basics of copywriting, which will prove to be invaluable throughout your career as a podcaster.

Let's take a look at Facebook and why it will work so well for you.

FACEBOOK ADS

Facebook ads are paid messages that are written in your voice to reach the people who matter most to you. When you create ads, you'll choose images, text, and an audience you think will help them build your listener base.

The reasons I use Facebook ads:

- Facebook ads are cheap and have a very high conversion rate for the price.
- The data Facebook collects is superior to most other platforms, especially as they are linked to Instagram.
- Facebook targets ads more specifically than most platforms so that the principles used here can be transferred to other platforms if needed.
- This method converts people to recurring listeners, not just a one-off listener.

WHY DO FACEBOOK ADS WORK SO WELL?

For a start, it is the cheapest form of advertising. All it takes is $5 to reach 1 000 people! Nowhere else on social media can you get this kind of return. It's not rocket science to figure that this is where you should be. Also, Facebook has 1.09 billion daily active users. That's a huge amount of people at any given time on this platform. If you get likes on your Facebook page, add those people to your Facebook group if they meet your requirements. They have to blend into your brand!

The point of Facebook ads is not to gain listeners directly to your podcast (although that may happen anyway) but to gain members for your Facebook group. The reason for this is simple – the conversion rate from a new listener to a regular listener, rather than being a once-off to a regular listener is much greater if added to a group and you are constantly engaging with them. Although you are not allowed to invite more than 50 people a day to a group, this is a very effective method of contextualizing your group with the right people through high targeting options.

～

WHY YOU SHOULDN'T RUN ADS DIRECTING TRAFFIC STRAIGHT TO YOUR PODCAST

When you send traffic straight to your podcast, the person seeing the ad will be seeing your brand for the first time, so they're not yet warmed up to your content. Think about it, you're asking a random person to go away and listen to your podcast. Even given that the episode being advertised is great and relevant to them, that's a lot to ask! Of course, if your advert is absolutely irresistible and it's seen by someone who's in the right time and place to go ahead and listen, it can work. But, generally speaking, it's really hard for you to capture that person and then retarget them. As soon as you stop paying for your ads, you've lost the traffic source for your podcast.

You may have a call to action at the end of the show directing them to your group, but as we know, very few people actually act on these things. So what will happen is at best, that person will consume your podcast content and usually never come back again. This brings up the question of "how can I ensure that if I'm going to spend money on ads, I'm actually capturing new listeners, retaining their interest and retargeting them with future episodes after the episode is done."

I'm proud to announce that this is where the PGL strategy comes into place. It allows you to seamlessly filter listeners from non listeners, potential listeners that like the idea of your show and brand, and potential listeners who aren't sold on your brand and purpose. The PGL strategy still allows you to send traffic instantly to your podcast, but also instantly captures that potential listener and allows you to go on to nurture your relationship, keep their interest, and get them to listen to all your future episodes.

THE PGL STRATEGY

PGL stands for page, group, listener. It brings people to the page, then to the group, then from there they become a regular listener.

So here is how it goes: You set up your advert with the purpose of getting your potential listener to like your page. Once they have liked the page you can then automatically invite them into your group. Once they are invited to the group, you have specific questions that act as a filter. These membership questions are awesome because you want the group to be filled with actual/potential podcast listeners, keeping the quality high, whilst still driving traffic to your show. Once they are in the group you will nurture the members, providing them with valued base content that align with your show's message. Finally, you can run promotional campaigns when you launch a new episode.

HOW TO CONSTRUCT YOUR AD

There's a lot that must meld to make a Facebook ad successful —you need the right targeting, a great image or video, and compelling copywriting. That's a lot to ask of someone who is not used to writing advertising copy – which, by the way, is a copywriter, the kind of person huge ad agencies pay a lot of money to get the right touch. The word 'copy' means a piece of writing. Read *How to Become a Copywriter* in this chapter. That will help you with your wordplay. Copywriters with a magic touch are in huge demand. However, don't despair. I can't teach you how to be a Booker prize writer, but you can learn the basics, and that's all that is needed here. Being a podcaster means that you have an inherent creative streak anyway, and that's a good starting point. Not many people have that. You just must transfer whatever is in your head when you are speaking, to your hand when you're writing. What you are learning here you can use over a range of platforms and on your web page. But this specifically is for your Facebook mission.

Your ad should have a one-line heading. It's got to be short enough and startling enough that people will read it, and then read it again. I see so many ads on Facebook that are just 'there', seemingly to fill a space. They do nothing for me, least of all make me want to read further. I think "Surely the creative person should have passed this ad?", but then the reality hits me that it was probably them who wrote it! I would certainly have nothing to do with whatever they're offering and the brand for me is so thin and translucent that it is like a mist that never clears. It's hazy and horrible. You certainly don't want that. Your ad has got to stand out and make a statement. Your branding must be brilliant. Brutal even. Don't forget that branding is emotive and that appeals to the senses. Not just a vague curiosity that tickles the mind for a while and then is gone, like it was never there to begin with.

IS YOUR AD IRRESISTIBLE?

It had to grab the person reading it so much that the call will be irresistible. That person reaches straight for the 'like' as if they had no option to do otherwise.

On a subliminal level, the ad has taken you to a place the reader wants to go to. On a much deeper level, that person is there already. That's the power of a headline and the copy that follows! It's like how you start your podcast. Don't say "Oh hello, it's me again", like so many do. I just switch off immediately. Grab them immediately with something that makes them want to hear more, read more. Don't forget that people these days have an intensely short attention span. If you haven't got them in the first couple of *seconds,* it's unlikely that you will have them at all. They will have moved on.'

In your ad, when you include 'like if....' think of 'like if striving to smash your week ahead', 'like if you've been down and gotten back up again!', 'like if you believe and have experienced the power of the law of attraction in your life'. If you're thinking of self-help, these likes are terrific. These are statements that will resonate with your audience, the kind of people that will gravitate automatically to your group.

There are two types of Facebook ads – the type that you see in your Facebook newsfeed (I like these) and the right-hand column ads, which is like a reminder ad, short and sweet, that you are still around. The first type of ad, in your newsfeed, is where you can display your creative prowess. With your writing, which we will talk about shortly, is the picture you chose to go with your writing. You must choose a high-quality stock image from the myriad stock pic libraries that abound on the Internet. There are many free websites (such as Pixabay.com and Pexels.com) and pay-for sites like Shutterstock. I would go for the paid-for sites as the choice is much better and you are more likely to find something you won't ever find on the free sites. Also, the fees you pay on sites like Shutterstock are minimal, so it's worth it.

DEMOGRAPHICS

Interesting to note that when you create a Facebook page (like you've done already), Facebook automatically creates an ad account for you. Go to the Facebook business sites and see what they offer there to help you get on your way. It's quite astounding!

Some of the ways that you can target your ad is based on:

- Location
- Gender
- Interests
- Behavior
- Language

And there are many more sub-groups, but you're more than likely will be overwhelmed by thinking "Oh my word, I've got to take a million things into account before doing my ad…. it's all just too much." Get out of that thinking. Firstly, think of the principal things – Facebook group attraction and podcasting. These are your predominant focus areas. Next, touch on the areas below. You'll have done most of this anyway.

For the location, only choose countries with English as the native language. Also, choose English as your language. For age, gender, and detailed targeting, what you chose will rely on the audience research you have done thus far. This goes for demographics as well. You'll have found out most everything already, like education, employment, lifestyle details, and behavior. You know your target audience backwards (remember all the research and surveys?), so you know how to target these ads. When you come to Interests, look at the people's interests, activities, pages they have liked and related topics. Naturally, you want to focus on interests like podcasting – what podcasts the ideal listener likes, anything you associate with your brand. Anything that is part of you, your show, and related interests. When it comes to behavior, target people based on purchase behaviors or intents, device usage and so on. Anything obvious. Note that some behavior data is available only for US audiences. Naturally, you also want to include here people who listen to podcasts or people who like audio.

LAW OF ATTRACTION

When choosing your audience targeting your Facebook ad account, you can browse between all the different demograph-ics, interests, and categories they have. Sticking to the self-help example, if you want to target people interested in, say, the law of attraction, then the interest category called 'Law of Attrac-tion (New Thought)' is your best choice. Based on all the data that Facebook collects, the ad would only show to people that Facebook has identified as likely to be new parents If you want to zoom in even further, a good choice would be the interest category called 'The Secret (book)'. The ad will show to people who have liked the page 'The Secret' and other related pages. Facebook has no way of knowing whether people have bought the book, which is why there is no demographic category, which only deals in certainties.

For a daily budget, I would suggest $3 -$5 a day. You should be able to reach 50 likes on your page every day. Don't spend more than that as you can only invite 50 people to join your group every day, and, also, you want to see how things pan out. If your budget only allows for $1 or $2 a day, that's fine as well. You obviously must work within your means.

TIP: Your Facebook page must be linked to your Facebook group for you to invite them. You can link them in the group settings.

SIFTING THROUGH THE RIFF RAFF

Now that you have your ad running, over the next few days and weeks you will get people liking your podcasts page and of course you will be immediately inviting them to join your closed group. However, as you can imagine, the sheer amount of people you're reaching combined with a question in the ad that everyone will say yes to, means that you will attract a fair amount of people who may not really be potential listeners, or suitable members of your community. To maintain a high quality of group, you need to set out membership questions that will let you know how engaged each member is or will be. The questions that you will have set up will also direct traffic to your podcast whilst at the same time capturing that potential listener's email. Marvellous.

The questions should have tickbox answers where possible, because the more writing people have to do, the more people will be put off.

1. What do you think about...(Proceed to insert your message/Massive Transformative Purpose)

Recommended tickbox selections:

This means a lot to me.

I agree with this.

I am looking to learn more about this.

This doesn't interest me.

2. How often do you listen to podcasts?

Recommended tickbox selections:

More than once a week.

1-4 times a month

Occasionally

Never tried.

I don't like podcasts.

3. Would you like to receive a link to an episode of my podcast, talking about (insert either your most popular or first episode, depending on which is most suitable)? If so, please type your email below:

(Open text box)

USING THIS AS A TEMPLATE WILL ENSURE YOU CAN OBTAIN THE data you need from people upon group entry, and be able to turn anyone down who doesn't align. You should only decline requests from people who say they don't like podcasts or aren't interested in your message and values. If they resonate deeply with your message and regularly listen to podcasts, then you have a winner! Any answers between these two opposites, you should still accept into the group. Obtaining people's emails is a bonus here. Even if they don't leave their email, this kind of person will have no other choice but to inevitably start to follow your podcast after they keep seeing your content within the group. If someone is 'looking to learn more' and only listens to podcasts occasionally, then as they continue being a member of your Facebook community they are still likely to end up listening sooner or later. This is the amazing thing about the PGL strategy - by employing a bit of delayed gratification you end up capturing the people who weren't immediately sold. Would this kind of person have clicked on a random ad to go and listen to a podcast they'd never heard of? No way! But soon enough you'll have them eating from the palm of your hand. The reason direct ads on any social media platform (directing traffic straight to the podcast) don't work as well as the PGL strategy is because you sacrifice the ability to later solidify them as a loyal follower through engaging within your community.

~

HOW TO BECOME A COPYWRITER

Have you ever listened to the podcasts on NBC? There are some truly great ones there and the ones that hook me are the dramatic ones. Of course, they use the trailer man for the voice, but you've got that tied up now too. What they do is very simple. They use a great picture on the cover, headline, a few lines of copy and a great tagline. Tell you what, I want to listen to that podcast more than anything.

Right, let's get to it.

What is copywriting? It's merely moving the words around so you end up with a sentence that will spur the people reading (or listening) to buy whatever it is you're selling – and in your case, it will be your podcast. I tend to be very dramatic or ethereal, but that's just me. You can just be yourself. Follow these steps and you'll be just fine at copywriting.

A quick note, people use the word 'copywriting' for anything these days, whether it be content writing, blogs, whatever. It's rarely used as it should be – a copywriter is someone who writes in a way that maximises conversions. Writing content and writing ads are two completely different things where different skills are needed.

THE SECRET SAUCE TO INCREASE CONVERSIONS

This is what copywriting is all about. It is the art of crafting words for the sole purpose of conversion. What differentiates good copywriting from bad copywriting is that good copy makes the takeaway irresistible. Bad copy makes it a take it or leave it scenario. Mainly, leave it. Another point to keep in mind. Brilliant copy may not sell anything. You may have writers and designers the world over fainting over your deathless prose, but the buyers, not much. You have got to be at the level just under that. Nowhere near bad, but just under brilliant. Most times, the ad is not emotive enough for the demographic in mind, or not correctly emotive for the demographic. *Point is, know your demographic.* Otherwise, you're dancing in the dark.

The salient points:

1. If it for business, you're going to appeal using the correct language for this demographic. Wall Street buzz works. Aspirational. To the point.

2. If it is for podcasters, it is imperative to use the language and emotive aspects that will draw in listeners. Clever, creative copy.

3. Spike curiosity without giving the game away. The heading "This changed my life." is enough to grab your attention. The smaller head under it: "And it didn't cost me a cent." will seal the deal before the writer has even read the body copy. If you're curious, we are talking about meditation. It's vital that you don't give away what the secret is. They have to listen or do whatever you want them to do to find that out.

4. You can deal with potential objections by thinking about them early on in your copy. And you can give answers too. "This will never work for me", "I'm not interested in this", "Not relevant"… these come up very frequently. Here's how you answer them: "Even this 71 year old grandma was able to turn a profit online doing this!" This would deal with the objection someone might have surrounding a money making tactic that may at first seem complicated or technically difficult. "I've seen results just from 10 minutes a day!" This deals with the obvious objection of the thing in question being time consuming.

5. Use numbers. They always add authenticity. "I did this for 90 days" quantifies better in someone's head than "I

did this for 3 months". "The 8 things you need to know before investing in your first bit of real estate" is better than "Important things you should know before…" And for some strange scientific reason, odd numbers are proven to convert better than even. So actually, "The 7 things you must know before investing in your first bit of real estate" is the best.

6. Use credentials. If you have a guest, give the credentials of that person. "Our guest today is Ravashanda Buja, best-selling author of "Buddha and the Bad Eye."

7. Use the language of the audience. Know your demographic! Use language that they can relate to. If you're talking to male bodybuilders, use words like "ripped" and "shredded" rather than "muscly" or "big". Build your body copy up so each bit reaches a climax until the pay-off line.

8. Give a clear and simple call to action. This is your chance to convert, so don't muck it up. Hit the heart and mind of the person with your pay-off line. I've said this before in this book; choose ONE action. Giving people a choice means they are more likely to do none at all.

9. On the podcast, feature your next attraction.

What I've given you here, you're probably not going to find in any other self-help book. This is what makes you different. This is what turns you into a copywriter to be reckoned with.

Go through this again. Embed it in your brain. It's practically the same thing, but with different words and styles. We are moving between the left brain-right brain hemispheres. Some of what you read serves to emphasise what you have already read, and some is new. Or is it? Like a tongue-twister, this is a mind-twister, to get your brain working on multiple levels with some 'secret sauce'.

THE IMPORTANCE OF COPYWRITING

This is the most vital part of your ad. It must stimulate, excite, and spur to action. You will use copywriting everywhere you can imagine. Your podcast title and description. Your social media posts (especially the attention grabbers like TikToks and reels). Your paid adverts. Anything that's in the slightest way promotional, anything that is remotely tied to gaining more attention on your podcast, smother it in that secret sauce. The emotive parts, as stated elsewhere in this chapter, are the most important parts of the ad. This all comes through your writing. If you say "The biggest news today! You've never seen anything like it", chances are people will run away. It's on the same level as "Buy a used car from honest Fred" (there's a picture of him too and he looks anything but honest), and anything that says, 'the biggest, the best, the brightest, the blockbuster', most probably means it's awful, more awful, the worst and the least likely.

People will not be duped. They are not stupid. Everyone has been using that copy since advertising first began. It may have worked in the 1950s, but it certainly doesn't work today. Today everything is more subtle, succinct. Sometimes, a picture and logo will convey everything you want to say. Mainly, though, you need that magical copy to go with the picture. You would have to find (or take) the most incredible picture you can think of, even if it's possible for you to think of, to run that alone without any copy. In any event, while you're still building your brand and it still is very much an unknown factor, best you spell it out.

That doesn't stop you though, from spelling it out in the most brilliant way. Your podcasts leave people breathless. Your writing should do too. Pretend that you're writing for your ideal listener. Just one person. Your avatar. Make that person the most valuable person on earth. You will do anything to woo that person, to bring that person over to your side. Your copy must reflect your passion, which is part of your brand. Your branding must bite. Your writing must feel that you've tasted a person's blood. It's metallic and it's marvellous. It's like you've run a marathon and as you stumble over the finishing line, you feel like you're on the verge of passing out. At that moment, and all the moments above, the delight and danger are sensorily sensational and spectacular. Am I getting to you here? You know the feeling when you've had an anaesthetic and you're asked to count backwards? In the time between then and dropping out, is the space filled with fear, excitement, falling, and total deliverance. It's so quick the time, but it is a rush of all these feelings. Write, write, write about these experiences. It will change the way you think forever. It'll change your writing forever. Even if you don't use any of it for ads, you'll have sparked that creative fire within you.

WHAT YOUR COPYWRITING WILL DO

This will move people to the abyss and then delight. Your writing will:

- Increase conversion of your ads.
- Increase the number of listeners that will follow through with your call to action.
- Will save you money and time.
- Will attract more listeners to your group.
- Make more people pay attention when you run your free promo.

The difference between copywriting and contact writing is the former is emotive and a call to action. The latter is more organic and straightforward. The sum of the whole is to engage with your audience on a myriad of levels and to build your base.

You are to practice the skill of copywriting until you are satisfied that you go into battle and that your armour is intact. "To dream the impossible dream…" said the Man of La Mancha, and, indeed, he made it possible. You can do that too. The scenario I have painted for you in this segment you're unlikely to find in many self-help books, which mainly stick to the absolute basics. But then, this book is special, and you are special and thus you are reading material not found in ho-hum books.

You'll notice when you start to get conversions from the people you long to have in your group and your podcast audience, that I have not been talking nonsense. I have been talking about the stuff of dreams and conversions, and the two do, indeed, go hand in hand, as you will discover.

Oh, how I long to read your writing and listen to your podcast. I know I will feel I am in the presence of greatness.

I salute you, friend.

CHAPTER TAKEAWAYS

- Use ads on Facebook for a fast conversion rate.
- The PGL strategy.
- How to write the most killer ads anyone's ever seen and you're so proud you tell everyone to go take a look (if they haven't already).
- What is copywriting, and how you are going to become one of the best copywriters anyone's known.

- How to target your ads on Facebook using demographics and your target audience knowledge.
- How to reach a huge audience with just a daily budget of $1-$3(see what I did there?)

CALL TO ACTION

DO YOU WANT TO JOIN OUR FACEBOOK GROUP CALLED *PODCAST Marketing Made Simple*? Make a post with your copy written description use the hashtag #copywritecheck, and myself and many like-minded podcasters will personally give your pointers and help you through this process, so you can convert in the most dramatic way possible.

BUILDING YOUR OWN PLATFORM AND BEING SEEN WITH SEO

"Believe you can and you're halfway there" – Theodore Roosevelt

Crew: Captain Michael Ork, USN
ISS Location: Low Earth Orbit
Earth Date: 4 July 2021
Earth Time (GMT): 13:30
C7 FROM THE CAPTAIN'S LOG

It's Independence Day down under, and I look at the beautiful drifting orb below me and I wish them Happy ID4! I would like to be with my family today, but my heart is with them, and that's all that I can do.

My last entry as Captain. It's a strange moment. I am so excited to tell everyone back on Earth what it's like being in the ISS, and I'm

really sad to be leaving my buddies on the ship. I suppose life is all like that. A lot of hellos and goodbyes. They're always the main things. The rest is just stuff happening which doesn't affect us much, we just carry on and do it. It's the hellos and goodbyes that get you. Anyways, I'm not going to get maudlin now. This is an amazing ship, and you have no idea just how state-of-the-art things are here. I guess for our research it must be, but still, some things never cease to surprise me.

From one thing to the other, but not really, someone asked me to fill this in just for interest's sake. He, like I, is also part of an MTP – Motivating Transformative Purpose initiative on earth – and this was an MTP assessment questionnaire. It went like this for the title:

What problem do you want to take on and solve?

1. *If at the end of your life you had made a significant dent in this area how proud would you feel?*
2. *Given the resources you have today, what level of impact could you make in the next three years if you solved the problem?*
3. *How well do I understand the problem?*
4. *How emotionally charged am I about this?*
5. *Will this problem get solved with or without you involved?*

It just made me realize that an MTP requires a different type of thinking. It requires a mindset and work environment that leans into complex problems and dares you to think big – really big. I love this kind of thing. I guess that's why I'm an MTP kind of person. Do you have this kind of leaning son? I know you're reading this because I'm going to take it home and share it with you.

I know my friend's daughter is in touch with you because she loves your podcasts. Isn't it amazing how we're all connected in some way?

Hope to catch up and say "hi".

Another hello.

HEY, FRIEND. GOOD TO SEE YOU AGAIN. HAT IN HAND LOOKING slightly glum. What's up? Oh, we're getting near the end. Ah, don't worry. It doesn't have to be sad getting near to the end. Especially doing all the podcasts that are going to set the world alight. Don't look suspicious, either! I'm being serious. Out of the class, I say that you're the one that's going to make it. Big time. I told you to trust me at the beginning. I have never let you down, never will. Stick to what you learned here, and you'll never go wrong. Okay, pal?

Now, the website thing! I've alluded at various points throughout this book to websites, and how it's important to have one. So, now, we're going to learn how to do one that's going to complement your podcasts brilliantly. Ready? Let's go.

WHY YOU SHOULD HAVE A WEBSITE

This is your home in social media. Someone may hear your podcast and want to find out more about you. Where do they go? To your website. Here you have all the details about yourself, your picture, and a theme (if you like). Careful that it does detract from your brand. It may blend in nicely (or not) and you're up and away.

Now, your podcast host probably has already given you a website, and that's great. It's kind of functional and suits the purpose but is hardly going to make Cruella de Ville rise from the dead.

So, you need to build your own with your brand and theme in mind, and whatever you'd like to grab people's attention. This is your home, and like your apartment or house, you decorate it the way that you want to. You know that saying, 'it's nice to come home to' must mean everything to you regarding your website. So, don't get rid of your host's website for you. You can send people that land there to your main website. The more there is about you, the better.

Now, regarding the writing. The copy on your site is very important as everything on there is the persona you have given yourself, so all the copy must reflect that. If you are going to write blogs for your website...say, expanding on themes that you introduced in your podcast, this is where you will do it. This is where you can have allied stories that will draw the reader in. Here, you will also feature what guests you have coming up on the show and little biographies of them all. Your page must be fun and exciting, and your writing must reflect that. You know from the previous chapter how vital writing must be, and since then you've become very inspired. Well done, hey. There's a reason you used to get A+ for your essays at school. It's all coming back to you know, like riding the proverbial bike.

The first thing, then, that the person will notice is the WOW of the page. Not too WOW but like *wow*! Caps may have the feeling of knocking you out, which defeats the whole exercise as you won't be compos mentis. Lower case *wow* much better, as it will be stunning, yet readable and…very important…. friendly to navigate!

If it has the effect of blowing you away, you may end up flat on your back. And navigating the thing is like trying to read *Homeus Opus* in small print Old English. You end up wanting to smash the computer to bits (this feeling is a common occurrence with most creatives). It just must be cool, with all the relevant info easy to find and exciting to read. Naturally, you'll have archived your podcasts here with easy to find episodes, complete with title, picture, and a few lines of body copy. Again, don't write a novel. People will get irritated and not only want to smash the computer to bits but you too!

THE THEME OF YOUR WEBSITE

Bottom line, use WordPress to help you build your website. When it comes to themes and functionality, they have got it down pat.

There are two themes that you can use – the first is Second-Line Theme, where you can build your website using your own branding. It's yours. You control it. Use it.

A theme is like a piece of skin or template that you put on your page that gives you the look and extra functionality. You can use whatever you fancy. As I said earlier, don't go wild and make the final product look something people want to avoid, like if you had a killer hangover and you're trying very hard to make sense of the function you had to attend. Not good.

It's got to be simple, easy to find, easy to use and leave you feeling refreshed. Because there are too many amazing-to-look-at sites out there that leave you feeling punch drunk and exhausted. You need a degree in how to navigate the darn thing. You must use the theme that is linked to your podcast – your brand. This theme is brilliant because it's built for podcasters and it's good to just plug and play. You're not interested in winning the Site of the Year competition, just having a functional website that suits your creativity and control. This, then, is for you.

It sets up everything for you, so the exhaustion rating is virtually 2. If that.

You need to have a 'subscribe to' podcast button, and it's done for you, as is the instant player, which is a great feature. It will sort out your back catalogue, and you can listen to it right there and then, no need to navigate to page 5 or anything. Everything about SecondLine is easy, which is what you want your readers to feel. Life is tough as it is so don't make your web page a grind as well. Let that be a welcome escape to brilliance and creativity, much like your podcasts. Then you get Divi, which is part of Elegant Themes (also from WordPress). With this, you will be able to super customize your site, but you have to build it yourself. You can have all the glitz and glamor that you want if it is part of your brand. If you want things to go Crackle! and Pop! In your head, this is the theme for you. It will naturally take you longer to create, which is neither here nor there if the result is pleasing. The theme is not tailored to podcasters like Second Line, but you can build podcast-specific items like the player. It comes with button widgets that will help you do all this. It's your choice, then. If you want a plug-and-play or a system builder, it's up to you. I would recommend Elegant Themes' Divi theme. The control that it gives you is worth your money in gold. Okay, the other is easier, but Divi gives you the satisfaction of knowing you have total control in theme and content. It's great to be able to put, say, the player exactly where you want it and not have to work around items that have been put in place before you get to work on the site. Divi ain't the deputy. He's the main dude. Trust me.

WordPress also has a podcast academy that will coach you in all the necessities of launching a podcast website. The prices are very reasonable and once you've completed that course, you will be a dab hand at the whole website thing – and more.

REASONS WHY HAVING A WEBSITE IS CRUCIAL

Don't forget this all comes back to marketing your podcast show and getting listeners. If it's a dull site, how many people will head over to the podcast? Would you?

1. A podcast is not visible, so what's to attract the eye? Your website, that's what. Hence the importance of your brand having a brilliant showing on your site, your archived material neatly in one place and the feel of the site being fascinating. It all makes for an interesting 'dig'.

2. Make your site a couple of pages, so you can go into a bit of detail about your archived podcasts. You can have in-depth profiles on upcoming guests, competitions, and maybe some titbits from podcasts all over the world. These pages must be just as interesting as your podcast! Make these pages like the landing page so you carry your theme through.

3. You take your website seriously, and it shows! This will also attract potential sponsors who are just

looking to get involved with someone like you. Do you know that sponsors rank having a great website as one of the important points to sponsorship?

4. Your podcast title is also vital to sponsor success. Not only does this attract listeners, it also attracts sponsors. We've been over this already in this book, but it's worthwhile harping on it. You will also have a title emblazoned on your website for your next attraction or a forthcoming attraction, so ensure it grabs the viewer who will convert to a listener. 'Open Cast Mining in Lithuania' is not going to do it. 'Find out who murdered Donny de Vallio' will most definitely. Get the picture?

5. Blogging your way to fandom. Blogging, as we've said before, is a must to keep your views and news up to date and fresh. Your site will have a ready-to-use platform where you can blog to your heart's delight. Don't, whatever you do, let your blogs go stale. There is nothing more off-putting than stale copy on a website. I'm amazed that people still do that. Big smack on the hand!

6. Easily accessible. Rather than having to hunt around on all the social media platforms to get info on your show, it's easily accessible in one place! From your website, you can direct people to the channels where your show will play.

7. On your website you can get people to subscribe to your mailing list. I could probably write a whole book

on the power of a mailing list so for now I'm just going to keep it brief. A mailing list is one of, if not the best way of keeping your listeners updated with new episodes and making sure they don't miss anything. It's certainly the best way to monetize your audience when you're ready to do that, besides any advertising done within the actual podcast episodes. Every person on your mailing list is going to be a platinum quality follower of your podcast and brand. They probably already were if they chose to give you their email, but having them on the list ensures they will never be anything less than highly engaged and receptive to your episodes and products.

TRENDING EPISODES

Make sure you add trending episodes and most listened to episodes to your website and highlight them as such. This is the only place where you can find them, so it makes perfect sense that this is where you will put them. I am really surprised that more podcasters don't do this. I know why. It's because they're not thinking about marketing. And it's also probably because they don't have a website.

Would-be sponsors will head straight here. Would-be listeners would head straight here. It's the one place where people get immediate insight into what your podcast's all about. And seeing as they're your trending podcasts, they're obviously among your best. Everyone will take immediate notice and be converted! This is what keeps the listener engaged. This is the flexibility that a website gives. There's nothing else like it that will capture the heart and mind so immediately, so inclusively.

This is the format that YouTube uses to great effect. "Ellen's Top Ten Most Embarrassing Moments" and so on. There's a myriad of them and they draw huge audiences. Your "Top 3" or "Top 10" would work the same way. Instead of listeners having to work their way through masses of sound, what they're really looking for is "the best of......" This will draw them to your live podcast without added effort.

Human behavior being what it is, it will always go for the best. No one has the time or energy to spend hours wading through pages or bites, as wonderful and creative as they may be, to get to the soul of the matter. Why is it that the compilation music albums and "best of" albums sell so well? It's because it's the best that the artists can give. What sold the most? What do people so many years later still talk about a particular album? Because it changed their lives. I must be honest, it's very rare to hear people talk about a podcast that changed their lives or one that still lingered all these years on. I'm sure there must be podcasts of this nature. It's just they're not marketed as such. Podcasters should do more in shouting about their success, the way that recording artists do. This will add to their legacy and give legs to their shows.

Do you know how a piece of music can take you immediately years back, to a certain time and moment? I've never known a podcast to be able to do that - yet! Words can have the same emotive power. *'Hasta la vista, baby'* did it. *'If I find you, I will kill you'* did it. There must be plenty others. Podcasters, use this in marketing campaigns, everywhere on your website. Make those sayings so popular that people will remember them years from now. Why did that episode work so well …? "Was it something that I said?" Yes! Yes! Yes! It was. That's a great tagline to use.

~

HERD BEHAVIOR

Social proof is a psychological and social phenomenon wherein people copy the actions of others in an attempt to undertake behavior in a given situation (Wikipedia) The term was used by Robert Cialdini in his 1984 book *Influence*.

Also known as herd behavior, this is where people act as one. If someone buys ice cream because it's the thing to do, everyone else will. Well, most everyone else. Taken to another level, people in London say if two people stand behind one another near to a bus stop, other people will line up behind them. They aren't even at a bus stop, but they say people are so obsessed with queuing they will queue anywhere where one person is behind another. It's everywhere, this phenomenon. "People are like sheep," one commentator said dryly. It's true, though. They are! In the podcasting biz, people are likely to click onto something trending. It must be very popular, so they'll click on it. No one will say, "I'd rather listen to one of his more obscure podcasts" (one or two might), because that's just how people behave.

You should use this as a test whether something's trending or not, just to see what happens. Choose something good, something that you think should be trending and get that news everywhere. You may soon have a stampede on your hands. Likely you will! Very much part of this trend is FOMO. Lots of social media drives people nuts because people are talking about this and what they found on social media whatever is trending, so the masses feel they must keep up. They will do anything to do that for fear that they may have missed out on something crucial to their existence. Or, heaven forbid, go somewhere where people are talking about a trending topic you don't know about. The shame! The hurt! As they would do at Marvel: "Sob!", "Choke!".

Anyway, we jest, but for some people (or rather a lot of people) this is kind of a life-and-death scenario. That's FOMO for you! This is why, knowing this, and using it in your advertising copy, you could whip up excitement about your podcasts.

HOW TO BUILD A WEBSITE

There are masses of website builders online but for my example, I have chosen WordPress, specialists in websites for podcasters.

1. You must have a hosting provider. You can rent space from this provider at small monthly rates depending on your needs.
2. You are offered a domain name (must have), great company service, and a platform where you are aided in establishing WordPress.
3. Pick a domain name from HostGator (you'll be directed), follow any other instructions at this stage and scuttle back to your site.
4. Install WordPress. This is done in a few minutes with easy-to-install instructions on https://www.hostgator. com/blog/need-website-podcast/ Just to mention that you don't have to be able to code or anything. It is so simple you'll be amazed.
5. Choose a WordPress theme. A pre-coded template will give your website a great look. Themes from WordPress include "simple podcast" and Podcaster SecondLine (we've just been speaking about this).
6. Install the correct WordPress plugins. ("What!" you say, startled. Don't sweat. It's easy) WordPress gives you the whole lowdown. You simply plugin and play! You choose plugins dependent on your needs.

7. When it comes to starting a podcast website, you'll want to look into plugins that startlingly display your podcast episodes. Here are other plugins you should check out: Smart Podcast Player, Seriously Simple Podcasting, PowerPress by Blubrry, Buzzsprout Podcasting, and Libsyn Publisher Hub. You'll have WordPress help all the way, including how to plug in the plugins!

8. Customize your podcast website. This involves site identity, menus, widgets and more. Follow the easy instructions on the site.

9. Publish your first podcast here. Okay, you'll be using this as a matter of course, but you will also be using the social media channels for your podcasts primarily. The platforms are where your audience is! Start slowly and build on the knowledge and experience that you gather here.

SEO AND ITS IMPORTANCE

I've touched on SEO throughout the book, and by now you must have a clue as to what it's about. It stands for Search Engine Optimization, basically using all the search engines to come up with what the reader or listener wants.

With blogging, or posting blogs on websites, the goal with SEO is to use keywords that Google recognizes and in its algorithm function and figures out where this story or blog should be placed. The top prize for any SEO blogger is the first story on page 1 in a Google search. This shows that you have used SEO correctly and that Google likes it. There's a lot of people studying the latest Google search algorithm updates! What we should concentrate on, though, is how SEO can help your podcast. The point to remember is that Google is now ranking podcasts, which is quite an innovation. You would use the same techniques for getting your blog ranked as you will getting your podcast ranked. Believe me, this is where listeners head to now, first off. What is ranking? Remember though, what Google is ranking mightn't be what's trending. A good podcaster will satisfy the requirements of both (ranking and trending) so that the listener doesn't have to hunt all over the place.

You must know the trending keywords and topics to build your podcasts. While you want a trending episode, you also want one that ranks. Many people follow the rankings before listening to the podcast, so this is where SEO helps. How do you know what keywords to select to drive SEO? Well, think of your topic and think of the words that relate to that topic, the ones that Google will recognise as keywords. Study algorithms and take your cue from there. The point is not just to use a keyword as often as you can. Think of intelligent keywords and use them sparingly. Have at least seven or eight to use. Okay, the point here is not to get befuddled and make your podcast pitiful in the process. Sure, SEO is important for rankings, but start with just making good podcasts, regardless of keywords. You'll learn, as time goes on, how to slot them in without losing that creative magic that flows through your podcast.

The Web is chock-a-block with SEO and keyword articles. Check them out, but, as I say, don't let them turn you from maestro to mouse! Just keep in mind that you are going to have to start using SEO at some point, so keep that in mind.

Here's in a nutshell, what SEO does:

- It generates free traffic from Google to your site should you comply with its keywords algorithm.
- What types of words do your listeners use? Know your audience! This is what the listeners will be looking for. So, it's keywords that are ranking with listeners and Google.
- Craft the episode around keywords. Just think about what people are interested in and use words that are related to that. Listeners will search Google for those words and end up at your podcast.
- Research the competition on what keywords are trending and then see on Google what words are ranking. Take your cue from there.
- Episode titles are super important. It would be great to use a keyword in the title. So, let the title reflect the keyword and the keyword reflect your podcast.

Subscribe to Buzzsprout on YouTube and you will find a host of videos on SEO and podcasting. It's a great channel and a must for the podcaster,

As I've stated, this takes time and practice. Don't think you're going to nail it from Day 1, but just keep this in mind as you go along. The main thing here is not to get bewildered and get turned off from podcasting. There are some for whom this has become a stumbling block. Don't let that happen to you.

Just keep slowly at it, and it will come naturally.

COMMON MISTAKES

- Don't have a date in your URL. This will date it! Google will relate to that date only and that's all that matters to them. Big no-no.
- Thinking of your site as the one and only. Link to others, build on keywords and in the end, your site will get big-time traffic.
- Thinking of SEO as just SEO. You must build a brand with SEO.
- Stale content is a big turn off to readers and Google. The big mistake people make is not to update their content to keep it fresh and new.
- Not thinking of the user first. A very common mistake is thinking of the topic first and not the user.

Comment on the typical user, then comment on the topic.

Wow, we've covered a lot of ground here. Whaddya think, pal? Okay, so you're not talking. You've got SEOs and keywords flying around in your brain. Oh, now you're smiling. Fooling me, huh? Remember, keep at it!

Your podcast is going to be a hit, come what may. Thanks for coming along with me on the ride, pal! It has been good knowing you. Here's seeing your name in lights!

CHAPTER TAKEAWAYS

- Why having a website is crucial – this is your "eyes" and people can see what's happening on your podcast.
- Writing great copy for your website is vital – If there's a lot of "guff", people will turn off. However, scintillating copy and must-know copy is a turn on!
- Choose the themes of your website carefully. Between SecondLine and Divi, a lot is going for you. Both are great!
- Constantly add new blogs to your website. Trending episodes are an absolute must.
- All about what part FOMO – Fear of Missing Out – plays in your attention and marketing of your podcast and website.

CALL TO ACTION

IF YOU DON'T ALREADY HAVE ONE, CREATE A WEBSITE. IF YOU DO, evaluate it now that you have read this chapter. How could you improve it?

BONUS CHAPTER

It takes a whole of guts, good thinking too
To make podcast power all the way through
You gotta take this, then take that, swirl it together in
    a vat
Add a touch of SEO and a pinch of magic mind
To have a product of a very different kind
A suitor would be the masses come to hear
Pulling in many listeners from far and near
Everyone amazed at the power of sound
The very thing they longed for, now found.

To wrap up this discourse on podcasting and how to get
going, you've realized that it takes a mighty amount of work to

get your podcast up and running. You're willing, though, to put in the work for the result – a podcast that's trending, that has drawn a great audience and the legacy that will have guests begging to be on the show. You woke up then, your coffee ice cold. "It's not so easy to be so bold," you thought, shivering.

Indeed. What is easy then? Not a lot. Sometimes just getting to the subway is a feat. Another day, another dollar. I hate that saying, but it's true. Get over it, and don't be blue, there's work to do if you want to make it through.

What was it that you wanted again? Ah, a podcast.

You can get Cousin Vinnie and Shirley to listen in. They've always said you've got a fine head and your speaking voice sends shivers down the spine. Who said that? Shirley? She couldn't have, she's your sister for Pete's sake. She thinks you're the original down-and-out from Beverley Hills. She hates your guts, so she couldn't have said that. Maybe it was Vinnie sending you up. Yeah, must have been that. You wake up again as the train pulls into your stop. Funny how the mind just knows these things. Funny, also, how you're going to spend the rest of your life going nowhere, doing the same thing, day after day.

Funny? Not so much. So, wake up. Dreams never become reality on the 7.32 from Brooklyn.

Dreams could start coming through when you're sitting in front of your computer in your studio apartment. A nice phrase for a cupboard. Which is what it is. Anyway, snap to it.

We're going to throw some tough love at you, buddy, because that's what you need. You must have heaps of discipline to get that commitment going. Okay, that sounds a bit harsh, but it's a reality.

That's not to say if your topic was really hot, you got a lot more people than Vinnie and Shirley to tweet, and you became an overnight sensation. Chances of that happening? Not much, but we're not dissing it either. The reality is that most people, including you, must pay your dues before hitting the big time.

All the stars in Hollywood? Brad Pitt used to dress like a giant chicken trying to lure prospective eaters in from the sidewalk into the Chicken Den, or whatever the place was called.

So, I mean, come on.

You got stuck for quite a long time but there's new blood here now, raring to go.

Take note of this story, y'all…

HARD WORK THE KEY TO SUCCESS

You must be prepared to put in some really hard work. You have got to know the business inside out. You have got to read this book at least twice. You must go onto sites online and read all the podcasting bits. This book puts humanity into what you're learning, so it complements the hard facts well. No excuse then not to read!

All the info you get will become like the holy grail, so store it in the recesses of your mind.

Be prepared to practice, practice and practice again.

Get used to the sound of your recorded voice. Can you improve on it? Of course you can, and this book tells you how.

Can you improve on what your 'studio' looks like for your pictures you can post on your website? Important! You can use a green screen and then download a great background to use on the screen.

Make sure your scripts are not epics. Once more people are hanging on to your every word, you can make them longer. I know a podcaster who started at 5 mins straight and kept it at that for quite a while. He had people thirsting for his next episode and that was his MO to gain listeners.

His script, though, was also excellent and knew how to end on a cliffhanger to get the people listening in. He's going great guns today and has come a long way from the 5 mins a day thing. He still practices his cliffhanger MO though and still knows how to reel the people in with this. You've got to be a great scriptwriter to pull this off, and most people don't fall into this category. Most just have to work darn hard!

He also follows all the organic marketing strategies that are spoken of in this book. He follows everything we've been talking about and he figures that this is the only way to build a successful podcasting business. He says you can split the business in half – half for the podcast and the other half for marketing.

You better make sure that you know what you're doing with your podcast first, though, and then get into marketing. And even before you get into all of that, you must commit to giving this all you've got.

COMMITMENT

Most people when they fail at podcasting, don't fail because of a lack of desire. They fail because of a lack of commitment.

There's a lot of commitment that is needed, and most podcasters when they start, be it as a part-time gig or full time, don't have a clue just how much is going to be needed from them. The point that you've all got to realise is that you can't approach this effort half-heartedly. You must give it your all, or not at all.

You'll have come to realize this truth while reading this book. Some of you will fall away, as is always the case, thinking it's just too much of an effort, but others will read it, be inspired, and go on to make great podcasting careers.

PODCASTING FOR BEGINNERS: VALUE EDITION

Why is it just such a lot? Because it is! That statement will probably drive you wild, like "it is what it is". That drives me wild, so I guess it does you, too. Whatever, it's true. You're not merely marketing a commodity (your voice), you are marketing your story. So, there's a three-point plug here. You have to be a creator and a communicator, firstly and secondly. And thirdly, you must be a marketer. That's quite a tall order that we have here, and this is where many shriek and run away back to their safe 9-5 gigs.

This is why it requires people who have the guts to commit. People who are willing to give their best and blow the others away. There are many people like this. Most find their way into acting, singing, and dancing. Though there's talent in abundance, it still takes guts and a commitment, especially if it's a musical, to perform for 8 shows a week.

When you start making it in podcasting, it will take that same kind of commitment.

Those performers didn't make it to Broadway overnight – it took many years of slogging away in dingy rehearsal rooms, honing their skills to the perfection that is needed to make it big time. Many don't make it. They've got the skills, sure, but there's so many trying out for the same part, if they don't have the X-factor, they will lose out. Not all have the X-factor, that special something. Most weren't born with it. It comes from practicing hard and learning new and difficult routines which may seem impossible. They prove it's possible with dedication and discipline, and they're the ones who blow the directors and producers away at auditions. It's the same with another sector of the creative arts – podcasting. This is an extremely creative business, and if you never knew that you were one (creative), don't let that scare you off either. You tell stories you've created, and you pitch them in a certain way using the dramatic skills that you thought you never had either. Your marketing is creative as well. You give pitches to marketing people for sponsorships. You thought you never had this talent too, but you do. There are many things hidden inside that have are now starting to blossom out.

Did you realize that it's harder for you than it is for actors? They are using their entire bodies to create something for an audience. You only have your voice, and you must use that to convey everything an actor does!

PERSEVERANCE, DEDICATION, AND HARD GRAFT

I'm not trying to make this scarier than you probably feel, but I'm painting the entire canvas of the podcasting landscape. Some qualities don't magically appear one day and say, "Take me, we're yours!". This needs perseverance, dedication, and hard graft. This is what the actors have in that rehearsal room before going to the dreaded audition.

This is what have, too, or rather, what you should have, too. These qualities are not born with you. They are developed. If you have no desire to develop these qualities or feel that it is just too much effort, this business is not for you.

You also, I'm sure, didn't wake up one day and say, "I'm going to be a podcaster". With most, it's something that's always been there. You maybe weren't sure how to assemble the thoughts, but the idea was there. Like virtually everyone, as you grew, the feeling did as well, but you never knew what all was involved. When you did find out, it didn't put you off. It strengthened you, because you love the challenge, no matter what you must do to get there. These are the people podcasting needs! It will take a lot of time as qualities such as these are developed in months or even years. To have aspirational ideation is a great idea but you must be realistic and practical about it. Some would-be podcasters even go for speech classes that help them to be able to project with confidence and flair.

The same podcaster I was talking about earlier went for speech classes even though I thought his voice was terrific. Thing is, he wanted it to be perfect and he was willing to go to any lengths to get that perfection. That is dedication and commitment. That's what turns mediocre podcasters into great podcasters!

BLOCKBUSTER YOUR BRAIN, BODY

The concept of input-output applies to every facet of life. Whatever you put in, you get out, and then some. How do you overcome hardship? By applying your mental prowess. You toughen your mind the same way as you toughen your body. You do physical exercises and mental exercises, so you grow them simultaneously.

How do you do mental exercises?

- Practice mnemonics. Absorb more and more information every day.
- Exploit your weakness. If you are not a morning person, try and become one, and work at it until you become socially acute early in the morning.
- Do small talk. Some people avoid functions entirely because they are too shy to make 'small talk'. Attend as many book launches and functions as you can and make as much 'small talk' as possible. Introduce more gravitas into small talk.
- Try out for an amateur theatrical production, even if the thought terrifies you.
- Read material that makes you extend your boundaries.

These are just some of the mental exercises that you can use to blockbuster your brain. This will turn you into someone you never knew, but the very person that is needed to push those boundaries to produce a breathtaking podcast. Try it. You will be amazed at the results.

When it comes to physical exercise, don't go for the run-of-the-mill run, walk type of thing. Get to the gym and start working out on those machines. They look like instruments of torture for a good reason. Your goal – to push harder, to increase the weight, see how the principle of mind over matter works. Naturally, you're not going to dive into anything that's going to cause harm. Get a trainer to put you through your paces. Tell him what you're doing it for and get working, even if you're only going to go for the real heavy stuff after a year or so. Just do it consistently. It's called commitment.

INNOVATION, MOTIVATION

When you are committed, you stick to your goals and your vision remains intact. Engagement and commitment are very important in companies. If you used to work at one, you would know how a good management team used to instil qualities of trust, innovation, and motivation. These make companies operate at the top level.

It was this that opened new doors, brought in new business, and make the company a tightly bound and secure unit, securing growth. You can apply the same principles to your business, and this will come naturally once you begin to push body and mind harder and build creativity and strength you never knew you had within you. You will find that it's truly amazing what commitment can do. You will find that this dedication to a cause – your podcasting – will take you to places that you never dreamt of.

As soon as you begin to unlock the mind and body, new thoughts, new aspirations, new vistas open up. It's almost as if the mind and body were obstructed with all sorts of baggage and muck and now you're cleaning it all out.

The point is, too, that you will need to sacrifice some things because those old things are now being replaced by new things. After a while, they won't seem like a sacrifice at all, and you'll wonder how you ever got by.

WHAT HAPPENED TO JOHN?

My friend John was in an accident at the construction site where he was overseeing a massive job for his boss. He spent two months in hospital and while he was there, he started to think about where he was in life and his future. He realized that he wanted to move on and do something different with his life.

While he was in the hospital, he listened to some podcasts and was amazed to find what was out there. The more he listened, the more he began to think that this was something that he would like to try and do. He became saddened at the fact that he wasn't a storyteller, so how would he get scripts done for a podcast of his own? He realized that a friend, Seth, who was a writer for a community newspaper, could help. He gave him a call; Seth came to see him in hospital, and they agreed to try and get something going. Seth seemed to be excited about the whole thing. Sadly, a couple of months later, the whole idea unravelled as John was too set in his old ways to commit to anything regular. He soon forgot about it, took a job as a sales rep, and went on to do well at his new job. The irony is that Seth started a podcast and is still going great guns.

After a year or so, John realized his mistake in giving up on a grand plan, thought long and hard and decided to give it a go again. In the meantime, he had begun to seriously date a girl who was a copywriter at an ad agency. She was sold on the idea! John knew that he would have to commit because of the work that was involved, and his girlfriend Julie was more than happy to see him stick to his plan and get some real discipline in his life. She would be doing the writing too. It's almost as if podcasting was determined not to let him go!

Two years on, he's now a full-time podcaster, doing most of the writing, and is married to Julie. They have never been happier, and his podcast is a great success.

He's so disciplined he drives Julie crazy.

LEARN HOW TO BE YOURSELF

This may sound like an odd thing to ask, but you have to learn how to be yourself. Many people when starting a podcast think they must do it in a different persona. That's probably the worst you can do.

Your audience needs someone real, someone they can trust. Few podcasters think of this. They want to turn themselves into superstars and think they must sound like a famous actor to sound plausible and get people to like them.

Fact is, people want to hear the real you. They can't put their trust and confidence in someone who is putting on a show. The audience is not easily duped. Don't even think of doing this. It's a completely different matter when you're trying to improve yourself – like deepening your voice, sounding more confident. You should always try and improve yourself, like improving the subject matter for your show.

Your listeners can tell a mile away if you're not being honest or trying to bulldoze them into believing something that's simply not true. Never, ever take your audience for granted. Your engagement with them is going to make or break you. Make sure it's solid, firm, and unbreakable. For this, you must be top-notch in what you're aiming for.

Do your homework before doing your show. Make sure what you're going to sprout forth is something people can build a foundation on to get them coming back. Ensure your facts are, indeed, facts and your story is airtight.

Also, never go attacking people on air just for the sake of it, thinking this is going to grow your base. What you give out, you get back (output-input). Are you able to handle that? Also, there is nothing wrong with questioning a person's motives in doing something questionable. But don't make it personal and always do it in the spirit of kindness.

I can see you're quite taken aback by that, but just think about it. What if were you in that position and you made a mistake and regretted it afterwards? Are people going to condemn you forever? You wouldn't cope with that easily, or at all, and could even drive you to start behaving in a manner you'll come to regret even more.

We all need love, and in an unforgiving world, even more than we ever did. Don't add to the hatred that is swirling around everywhere. Become a shining light and add a great dollop of forgiveness into your message. This will draw listeners by the mass. They need to be taken care of, to be loved and listened to without fear of rebuke or censure.

Your audience will do the same for you. The world is a hard, cruel place. You can certainly take people to task, but after you've given them a whack on the hand, forgive them and give your reasons for doing so. You'll find those answers in your heart. Your people will love you even more for doing so.

I'll leave you with that thought and missive.

I trust that you have learned a lot in your quest to be a podcaster of note. Just remember, it takes time. It takes delving into yourself and looking hard at what you see before looking out at others.

Remember to love your audience. Without them, you'd be lost. Which is something that we don't want for you. Ever.

Enjoy your vocation, my friend. You have a wonderful future ahead.

~

CHAPTER TAKEAWAYS

- Hard work is the key to success. Oh, what a cliché but oh, how real. If you don't do it, no one is going to do it for you.
- Discipline yourself to be in the enviable position of being able to make sacrifices easily to make your vocation sure.
- Commitment is the thing that pulls it all together. If you can't commit to seriously hard work, you'll come to loathe what you're doing and will quit.
- Push your mind and body to levels that you have never done before, and you will find joy and insight for your podcasts that might have passed you by.

- Love your audience. There's not a lot of it in the world and we could all use lots of it. Don't add to the hatred which can be found in abundance!

CALL TO ACTION

START EXERCISING. YOU'LL FIND IT WILL TAKE YOU TO PLACES you've never been before. Keep notes of your progress and your discoveries.

CONCLUSION

This book for me is a great journey. Sure, there's a lot of facts and how-to methods handed out, as there should have been, but there is more than that. This book has heart, something lacking in so many how-to books. Every step for me is a revelation, even though I knew the answers. I trust that you felt that there was something more than learning going on here. Did you feel that spark ignite as you progressed through the book? That's the essence that will carry you throughout your podcasting journey.

Right, let's wrap with some key reminders of what you learned, going through the book.

∾

I promised to give you a clear blueprint to follow to feel confident in consistently growing your podcast. There's so much information in each chapter, it's probably nothing short of overwhelming! So, if you got this far, absorbed all the information but aren't sure where or how to start, here's the most concise step by step summary I can possibly give you:

1. Niche down using *Bonus 1* and refine your show so that it resonates deeply with a specific group of people, rather than loosely with the masses. Create a target avatar that is the embodiment of this group of people. Eliminate the idea that a specific group of people is too small or that there aren't enough of them around to gain a colossal podcast following. It's not true.

2. Create your MTP using *Bonus 4* to keep you motivated, give you a sense of direction and have a message that attracts the right listeners for your show and gets them emotionally invested in your podcast.

3. Critically analyze your metrics and analytics. How can you adapt your show to best suit the listening habits of your audience? The aim is to maximize retention time, perceived value, conversions with calls to action, content for your audience, recurring listeners.

4. Given your new data on your target audience, hone down on the single most relevant social media platform.

5. Learn how to create content for your chosen platform using Chapter 5 and create a posting schedule

(modelled off the magic formula) that is sustainable for you.

6. Start to batch create content using *Bonus 3* ensuring you integrate your branding to it. I.e, colour scheme, messaging, type of content (education/entertainment/encouragement). Schedule the content for some time ahead (recommended: 4 weeks) so this isn't using up your time and energy on a regular basis.

7. Start the Growth & Hibernation Cycle. As you embark on your journey to podcasting success through social media, ensure you are doing things to create a positive ecosystem between the online community and podcast.

8. Identify your powerful story, find shows relevant to your podcast and run your quality check. If they qualify, start pitching. Once you have guested on shows, told your origin story and painted a picture of the future you're trying to create with your show, ensure you engage within hosts' online community to gain maximum exposure.

9. Build up your podcast network with podcasts related to your niche. Your network is your net worth! If you can, join a mastermind.

10. If relevant, run a Facebook ad campaign following the PGL strategy tailored to your budget, to scale the growth of your online community (and therefore podcast).

11. Create/refine your website using Chapter 7.

12. Use Chapter 7 to refine your use of SEO and improve your podcast's visibility.

If you do take action in the order of the chapters, you won't be far off - it will mostly just mean you won't get your community off to as seamless a start with the Growth & Hibernation Cycle as you would if you did the steps I've put before it above. This isn't a fiction book and each of these chapters can stand alone. Re-read to your heart's content! The main thing is that you absorb and apply everything here consistently, over time, at your own pace.

Putting together a successful podcast business takes **discipline, motivation and** mostly **commitment**. Staying fixed on these qualities will prove to be the key to your success. Many people on the journey fade away (called podfading) once they realize the amount of commitment that is needed. This is ubiquitous among podcasters and it's, indeed, sad to see how many people succumb to this. Don't let it happen to you! Take as many breaks as is needed. You are not running a race!

Also, **start exercising** and this will clear your mind and provide an important breather!

Above all, you must enjoy your journey, otherwise what's the point?

Podcasting is not your run-of-the-mill job. It's unique, it's creative and it's fun.

Be aware of the triggers that cause podfading and work around them.

If you do this, you'll have the time of your life!

Daniel Larson

I hope you've enjoyed reading this book. If you would like to work with me 1-on-1 to get help implementing the strategies you have learned, it would be delightful to set up a free evaluation call to see where you are and where you would like to take things with your show. Click the link below to get yourself booked in.

https://calendly.com/atpublishing/ertqualifier?month=2021-07

BONUS #4

If you're reading this as a paperback, visit this link to access your bonuses: https://daniel-larson.com/pmbonus

DEAR VALUED READER...

Discover how my friend Jake got to 300k/monthly downloads in under 7 months without using social media via the link below, and get a discounted **80% off** the 15 video training series I compiled, showing you how to do the same.

https://daniel-larson.com/reader-special-offer

Daniel Larson

RESOURCE LIST

A special thanks to sound engineer Jake Fielding for his lending me his expertise for chapter 4. Visit www.jakefielding.com for expert production for your project.

10 Ways to Learn About Your Target Audience. Entrepreneur. (2016). Retrieved 15 March 2021, from https://www.entrepreneur.com/slideshow/307880.

4 Strategies to Turn Casual Listeners into Raving Fans. Buzzsprout.com. (2018). Retrieved 7 July 2021, from https://www.buzzsprout.com/blog/listeners-to-fans?utm_source=buzzsprout&utm_medium=blog&utm_campaign=50-growth-tips.

5 Reasons Why Having a Website is Vital to Your Podcasting Success - Podcast Websites. Podcast Websites. Retrieved 7 July

2021, from https://podcastwebsites.com/2018/08/5-reasons-why-having-a-website-is-vital-to-your-podcasting-success/.

7 Benefits of Using Facebook Groups for Business | CS Agents. Social App Support. (2019). Retrieved 14 March 2021, from https://cs-agents.com/blog/7-benefits-facebook-groups-for-business/#:

7 Benefits of Using Facebook Groups for Business | CS Agents. Social App Support. (2019). Retrieved 7 July 2021, from https://cs-agents.com/blog/7-benefits-facebook-groups-for-business/#:

9 Listener Experience Tips for 80% more Clients and Business. Improve Podcast. Retrieved 3 April 2021, from https://improvepodcast.com/podcast-listener-experience/.

Branding Your Podcast: What Sets You Apart From Other Podcasts. Theshanman.com. (2018). Retrieved 12 April 2021, from https://www.theshanman.com/blog/branding-your-podcast-what-sets-you-apart-from-other-podcasts.

Breunissen, M. 5 Simple Tips For Improving Your Podcast Sound Quality | We Edit Podcasts. We Edit Podcasts | The fastest podcast editing service online, all within 48 hours. Retrieved 15 May 2021, from https://www.weeditpodcasts.com/5-simple-tips-for-improving-your-podcast-sound-quality/.

Bullock, L. (2019). How to Create an Instagram Content Plan for Your Business. Retrieved 7 July 2021, from https://www.

socialmediaexaminer.com/how-to-create-instagram-content-plan-for-business/.

Butler, N. How to Create a Powerful Brand Identity (A Step-by-Step Guide). Column Five. Retrieved 9 February 2021, from https://www.columnfivemedia.com/how-to-create-a-brand-identity.

Carbary, J. Relationship Marketing: 23 Ways to Nurture Relationships with Your Podcast Guests. Sweet Fish Media. Retrieved 4 June 2021, from https://sweetfishmedia.com/rela tionship-marketing-podcast-guests/.

Cattoni, A. (2019). What is Copywriting? The ABCs of Copywriting for Beginners. Youtube.com. Retrieved 7 July 2021, from https://www.youtube.com/watch?v=k5uI0yoKnF4& t=20s.

Caylor, B. (2018). Where Your Audience Is Hanging Out on Social Media | Caylor Solutions. Caylor Solutions. Retrieved 18 March 2021, from https://www.caylor-solutions.com/audi ence-hanging-social-media/.

Cell, E. How to Use Instagram Stories to Build Your Audience. Social Media Marketing & Management Dashboard. Retrieved 7 April 2021, from https://blog.hootsuite.com/how-to-use-instagram-stories/.

Ciccarelli, S., *Voices,* The 4 Different Types of Podcasts. (30 October, 2019.) https://www.voices.com/blog/4-different-types-podcasts/

Cider, A. (2021). How To Grow FAST On TikTok 2021 (TikTok Algorithm EXPOSED). Youtube.com. Retrieved 7 July 2021, from https://www.youtube.com/watch?v=vF7KJEeciIw.

Commitment to work: Definition, importance and tips to improve work commitment | QuestionPro. QuestionPro. Retrieved 7 July 2021, from https://www.questionpro.com/blog/commitment-to-work/.

Cooper, P. (2020). How to Use Instagram Stories to Build Your Audience. Social Media Marketing & Management Dashboard. Retrieved 3 March 2021, from https://blog.hootsuite.com/how-to-use-instagram-stories/.

Cummings, A. (2020). How to Build Your Podcast Website (& Why You Need One) | HostGator. HostGator. Retrieved 7 July 2021, from https://www.hostgator.com/blog/need-website-podcast/.

Doyle, M. Where's Waldo | Building Trust through the Red Shirt. Come Alive Creative. Retrieved 23 March 2021, from https://comealivecreative.com/build-trust-with-a-podcast/.

Enns, J. (2018). How To Build A Community Around Your Podcast | Counterweight Creative: Podcast Strategy & Production. Counterweight Creative. Retrieved 7 July 2021, from https://counterweightcreative.co/build-podcast-community/.

Fennell, C. (2018). The Importance of Understanding Your Target Audience | SPEED. Enterprise Action. Retrieved 7 July

2021, from https://www.speedstartup.org/blog-post/impor tance-understanding-target-audience/#:

Fleishman, H. (2019). How to Master Non-Awkward, Effective In-Person Networking. Blog.hubspot.com. Retrieved 7 March 2021, from https://blog.hubspot.com/marketing/the-ulti mate-guide-to-non_awkward-effective-networking.

Captivate.fm. (2020). Podcast Analytics And Stats: How to Measure Your Success | Captivate. Captivate Unlimited Podcast Hosting & Analytics. Retrieved 7 July 2021, from https://www.captivate.fm/blog/podcast-analytics-and-stats/.

Gray, C. (2020). Before you continue to YouTube. Youtube.-com. Retrieved 7 July 2021, from https://www.youtube.com/watch?v=HXUf3L1Hg1Y.

Hall, J. Your Content Strategy Needs More Consistency. Blog.hubspot.com. Retrieved 15 April 2021, from https://blog.hubspot.com/marketing/create-content-strategy-that-works.

Hayden, B. (2014). Warren Buffett Knows It. Reinvesting in Your Business Can Lead to Huge Growth.. Entrepreneur. Retrieved 7 July 2021, from https://www.entrepreneur.com/article/241196.

Herrera, A. Podcast Networks: Should you join a network to grow your podcast?. Buzzsprout.com. Retrieved 16 January 2021, from https://www.buzzsprout.com/blog/podcast-network.

Herrera, A., & Herrera, A. Podcast Communities You Should Be A Part Of. Music Radio Creative. Retrieved 12 April 2021, from https://producer.musicradiocreative.com/podcast-communities-part/.

Hicks, K. (2020). Using Newsjacking and Trending Topics in Your Marketing - Velocitize. Velocitize. Retrieved 7 July 2021, from https://velocitize.com/2020/11/04/using-newsjacking-and-trending-topics/.

How to Create a More Consistent Content Strategy. Geek Chicago. Retrieved 7 July 2021, from https://www.geekchicago.com/blog-categories/how-to-create-a-more-consistent-content-strategy.html.

How to Create Winning Headlines in 9 Simple Steps. The Daily Egg. (2020). Retrieved 7 July 2021, from https://www.crazyegg.com/blog/headlines-9-steps/.

Hubbard, L. (2019). Why Is Identifying the Target Market so Important to a Company?. Small Business - Chron.com. Retrieved 17 April 2021, from https://smallbusiness.chron.com/identifying-target-market-important-company-76792.html.

Lance, K. 10 Tips for Creating Consistent Content - Katie Lance Consulting. Katie Lance Consulting. Retrieved 7 July 2021, from https://katielance.com/consistent-content/.

Langdon, S. (2016). 3 Reasons You Should Be Hanging Out With Your Target Audience. Entrepreneur. Retrieved 9

March 2021, from https://www.entrepreneur.com/article/
276411#:

Lee Dumas, J. (2014). Finding your perfect customer (your
avatar).   https://www.eofire.com/finding-your-perfect-
customer-your-avatar/. Retrieved 7 July 2021, from https://
www.eofire.com/finding-your-perfect-customer-your-
avatar/.

Masterclass, V. (2021). Voice Training Exercise | Easy steps to
improve the sound of your voice. Youtube.com. Retrieved 21
March 2021, from https://www.youtube.com/watch?v=
aeyn3kLd1Y0.

Maziriri, E. (2017). (PDF) The Influence of Brand Trust, Brand
Familiarity and Brand Experience on Brand Attachment: A
Case of Consumers in the Gauteng Province of South Africa.
ResearchGate. Retrieved 5 March 2021, from

https://www.researchgate.net/publication/
314980923_The_Influence_of_Brand_Trust_Brand_Familiari
ty_and_Brand_Experience_on_Brand_Attachment_A_
Case_of_Consumers_in_the_Gauteng_Province_of_South_Africa.

McLean, M., *The Podcast Host*, 7 Podcast Tips to Build a
Successful Show that Thrives. (3 December, 2018) https://
www.thepodcasthost.com/planning/how-to-make-a-success
ful-podcast/

McLean, M. (2021). Growth Through Networking for
Podcasters. The Podcast Host. Retrieved 26 February 2021,

from https://www.thepodcasthost.com/promotion/growth-through-networking-for-podcasters/.

Messitte, N. (2018). Five Considerations for Sound-Designing a Podcast. B&H Explora. Retrieved 21 April 2021, from https://www.bhphotovideo.com/explora/pro-audio/tips-and-solutions/five-considerations-for-sound-designing-a-podcast.

Millie, M. (2020). How To Grow FAST On Instagram Using Reels | 10,000 Followers In ONE MONTH. Youtube.com. Retrieved 7 July 2021, from https://www.youtube.com/watch?v=D-oETDVZOdE.

Millie, M. (2021). GB how to grow on instgram Avatar image HOW TO GROW ON INSTAGRAM IN 2021 | My Instagram Strategy If I Had To Start At 0 Followers!. Youtube.com. Retrieved 7 July 2021, from https://www.youtube.com/watch?v=TzgOZf444HY&t=2s.

Millie, M. (2021). HOW TO USE INSTAGRAM HASHTAGS 2021 | Ultimate Hashtag Strategy EXPOSED!. Youtube.com. Retrieved 7 July 2021, from https://www.youtube.com/watch?v=FM465vbNRic.

Multichannel marketing: What it is and why it matters. Sas.com. Retrieved 7 July 2021, from https://www.sas.com/en_us/insights/marketing/multichannel-marketing.html.

Nikolaeva, B. (2016). How to Build Strong Brand & Visual Identity | GraphicMama Blog. GraphicMama Blog. Retrieved 6

July 2021, from https://graphicmama.com/blog/stong-brand-visual-identity/.

Patel, N. (2019). #SEO #NeilPatel #DigitalMarketing 5 Beginner SEO Mistakes That Are Ruining Your Website Traffic And What You Should Do Instead. Youtube.com. Retrieved 7 July 2021, from https://www.youtube.com/watch?v=yX20m5mprCE.

Podcast Networks: Should you join a network to grow your podcast?. Buzzsprout.com. (2018). Retrieved 3 April 2021, from https://www.buzzsprout.com/blog/podcast-network.

Podcast.co, 9 Tips for Conducting Better Podcast Interviews. https://www.podcast.co/create/tips-for-better-podcast-interviews

Roth, C., *Entrepreneur,* Customer Loyalty 3.0 Is Never About Transactions. It's About Getting to Know Your Customers. (11 April, 2016.) https://www.entrepreneur.com/article/273761

Ruoff, M., Osborne, S., & Ruoff, M. (2021). 13 Creative Podcast Segment Ideas. The World's Audio. Retrieved 4 March 2021, from https://live365.com/blog/13-creative-podcast-segment-ideas/.

Schad, K. 8 Key Reasons Why Branding Is Important & 1 Why It Isn't. Imaginasium.com. Retrieved 5 April 2021, from https://imaginasium.com/blog/why-is-branding-important/.

Single-Channel vs Multi-Channel Marketing: The Numbers Are In. Kasasa.com. (2020). Retrieved 14 April 2021, from https://www.kasasa.com/articles/single-channel-vs-multi-channel#:

Social proof - Wikipedia. En.wikipedia.org. Retrieved 7 July 2021, from https://en.wikipedia.org/wiki/Social_proof#:

Software, S. (2021). What Is Multichannel Marketing and Why It Matters – The SAS Point of View. Youtube.com. Retrieved 7 July 2021, from https://www.youtube.com/watch?v=cFC9Xb07Ye8.

Todd, J. (2020). Give Me 10 Minutes And I'll Grow Your TikTok Account (Viral Video Structures). Youtube.com. Retrieved 4 March 2020, from https://www.youtube.com/watch?v=vF7KJEeciIw.

Todd, J. (2021). Before you continue to YouTube. Youtube.com. Retrieved 4 April 2021, from https://www.youtube.com/watch?v=lwSQwMRLUXg.

Weeks, M. (2020). Do You Even TikTok?! - The Daily Rind. The Daily Rind. Retrieved 4 March 2020, from https://dailyrindblog.com/do-you-even-tiktok/.

Winn, R., *Podcast Insights,* Best Podcast Recording Software (For Mac & PC). (20 May, 2020.) https://www.podcastinsights.com/best-podcast-recording-software/

Winn, R. (2021). How To Make Money Podcasting: 11 Ways To Monetize A Podcast. Podcast Insights®. Retrieved 14 April 2021, from https://www.podcastinsights.com/make-money-podcasting/.

Made in the USA
Middletown, DE
10 September 2024

60703355R00229